Social Policy, Service Users and Carers

Clive Sealey • Joy Fillingham
Peter Unwin
Editors

Social Policy, Service Users and Carers

Lived Experiences and Perspectives

Editors
Clive Sealey
School of Allied Health and Community
University of Worcester
Worcester, UK

Joy Fillingham
Department of Social Work and Social Care
University of Birmingham
Birmingham, UK

Peter Unwin
School of Allied Health and Community
University of Worcester
Worcester, UK

ISBN 978-3-030-69875-1   ISBN 978-3-030-69876-8   (eBook)
https://doi.org/10.1007/978-3-030-69876-8

This Palgrave Macmillan imprint is published by the registered company Springer Nature Switzerland AG.
The registered company address is: Gewerbestrasse 11, 6330 Cham, Switzerland

Acknowledgements

This book would not have been possible without the invaluable contribution of the chapters' service users and carers. As editors, we know that this has involved a huge commitment in terms of time and resources, sometimes involving re-visiting painful memories. The editors have been inspired and enthused by working with all of our contributors, and we hope that you are too.

About the Book

This book is primarily about providing a greater understanding of the real lived effect that social policies have on service users and carers. While service user and carer involvement has become more and more prominent in social policy over recent years, it is rarely the case that the perspectives of service users and carers go beyond consultation to true and meaningful involvement. The key aim of the book is to provide a greater understating of the real lived experience that social policies have on service users and carers, which hopefully provides the impetus towards changes to make such social policies better for service users and carers. This book is firmly rooted in the belief that experiential knowledge contributes meaningfully to the beneficial development of services and provision.

We have written this book with an emphasis on the co-production of knowledge between all contributors, be they academics, service users or carers. The key rationale for service user and carer involvement in this way is to utilise the lived experiences of service users and carers as the basis for the development of social policies more relevant to service user and carer needs and experiences. There are nine co-produced chapters, which are divided into three main thematic sections, for clarity of understanding. The first thematic section presents accounts from service user and carers focused on being in and leaving care. The second thematic section presents accounts from service users and carers focused on the impact on them of having to live within the specific strictures and structures set by policy. The third thematic section presents accounts from service users and carers focused on the specific limitations of policy and practice and which highlight the significant changes that need to be made.

The book concludes with a consideration of what social policy and practice learn from service users and carers. This chapter draws on the previous chapters to highlight key lessons that are relevant to social policy. This will relate not only to policy and practical issues highlighted by authors but also to theoretical issues. We hope that this will provide a greater understating of the real lived experience that social policies have on service users and carers, as well as an impetus towards changes to make such social policies better for service users and carers. We hope that this book will be relevant to the academic, to policy and practice context and, perhaps most importantly, to service users and carers themselves in relation to the impact that it can have on service delivery and policy outcomes.

Contents

Notes on Contributors

Bob Conner is a carer for his wife who is in residential care and a member of the IMPACT service user and carer group at the University of Worcester.

Francesca Crozier-Roche is a qualified youth and community practitioner and a parent with experience of the care system. She is a member of the University of Birmingham's service user and carer group.

Dionne is a qualified social work, practitioner, mother and care leaver. She is a member of the University of Birmingham's service user and carer group.

Dorothy is a twin to Dionne and has experienced the care system and some mental health challenges. She is a member of the University of Birmingham's service user and carer group.

Charles Mark English-Peach is a care leaver and student at Newman University, Birmingham.

Eva is a survivor of domestic and sexual violence and a member of the IMPACT service user and carer group at the University of Worcester.

Joy Fillingham is a lecturer in the School of Social Policy at the University of Birmingham and the Lead of Lived Experience of Service User and Carers within the Social Work Programmes of the University of Birmingham.

David John Sambrook Gowar is a survivor of domestic and sexual violence and a member of the IMPACT service user and carer group at the University of Worcester.

Chantele Harvey Head is a mother and wife who has lived with Crohn's disease and a bipolar mental health condition for many years. She is a member of the University of Birmingham's service user and carer group.

Janine is a survivor of domestic and sexual violence and a member of the IMPACT service user and carer group at the University of Worcester.

Joanne is a recently qualified social worker with experience of the benefits system.

Mark Lynes works as an Expert by Experience at four universities, including the University of Birmingham and the University of Worcester.

Becki Meakin is a disabled person and General Manager for Shaping Our Lives National Network of Service Users and Disabled Persons.

Jon Andrew Powton is a disabled foster carer for the National Fostering Agency.

Barbara Pugh is a carer and member of the IMPACT service user and carer group at the University of Worcester.

Christine Ransome-Wallis cared for her mother and is a member of the University of Birmingham's service user and carer group.

Clive Sealey is a senior lecturer in Social Policy and Theory at the University of Worcester.

Julia Louise Therese Smith is a qualified social worker who is now medically retired due to her impairments.

Vivienne Tongue is a mother, wife and therapeutic foster carer. She is a member of the University of Birmingham's service user and carer group.

Peter Unwin is Principal Lecturer in Social Work at the University of Worcester and facilitator of the IMPACT service user and carer group.

Abbreviations

ACEs	Adverse childhood experiences
ADHD	Attention deficit hyperactivity disorder
BAME	Black, Asian and minority ethnic
BDRG	Birmingham Disability Rights Group
CAMHS	Child and Adolescent Mental Health Services
CBT	Cognitive behavioural therapy
CPN	Community psychiatric nurse
CQC	Care Quality Commission
CSEW	Crime Survey for England and Wales
CYP IAPT	Children and Young People Improving Access to Psychological Therapies
DA	Domestic abuse
DBS	Disclosure and Barring Service
DHSC	Department of Health and Social Care
DLA	Disability Living Allowance
DoH	Department of Health
DP	Direct Payments
DV	Domestic violence
DWP	Department for Work and Pensions
EHC	Education, Health and Care plan
GP	General practitioner
IAPT	Improving Access to Psychological Therapies
IFA	Independent Foster Agencies
ILF	Independent Living Fund
IPV	Intimate partner violence
IRO	Independent Reviewing Officer
JNC	Joint Negotiating Committee
LA	Local authority, that is local council or similar
LGBTI	Lesbian, gay, bisexual, transgender, intersex
NAO	National Audit Office
NEET	Not in employment, education or training
NHS	National Health Service
NICE	National Institute for Care and Health Excellence
NSPCC	The National Society for the Prevention of Cruelty to Children

OFSTED	Office for Standards in Education, Children's Services and Skills
ONS	Office for National Statistics
OT	Occupational therapist/therapy
PA	Personal advisor
PAs	Personal assistant
PIP	Personal Independence Payment
PTSD	Post-traumatic stress disorder
SCIE	Social Care Institute for Excellence
SWA	Social work assistant
UC	Universal Credit
UNCRC	United Nations Convention on the Rights of the Child
VAWG	Violence Against Women and Girls
WHO	World Health Organisation
YTS	Youth Training Scheme

List of Key Learnings

List of Tables

Clive Sealey, Peter Unwin, and Joy Fillingham

Service user and carer involvement has become more and more prominent in social policy over recent years, as the value of learning from the people who use services has become increasingly recognised and valued. However, it is rarely the case that the perspectives of service users and carers go beyond consultation to true and meaningful involvement. This book is unique in that it provides first-hand accounts of the real-life experiences of social policy. The key aim of the book is to provide a greater understanding of the real lived experience that social policies have on service users and carers, with the hope that this will provide the impetus to inform and improve social policy. The terminology surrounding service users and carers is contentious and has developed over time, some preferring 'people with lived experience' or 'experts by experience' (Grant et al. 2020). We have chosen to use the term 'service users and carers' in this book as this is still the most common usage in the UK and, specifically includes carers, whose practice and policy needs are often overlooked.

Social policy is a term that you may not have come across, but which nonetheless has a huge impact on your everyday life. We can define social policy as policies which aim to improve the social and economic well-being of individuals and society. For example, social policies can have an impact on your health, your wealth and your living conditions. This is because social policies are concerned with the levels and quality of healthcare you receive, the type of education that you receive, the

C. Sealey (✉) • P. Unwin
School of Allied Health and Community, University of Worcester, Worcester, UK
e-mail: c.sealey@worc.ac.uk; p.unwin@worc.ac.uk

J. Fillingham
Department of Social Work and Social Care, University of Birmingham, Birmingham, UK
e-mail: j.fillingham@bham.ac.uk

C. Sealey et al. (eds.), *Social Policy, Service Users and Carers*,
https://doi.org/10.1007/978-3-030-69876-8_1

quality of housing that you live in, the amount of income that you receive and the type of social care that you receive. Defining social policy in this way enables us to analyse how social policy works and functions and also enables us to consider the relevance of social policies to you and your family, friends and community. It also shows us that the key aim of social policy is to find answers and solutions to social problems that affect us all, in order to make improve our social and economic well-being. However, as the lived experiences and analyses in this book will illuminate, social policy can also be used as a form of control and rationing, with many people being disadvantaged, rather than advantaged, by social policy changes.

The book originates from the writing of a previous book that was not primarily focused on service users and carers but did have one chapter that was co-produced with a service user. This was a chapter written in Sealey (2015) by Simon Heng. The feedback provided for this chapter was consistent in its emphasis that such a real-life account of someone on the receiving end of social policy had great impact on readers. Additionally, the chapter did not only have an emotional impact but also a real-life impact, in relation to the British Association of Social Workers (BASW) using it to help create policy. This led to a discussion as to whether something similar could and should be undertaken with other service users and carers. The book is the outcome of this discussion which led to collaboration between the Universities of Worcester and Birmingham, as discussed in the next chapter.

In writing this book, we are aware that there have been a variety of approaches from academia when working with service users and carers. This book aims to be different from previous academic works which are predominately books written about service users and carers by academics and so do not have the authenticity of lived experience. In contrast, the primary focus of this book is working *with* service users and carers, rather than the historical precedent of working *on* service users and carers. Table 1.1 summarises the differences in methodology, methods and outcomes of traditional research (*research on*) and service user and carer research (*research with*).

Table 1.1 shows that there are key differences in perspectives in these two approaches. In particular, while traditional research is clear in its focus on the researcher at the heart of the process, by contrast, service user and carer research puts service user and carer values and experiences at the heart of research, based on the belief that these values and perspectives can and do make an invaluable contribution to understanding theory, policy and practice.

Table 1.1 Traditional research versus Service user and carer research

	Traditional research	Service user and carer research
Methodology	Research as value free	Research as value/power laden
Methods	Process driven (ignoring power dynamics)	Inclusive (to overcome power dynamics)
Outcomes	Production of knowledge	1. Enabling individuals to confront and challenge power 2. Better quality knowledge, evidence and practice

This shows that this preference for *with* rather than *on* provides an important point of distinction between involvement that foregrounds the expert knowledge of objective scientific research versus involvement that foregrounds the experiential knowledge of service users and carers (Beresford 2007). Hence, the approach adopted here explicitly recognises that the lived experiences of service users and carers complements and enhances professional expertise and vice versa (Durose et al. 2012). This has some linkage to Arnstein's (1969) 'degrees of citizen participation', often presented as a ladder of participation with 'manipulation' at the bottom and 'citizen control' at the top. This book is firmly rooted in the latter, in the belief that experiential knowledge contributes meaningfully to the beneficial development of policies and services, wherein the individual 'is the only witness to all his or her care experiences, making him or her an essential source for information across services and care settings' (Foot et al. 2014, p. 49). This highlights that the book has an explicit focus on the co-production of knowledge, as detailed in the next chapter.

Who Is This Book For?

This book is primarily about how policy directly affects service user and carers. We hope that this book will be relevant to the academic, policy and practice context and, perhaps most importantly, to service users and carers themselves.

In the academic context, there are numerous degree courses at both undergraduate and postgraduate level where understanding the lived experiences of services user and carers is embedded as part of students' learning. This includes a range of applied degrees directly linked to health and <u>social care</u>, youth work and social work. This also includes degrees which have a direct impact on the outcomes for services users and carers, such as social policy, community development, housing and allied health courses such as occupational therapy and physiotherapy. The book will hopefully provide invaluable learning to enhance students' understanding of service users and carers in these and other related degrees.

▶ **Key Learning: Social Care** Social care is an all-inclusive term for a broad range of services designed to meet the practical daily living needs of individuals both inside and outside the home. These daily living needs can be specific such as washing, feeding, dressing, mobility and toileting. Daily living needs can also be more abstract such as maintaining independence and social interaction, enabling the individual to play a fuller part in society, protecting them in vulnerable situations, helping them to manage complex relationships and (in some circumstances) accessing a care home or other supported accommodation. For this reason, social care includes working with a very broad range of individuals including children, older people, people with mental health problems, people with learning disabilities and disabled people. It is estimated that 1.6 million people work in social care, which is approximately the same amount that work in the NHS.

This book is also relevant to those who make policy that affects service users and carers. As set out later in this chapter, service user and carer involvement has become a prime focus of policy over recent years, this book providing detailed experiences of how they are affected, both positively and negatively, by such policies. The chapters also provides some specific analysis of how policy could be improved, in terms of both processes and measures, which should be of relevance to policymakers.

The book should also be relevant to practitioners who are required to implement policy and so affect the lived experiences of service users and carers most directly. The experiences presented in the chapters highlight how important the relationships between practitioners and service user and carers are to enabling beneficial policy outcomes. We hope that this book offers practitioners significant insight into best practice.

Perhaps most importantly, this book is also for service users and carers, who have rarely, if ever, had the chance to articulate their lived experiences in the way that this book allows. It is hoped that the book will inspire others to be more involved in similar projects. The chapters detail lived experiences of social policy as written by service users and carers, or where this was not possible with the assistance of the book's academic authors. Each chapter explicitly has co-production at its heart, as it is believed that highlighting service users and carers as authors of equal standing alongside academic authors is an important statement. This is an almost unique approach to understanding the lived experiences of service users and carers, with a notable exception being Hughes' (2019) recent account of social work interventions. However, an important distinction between this book and Hughes' book is that the focus of Hughes' book is specifically on social work interventions and social work legislation, and so is written almost exclusively for social workers. In contrast, this book takes a significantly wider focus on social policy and considers the wider implications of the lived experiences of service users and carers in a social policy context. We believe that this approach enables and provides a more comprehensive analysis of the social policy issues facing service users and carers.

What Do We Mean by Service Users and Carers?

For the purposes of this book, we define service users in a broad sense as referring to people who use or receive social policy services and provision. The key implication of this broad definition is that the concept of service user is not static but can change over time due to circumstances. For example, getting a diagnosis of mental ill-health can transform an individual from being a non-service user to a service user almost instantaneously. The reality is that we are all service users of social policy in some sense, as argued in Sealey (2015), and so the significance of this broad definition is to highlight its relevance to all of us.

The definition of 'carers' is taken from Carers UK (2019) as anyone who provides unpaid care by looking after an ill, older or disabled family member, friend or partner. This excludes those who provide care for formal payment, such as through employment, but does include carers who receive <u>Carer's Allowance</u>, as this is not formal payment for caring. On this definition, there are approximately 6.5 million carers in the UK (Carers UK 2019), which is a substantial number. The Government Office for Science (2016, p. 11) stated that 'Between 2007 and 2032, the number of people aged 65 and over who require unpaid care is projected to have grown by more than one million'. This number is likely to be an underestimation, as the number of people needing care is predicted to continue to increase over the coming years.

Why Is It Important to Distinguish Between Service Users and Carers?

Service users and carers are often facing challenges together, in accessing services and information, in negotiating with government structures and in dealing with the day-to-day experiences of their impairments (or life experiences). However, the legal requirements and societal expectations placed upon service users and carers are quite different. Whilst a raft of legislation outlines responsibilities of professionals when working with service users, there are extremely limited requirements or references of statutory responsibilities to carers. A prime example of this is the *Health and Social Care Act 2012*, a key piece of legislation that supposedly covers both health and social care, but which makes references to carers only twice in its provisions but refers to (service) users 25 times.

Additionally, legislation which may appear to apply specifically to carers' day-to-day experiences of care such as the *Care Act 2014* is a huge misnomer as it does no such thing, as the legislation is about neither the quality nor nature of the support provided to carers or the carer. Indeed, it does not even define what care is! Instead, its focus is on the legal structures of the way in which statutory care is provided.

The views of carers are also seldom formally required to be taken into consideration. Yet expectations are often placed upon carers to undertake activities associated with the long-term care of loved ones. Some service users have argued that the need for unpaid carers to support them limits their opportunities and creates a level of dependency which is unwarranted (Picking 2000). This shows that the experiences of service users and carers are quantitatively and qualitatively different and so need to be recognised as such, in both policy and practice. Some people of course will also inhabit both roles and at times simultaneously, but it is helpful to situate and recognise the pushes and pulls placed upon both service users and carers in the current political context of social policy.

What Is the Current Political Context of Social Policy for Service Users and Carers?

The economic context within which this book is being published is something that cannot be ignored, for the simple reason that over the last decade or so, the policy of austerity in social policy has had a significant impact on the scope and level of social policy provision for service users and carers. This has been felt at both the national and local levels.

> ▶ **Key Learning: Austerity in Social Policy** Austerity in social policy refers to the cuts in both the funding and scope of social policies from 2010 to the present, especially those that impact on services users and carers. The key reasoning for austerity within this period has been the claim that there is not enough money to fund services to their previous level, and this has primarily resulted in the cutting of services and/or eligibility criteria being changed. As an example of this, the increase in higher education tuition fees to £9200 and the cuts in grants to students in 2012 was outlined as occurring due to the fact that the government could not afford to fund the finances required to pay for all students who wished to go to university. Therefore, austerity in this context refers to the cuts by the government since 2010 to the funding and scope of social policies.

As examples of austerity social policies at the national level, various benefits changes have either limited who can claim (such as Child Benefit), been frozen (such as Income Support and Job Seeker's Allowance) or had limited increases (such as Housing Benefit). Some benefits have also been abolished, such as the Education Maintenance Allowance, or completely redesigned, such as the change from Disability Living Allowance to Personal Independence Payment and the introduction of Universal Credit. The clear trend in these changes have been attempts to limit and cut benefits and benefit levels, and the clear outcome has been that the incomes of those reliant on such benefits have fallen, with a connected fall in their living standards (Bourquin et al. 2019).

At the local level, Amin-Smith and Phillips (2019) note that local government spending on services has fallen 21% in real terms since 2009–2010. Even more significant is their observation that these cuts have been larger for councils serving more deprived communities than for those serving less deprived communities. This is particularly relevant to social care provision, as it is local authorities who provide the bulk of social care across the lifespan, such as Sure Start centres for early years, children's social services, youth work provision, care for older people and care for disabled people. Local authorities also have important responsibilities for other social policy areas such as in relation to social housing, and education in relation to local authority-maintained schools. Perhaps not surprisingly, some of these services have seen significant cuts in levels of spending over the last decade of austerity, most notably within youth work and social housing, which have undoubtedly had a major impact on the outcomes for service users and carers across a wide range of ages and needs. These changes have certainly had significant impacts on people who rely on them, as the chapters in this book illustrate. However, the aim of this book is not to chart the impact of austerity per se, but to consider the lived experiences of service users and carers as a result of such policies. Specifically, this book takes the position that the outcomes from social policies could be improved by listening to lived experiences, something which has been notably absent in the austerity policy changes that have been made over the last decade. This is also somewhat ironic bearing in mind the professed changing perspectives over the last 20 years or so towards service users and carers, as detailed below.

What Is the Rationale for Service Users and Carers' Involvement in Social Policy?

The rationale for service user and carer involvement in social policy is to enable their lived experiences to provide a basis for the development of social policies more relevant to their needs and experiences. This relates to the impact that it can have on service delivery and policy outcomes. Omeni et al. (2014) outlined a number of benefits of such involvement, for example, improving the information and accessibility of services and improving the coordination of care, and in the relationships between clinicians and those receiving treatment. Such changes correlated to positive clinical outcomes, such as improved self-esteem and confidence, and demonstrated therapeutic benefits resulting from increased social interaction.

This rationale is also rooted in the negative consequences of not involving service users and carers, identified by Glasby and Beresford (2006, p. 274) as related to:

- The existence of unequal power relationships between academics and service users and carers, resulting in either hostile or paternalistic understandings.
- An inadequate awareness from academics of their position in relation to other people's experience, cultures and perspectives;
- This leads to the possibility of discrimination, either directly or indirectly, by the academics relating to class, race, gender and other forms of difference,
- The academic having a commitment to ideologies, agendas and values which limit their ability to value people and being able to appreciate the other person and their experience.

Furthermore, Beresford (2004) observes the possibility that academics are socialised into a reliance on models of understanding which subordinate and pathologise people, such as through medical models of 'mental health'. These limitations are reinforced by the perception of the worth of research with service users and carers, as outlined by Glasby and Beresford (2006). This shows that in the hierarchy of research evidence, objective scientific research is at the top of the hierarchy, while expert opinion that includes the views of service users and carers is at the bottom of the hierarchy.

There have been some notable attempts in policy to incorporate the voices of service users within a service improvement framework in health and social care (Omeni et al. 2014). For example, the recent NHS Long Term Plan (NHS 2019, 1.35) makes a specific pledge that 'People will get more control over their own health and more personalised care when they need it', with specific reference to person-centred care. It is perhaps the introduction of Healthwatch in England from the *Health and Social Care Act 2012*, which describes itself as 'the independent national champion for people who use health and social care services', which exemplifies most significantly this move towards inclusion.

▶ **Key Learning: Healthwatch** Healthwatch is an organisation set up as an independent consumer group for health and social care service users in England. Its aim is to champion the needs and views of service users. It does this by inspecting health and social care facilities and asking service users their views on services. It uses the information gathered within these processes to make recommendations for changes where necessary. It should be noted that unlike the Care Quality Commission, Healthwatch does not have any legal enforcement powers, and it principally relies on agreement and negotiation to achieve its desired aims. In Wales, the equivalent functions of Healthwatch are undertaken by Community Health Councils and in Scotland by the Scottish Health Council.

A key point to note in relation to Healthwatch is that it is primarily constituted as a 'consumer champion', meaning that its focus is on ensuring that the prevailing health and social care market functions as designed, rather than necessarily focusing on changes which are in the best interest of service users and carers (Carter and Martin 2016). As an example of this, while it is a statutory responsibility for the local Healthwatch to seek the views of local people, the powers that they have to enforce changes are very limited, and proposed changes are typically expressed as aspirations rather than a requirement.

What Are the Beneficial Outcomes of Service User and Carer Involvement in Social Policy?

The first beneficial outcome of service user and carer involvement in social policy relates to service and carers themselves, in terms of their personal engagement that can flow from their meaningful involvement. Foot et al. (2014) observe how such involvement has been important in challenging power differentials, highlighting poor care and neglect, inclusion, autonomy and independence. The ultimate upshot of this has been a seismic change of perspective of service users and carers, away from the impairment focused medical model of disability and towards the social model of disability in policy (Foot et al. 2014), which ultimately have led to improvements in social policies. A practical example of this is the emphasis on person-centred care in legislation such as the *Care Act 2014* and in policy such as in relation to dementia care.

There are various other benefits that can occur from the involvement of service users and carers. These include but are not limited to:

- Offering new types of evidence on which to base practice.
- Providing fresh insights from the inside bringing an enhanced validity to the research.
- A shorter distance between direct experience and its interpretation, meaning that the resulting knowledge is less likely to be inaccurate, unreliable and distorted.
- Bringing an ecological or real-world validity to research, focusing on subjective, lived experience in contrast to the objectivities offered by the natural science type approach to research that generally informs evidence-based medicine.
- Marrying expertise by experience with expertise by profession: collaboration between the service user and the traditional clinical, academic researcher, which corrects a distortion or imbalance in current research.
- The potential for the making of broader social and political change.
- A catalyst for more equal social relations of research production.
- The potential empowerment of service users and carers (Gillard et al. 2010).

These beneficial outcomes should not be seen as mutually exclusive, but as intrinsically linked together. For example, taking the last of these outcomes, where research does empower service users and carers, this can be a catalyst for more equal social relations not just in relation to research but also within wider society. Furthermore, where such a transformation does occur, this has the potential to be the further catalyst for broader social and political change. The most obvious example of this is in relation to the challenge and rejection of the medical model of disability by disabled people and their adoption of the social model of disability. This has had a huge impact on the provision of services within and outside of social policy, such as in relation to the emphasis in the *Equality Act 2010* on reasonable adjustments for disabled people. The key point about this approach is that rather than seeing service users and carers as people deserving of sympathy, it sees people as experts by experience, able to make a meaningful contribution to social policy and the provision of services and provision as experts.

The Structure of the Book

As detailed above, we have written this book with an emphasis on the co-production of knowledge between all contributors, be they academics, service users or carers. In the next chapter, we discuss and analyse what co-production is and how it relates to this book. This includes an analysis of the key benefits of co-production and how it can work. The chapter concludes with a summary of the key differences between production and co-production.

Chapters 3, 4, 5, 6, 7, 8, 9, 10 and 11 put the principle of co-production into practice with co-produced chapters. These chapters have been co-produced through close working between service users, carers and editors, and this is made clear in the title page of each chapter. Most authors have chosen to use their real names, but some have requested anonymity, and where this is the case, we have used an asterisk (*) to denote this.

As a book co-produced by multiple authors with varying experiences of writing, there are inevitable difference in style within the chapters. With the agreement of service user and carers, the chapters have been written to be as similar as possible, but in some instances, this has not been practicable or desirable. These co-produced chapters also contain a commentary of key issues raised in the chapter, written by the chapter's academic editor, and reflective questions for discussion and debate.

The co-produced chapters are divided into three main thematic sections, for clarity of understanding. However, it should be noted that these themes are fluid iand could have been interpreted differently. The thematic sections and chapters are as follows.

- Section 1: Experiences of Care Services in Childhood and Beyond

This section presents accounts from service users and carers focused on being in and leaving care. The three chapters in this section are as follows:

– Chapter 3: Living with Care Orders: Turning Pain into Passion

This chapter presents the personal experiences of having a child taken into care. The chapter will relate personal experiences of how and why this occurred and the lengthy and complex process required to eventually have the child returned from the care system. The chapter will also consider the impacts that this has had both in relation to parent and child. It will conclude by outlining some possible improvements that could be made when a local authority initiates a care order.

– Chapter 4: Improving Transitions for Independence to Adulthood for Care Leavers

This chapter outlines the experience of the transition from leaving care into independent adult life. It describes how the transition into independent adulthood is fraught with additional difficulties and complexities for a number of specific reasons that arise from being in care. This chapter provides a first-hand account of the impact and outcomes of the main policies that exist for care leavers and changes that could be made to improve the system.

– Chapter 5: The Realities of Fostering in a Flawed System

This chapter details the experiences applying for and becoming a foster family. It outlines the skills required to be an effective foster parent, particularly when dealing with vulnerable children and young people who may have challenging

behaviour. It draws particular attention to approaches which may negatively impact
on both children in the care system and prospective foster carers.

- Section 2: Negotiating the Strictures and Structures of Being a Service User
  and Carer

This section presents accounts from service users and carers focused on the
impact of having to work within the specific limits set by policy and practice. The
three chapters in this section are as follows:

– Chapter 6: Benefits and Employment Support for Disabled and Marginalised People

This chapter presents the experiences of individuals subject to key recent policies
which were designed to help disabled and marginalised people to become part of the
workforce. These policies will be critiqued from the perspectives of people with
lived experience in this field and recommendations made for improving the employment opportunities for unrepresented groups in the workplace.

– Chapter 7: Living with Long-Term Disability and Care: A Perspective on the
  Adequacy of Provision and Areas for Improvement

This chapter presents the experiences of receiving long-term care from the perspective of an individual who has personally lived with an acquired physical impairment for close to four decades. The chapter details that over this period, there have
been many significant events in terms of the care and support received or not
received. In particular, there have been marked changes in the structure of the social
care sector and organisations which have affected the roles of the people working
within them and which in turn have impacted to varying degrees on the care and
support received.

– Chapter 8: Direct Payments: Rationalising, Processes and Improving

This chapter presents a personal rationale and understanding of receiving Direct
Payments. It outlines how the key concepts related to Direct Payments of choice,
control and flexibility have had direct relevance to the author. The chapter then outlines the practicalities experienced related to the process of receiving, and the outcomes experienced, from Direct Payments. It concludes by outlining some possible
improvements that could be made to Direct Payments.

- Section 3: The Lived Experiences of limiting and limited policy, practice and
  services

This section presents accounts from service users and carers focused on areas of
policy and practice where their experiences highlight that significant changes need
to be made. The four chapters in this section are as follows:

- Chapter 9: Children in Need/Looked-After Children: Analysing the Adequacy of the Care System

The chapter presents the dual perspective of twins who had similar reasons for being in need, but individualised experiences of being looked after by the local authority. The key aim of this chapter is to consider how practice could be improved when working with children identified as a 'child in need' and a 'looked after child' by the local authority.

- Chapter 10: Mental Health: Services and Struggles

This chapter presents the long-term lived experiences of a mental health survivor. The account highlights in particular the impact that living with an undiagnosed mental health disorder over a long period of time can have on an individual and considers the effectiveness of services tasked with providing treatment and support to people living with a mental health disorder.

- Chapter 11: Lived Experiences of Domestic Abuse, Domestic Violence and Intimate Partner Violence

This chapter present the experiences of three survivors of domestic violence and abuse, two female and one male. The focus is on issues related to accessing support from domestic violence services and reflecting on professionals' attitudes. This chapter relates these experiences to societal attitudes and UK Government policy and makes recommendations for future best practice and policy.

- Chapter 12: Informal Carers and Caring

This chapter explores the lived experiences of carers, within a system and set of policies in which they are both required to take part, but where their insights are often disregarded. The experiences present that while the role of informal carers is recognised and valued in contemporary society, the necessary support systems are not in place, and many informal carers make financial and personal sacrifices to the detriment of their own health and well-being.

The book concludes with a consideration of what social policy and practice can learn from service users and carers. This chapter draws on the previous chapters to highlight key lessons that are relevant to social policy. This will relate not only to practical issues highlighted by authors but also to theoretical issues. We hope that this will provide a greater understating of the real lived experience that social policies have on service users and carers, as well as creating an impetus towards changes to make such social policies better for service users and carers.

Diversity of Authorship Within This Book

Each chapter author has defined and described themselves as they wish to be represented. The authors and editors are diverse in terms of their gender, ethnicities, disabilities and caring responsibilities in addition to their roles as academics, practitioners and citizens. We recognise the importance of reflecting a range of views, personal circumstances and life experiences to both acknowledge and facilitate further diversity within the voices of service users and carers and future developments in social policy.

The Use of Key Learning Boxes

We have used Key Learning boxes to make key issues and concepts clearer. Where an issue or concept has a Key Learning box, this is shown by the concept or issue being underlined in the text like this. In many instances, Key Learning boxes will be found to appear in another chapter in the book. Where this happens, you should refer to the List of Key Learning Boxes to see in which page it appears.

References

N. Amin-Smith, D. Phillips, *English Council Funding: What's Happened and What's Next?* IFS Briefing Note BN 150 (Institute for Fiscal Studies, London, 2019)

S. Arnstein, A ladder of citizenship participation. J. Am. Plann. Assoc. **35**(4), 216–224 (1969)

P. Beresford, Where's the evidence?: comparing user controlled with traditional research. Mental Health Today February:31–4 (2004)

P. Beresford, The role of service user research in generating knowledge-based health and social care: from conflict to contribution. Evid. Policy **3**(3), 329–341 (2007)

P. Bourquin, J. Cribb, T. Waters, et al., *Living Standards, Poverty and Inequality in the UK: 2019* (The Institute for Fiscal Studies, London, 2019)

Carers UK, Facts about carers, Policy Briefing August 2019 (2019). https://www.carersuk.org/for-professionals/policy/policy-library?task=download&file=policy_file&id=6775. Accessed 5 Dec 2019

P. Carter, G. Martin, Challenges facing healthwatch, a new consumer champion in England. Int. J. Health Policy Manag. **5**(4), 259–263 (2016)

C. Durose, Y. Beebeejaun, J. Rees, et al., *Towards Co-Production in Research with Communities* (AHR, Swindon, 2012)

C. Foot, H. Gilburt, P. Dunn, et al., *People in Control of Their Own Health and Care: The State of Involvement* (The King's Fund, London, 2014)

S. Gillard, R. Borschmann, K. Turner, et al., 'What difference does it make?' Finding evidence of the impact of mental health service user researchers on research into the experiences of detained psychiatric patients. Health Expect. **13**, 185–194 (2010)

J. Glasby, P. Beresford, Who knows best? Evidence-based practice and the service user contribution. Critical Social Policy **26**(1), 268–284 (2006)

Government Office for Science, *Future of an Ageing Population* (Government Office for Science, London, 2016)

S. Grant, R. Allen, G. Nosowska, et al., Editorial: resilient, steadfast and forward-looking: the story of social work in the UK told through 50 years of the British Journal of Social Work. Br. J. Soc. Work **bcaa137** (2020). https://doi.org/10.1093/bjsw/bcaa137

M. Hughes, *A Guide to Statutory Social Work Interventions: The Lived Experience* (Red Globe Press, London, 2019)

E. Omeni, M. Barnes, D. MacDonald, et al., Service user involvement: impact and participation: a survey of service user and staff perspectives. BMC Health Serv. Res. **14**, 491 (2014)

C. Picking, Working in partnership with disabled people: new perspectives for professionals within the social model of disability, in *Law, Rights and Disability*, ed. by J. Copper, (Jessica Kingsley Publishers, London, 2000), pp. 11–32

C. Sealey, *Social Policy Simplified* (Palgrave Macmillan, Basingstoke, 2015)

Co-production: Rationale, Processes and Application to this Book

Clive Sealey, Joy Fillingham, and Peter Unwin

In this chapter, we discuss and analyse what co-production is and how it relates to this book. This is highly relevant as we have written this book through an emphasis on the co-production of knowledge between all contributors, be they academics, service users or carers, or a combination of these prescribed roles. This chapter analyses the key benefits of co-production and how it can work. The chapter concludes with a summary of the key differences between production and co-production, and how co-production has been applied to this book.

The main aims of this chapter are to:

1. Provide an introductory account of the concept of co-production.
2. Consider some of the challenges that co-production presents.
3. Outline a rationale for using co-production within this book.

What Is Co-production?

The application of co-production is something that is now in vogue as an uncontroversial and common-sense shift to delivering public services (Paget 2014; Durose et al. 2017), and according to Horne and Shirley (2009), co-production is more

C. Sealey (✉) • P. Unwin
School of Allied Health and Community, University of Worcester, Worcester, UK
e-mail: c.sealey@worc.ac.uk; p.unwin@worc.ac.uk

J. Fillingham
Department of Social Work and Social Care, University of Birmingham, Birmingham, UK
e-mail: j.fillingham@bham.ac.uk

© The Author(s), under exclusive license to Springer Nature
Switzerland AG 2021
C. Sealey et al. (eds.), *Social Policy, Service Users and Carers*,
https://doi.org/10.1007/978-3-030-69876-8_2

common in the UK than other European countries. The focus towards co-production has been rationalised as 'a radical new approach to public services', which 'overturns the conventional passive relationship between the 'users' of services and those who serve them' (Boyle et al. 2010, p. 3). There has been a distinct trend towards co-production in the UK over the last 20 years or so, as evidenced by the fact that within most new health and social care legislation, there is a reference to the need to involve people who use services and carers (Pieroudis et al. 2019). This is evident from the fact that co-production has become apparent in a vast array of policy initiatives, including health (family nurse partnership, Headway), education (nursery schooling), criminal justice (community justice panels), social care (residential homes), employment (as through the Richmond Fellowship charity), and housing (as through the KeyRing charity) (Boyle et al. 2010). More recently, the personalisation agenda, as expressed through Direct Payments and individual budgets, has come to be seen as 'the most common form of co-production' (SCIE 2015), due to the fact that they both focus on incorporating the 'lived experience' of service users (Needham 2013). Of particular relevance here is the recent research by the Social Care Institute for Excellence (2019) which suggests that there is a real appetite from those working in the social care sector, carers and service users to see co-production put into practice. Furthermore, as Oliver et al. (2019) argue, the authors of this book believe that a focus on experiential learning and knowledge is an important component of evidence-informed policy, as a way to ensure that the work of academics has an impact beyond academia itself.

▷ **Key Learning: The Personalisation Agenda** The personalisation agenda is an approach to providing care that aims to the give individuals receiving care a high level of choice and control over how their care and support is provided. This requires that care and support be 'personalised', meaning that it is specifically tailored to meet the wishes and needs of the individual, rather than having services which are the same for everyone. The crucial emphasis is that services are designed with the involvement of those who require them and not simply imposed upon them. Key elements of involvement are giving people a clear understanding of how much is to be spent on their care and support and allowing them to have a choice over the provider and/or the type of care that is provided. Specific policies associated with the personalisation agenda include direct payments, personal budgets and personal health budgets. There are also a number of related terms used which reflect the personalisation agenda. These include person-centred planning, person-centred care, person-centred support, independent living and self-directed support.

Further evidence that co-production is now a topic of mainstream interest is the fact that the *Care Act 2014* is 'one of the first pieces of legislation to specifically include the concept of co-production in its statutory guidance' (SCIE 2015, p. 1). As a consequence of this statutory guidance, there is now a requirement for local authorities to develop and implement their information and advice services, with a minimum requirement that a local plan is developed which 'adopt[s] a 'co-production' approach to their plan, involving user groups and people themselves, other appropriate statutory, commercial and voluntary sector service providers, and make public the plan once finalised' (Department of Health (DoH) 2017). Perhaps more significantly, the guidance provides an updated definition of co-production, as:

> Co-production' is when an individual influences the support and services received, or when groups of people get together to influence the way that services are designed, commissioned and delivered (DoH 2017).

A potential benefit from this explicit articulation and definition of co-production in legislation is that it provides a legal basis from which co-production has to be applied, which is a change from the past. For instance, the definition emphasises that co-production relates to the design, commission *and* delivery of services. Furthermore, it also makes clear the co-production process should primarily involve service users, carers and the community that they live in (SCIE 2015, p. 12).

However, SCIE (2015) notes that the DoH definition of co-production is limited by the fact that, in contrast to other definitions, it only requires people who are using services to be involved in the process of co-production. This can exclude many carers, including those who may want to use the services in the future or who have experienced services in the past. Co-production in these terms, then, is limited and appears to exclude a range of groups and individuals who have an active interest in improving provision for all service users and carers.

Additionally, the DoH guidance references Derby City Council, as a good example of co-production in their development of clear and easy-to-use customer information to support their new customer journey for self-directed support (DoH 2017). However, a closer analysis of this example highlights the fact that the level of engagement with service users is not very high and the exemplar of self-directed support also suggests that emphasis within legislation is on co-production as a means to a financial end and not a new way of thinking. For example, taking into consideration what we know about the financial impetus that drives the personalisation agenda, it is perhaps not surprising to note that the interest in co-production from policy-makers has been motivated by the ongoing pressure to cut costs. This means that the acknowledgement that co-production can have a significant role in achieving positive outcomes from public services is often of secondary consideration in policy (SCIE 2015, p. 2), and this is what seems to be evident in the Derby City Council example.

As well as the legal definition of co-production above, there are also other definitions that have been made by organisations, academics and other groups. We have highlighted three definitions below to draw out some key general points in relation to when co-production can be used:

> Co-production means delivering public services in an equal and reciprocal relationship between professionals, people using services, their families and their neighbours. Where activities are co-produced in this way, both services and neighbourhoods become far more effective agents of change (Boyle and Harris 2009, p. 11).

Co-production is a mechanism for actively involving people who are the direct beneficiaries of a service, product or piece of research. It aims to work with communities, offering opportunities to shape the development process, thereby ensuring a relevant outcome (Bunning et al. 2017, p. 2).

Co-production is a relationship where professionals and citizens share power to plan and deliver support together, recognising that both partners have vital contributions to make in order to improve quality of life for people and communities (National Co-production Critical Friends 2013).

The similarities that are evident in these definitions are their emphases on some level of engagement between the service provider and the recipient. Also, the emphasis within the definitions is on co-production as effecting a positive change in the outcomes for recipients.

However, it is possible to observe some distinct differences in emphasis in these definitions. Evident from the first definition is an emphasis on simply delivering public services, while the second definition goes beyond this to include the development of a services, and the third definition specifies planning and delivering together. Another key point of difference is the emphasis on 'active engagement', as evident in second and third definitions, but not in the first. However, there are different emphases in the second and third definitions, wherein the third definition 'requires that people who use those services are involved 'from the design stage onwards'' (Equal Citizens Services 2011, p. 12), meaning the planning and design of services and not just its delivery.

These differences make relevant the observation from Bown and Raines (2014, p. 8) that 'co-production is renowned for its 'excessive elasticity' in the ways in which it has been defined and interpreted'. This elasticity can make co-production an attractive option for many professionals and policy-makers, as how co-production can take place and its depth and level of inclusion can all be varied.

Furthermore, it is important to distinguish between co-production and participation, as the two are often confused. According to SCIE (2015, p. 6), there is a clear difference between the two, wherein 'participation means being consulted while co-production means being equal partners and co-creators'. Additionally, while personalisation's main concern is with tailoring services, co-production goes well beyond that, to demand 'active involvement and decision-making by the person using a service' (ibid.: 8). Table 2.1 presents a summary of these key differences between production and co-production as discussed above.

Which Services Is Co-production Possible In?

Whilst acknowledging that co-production is not possible in all types of services, Boyle et al. (2010) outline the potential for co-production to have real changes in areas such as the following:

- Adult social care and elderly care
- Healthcare

Table 2.1 A summary of the differences between production and co-production with service users and carers

	Production	Co-production
What?	Delivery of services *to* those using the service	Planning *and* design *and* delivery of services *by* those using the service
When?	At the end	At the beginning
	Short term	Long term
Which?	Transactional services	Relational services
Who?	Professionals	Non-experts: Services users, the community, all stakeholders
How?	Passive recipients	Active engagement
	Deficit approach	Strengths-based approach
	Top-down	Bottom-up
	Bureaucracy	Relationship
	Structure	Agency
	Nonparticipation/tokenism	Partnership/engagement
	Hierarchical	Egalitarian
Why?	Curative	Preventative
	Cheap in short term, more expensive in longer term	Expensive in short term, cheaper in longer term
	Equality of opportunity	Equality of outcome
	Power domination	Redistribution of power
	Re-production of conditions	Transformation of conditions
	Uniformity of views	Diversity of views

- Mental health services
- Supported housing
- Criminal Justice and community policing
- Education, early years, youth services, childcare and families
- Welfare to work
- Regeneration

This reflects a recurring theme within the co-production literature that it is best suited to those types of services which are 'relational' in nature (Sherwood 2013). This refers to services where 'there is frequent contact between people and professionals' (Boyle et al. 2010, p. 14), and 'less emphasis on 'transactional' approaches to delivery' (Equal Citizens Services 2011, p. 13), and 'where the benefits outweigh the risks', such as in early years, education, long-term health conditions, adult social care, mental health and parenting (Horne and Shirley 2009, p. 25). A key feature of this aspect of co-production is that this is a service that 'starts with the client and what they really want, rather than trying to fit them neatly into specific service packages or predetermined outcomes. It is about relationships, not about 'services'' (Boyle et al. 2010, p. 7).

Who Should Co-production Involve?

A fundamental feature of co-production is the use of 'lay partners', which refers to non-professionals such as service users, carers, stakeholders and the wider community. The original roots of co-production from the 1970s reinforce the importance of non-professional voices to its functioning. Firstly, the work of Elinor Ostrum and colleagues (Ostrum et al. 1978) observed that crime rates increased when local police started driving around in patrol cars instead of walking on the beat fighting crime, from which she coined the term 'co-production' as a way of explaining how co-operating and collaborating between the police and local people was essential to maintaining a safe community and reducing crime rates. This is because such co-operation and collaboration provided valuable information to the police about what was going on in the neighbourhood, information which only members of the local community could know and which enhanced the information held by the police. This highlights how non-professionals can offer new types of evidence on which to base practice, thereby providing fresh insights from the inside and meaning that the resulting knowledge is less likely to be inaccurate, unreliable and distorted (Glasby and Beresford 2006). This highlights the importance to co-production of collaboration between those in receipt of/affected by services and service providers.

How Should Co-production Work?

Following on from Ostrum and her colleagues' work, the civil rights lawyer Edgar Cahn in his book *No More Throwaway People: The Co-production Imperative* (Cahn 2000) drew on his own experiences of ill health and passive receipt of services during this time. In particular, it was 'the expectation that he couldn't, shouldn't or wouldn't do or decide anything for himself' which particularly struck Cahn (Paget 2014, p. 50). His subsequent development of the notion of timebanking arose from this experience of the wastefulness of the 'passive' service user and linked to notions of 'power redistribution, (between institutions and communities; national and local; professionals and people) and organisational development notions of distributed leadership, systems change, and networks' (Malby 2014, p. 7). What this suggests is that the current ways in which public services (and co-production usually refers only to public services, not the private market) are delivered is problematic, primarily because of their top-down approach, and wherein 'the conscious or unconscious maintenance of service users as passive recipients is not just a waste of their skills and time; it is also the reason why systemic change doesn't happen' (Boyle and Harris 2009, p. 11). More specifically, 'the central idea in co-production is that people who use services are hidden resources, not drains on the system, and that no service that ignores this resource can be efficient' (Boyle and Harris 2009, p. 11). For this reason, a key rationale for a shift towards co-production is to 'provide public services that rest on an equal and reciprocal relationship between professionals, people using services, their families and neighbours' (Boyle et al. 2010, p. 3).

▷ **Key Learning: Timebanking** The concept of timebanking is that services are provided based on the mutual exchange of skills rather than through the exchange of money. So, for example, a lawyer may provide legal services for free to an individual, and the time spent doing this is lodged with a time bank as credit. When this lawyer needs a service to be provided, for example a plumber, the credit built up in the time bank can be used to access services, without payment. The key point about time banks is that there is no hierarchy of services and skills, so the time provided by the lawyer is equally valued as the time provided by the plumber. So timebanking is a way to provide services without a specific emphasis on monetary capabilities.

Hatton (2016) has identified that one of the key issues when trying to incorporate co-production is the speed of actions required, wherein there is often an impetus to proceed at a very fast pace; he argues that co-production should proceed 'a little at a time', in order to enable participants to keep up to speed with the process. Additionally, Stevens (2010) highlighted incorporating the following features into practice as a key requirement for co-production to work:

- A strengths-based approach
- Reciprocity and mutuality
- Building support networks
- Limiting hierarchies and structures between professionals and non-professional
- Enabling co-production that facilitates services rather than simply delivers services
- The active rather than passive involvement in service design and delivery

Why Should Co-production Be Used?

The key rationale for co-production is the variety of positive outcomes that occur from it (Malby 2014). According to the SCIE (2015, p. 17), these benefits can be divided into two types:

- *Instrumental benefits*—the use of people's experience and expertise, which can contribute to a more efficient use of resources.
- *Intrinsic benefits*—an increased sense of social responsibility and citizenship and benefits to the wider community (sometimes defined as social capital), particularly to improved health and wellbeing.

In relation to instrumental benefits, there is a variety of evidence about the financial benefits that occur from co-production. For example, according to Boyle et al. (2010, p. 4), co-production provides 'savings of up to six times the investment made in new approaches'. Furthermore, they argue that evidence from the Family Nurse Partnership in the US shows that 'for every $1 invested, research shows that between

$2.88 and $5.70 is saved from future public expenditure across health, criminal justice and social support services, and the savings are greatest for those defined as 'high-risk" (Boyle et al. 2010, p. 8).

Additionally, Stevens (2010, p. 3) has observed that:

> there is considerable evidence that co-production helps to prevent people getting ill, increases their wellbeing and involves those who are seldom heard in society. Co-production is designed to prevent needs arising in the first place, by maintaining and improving the quality of people's lives and extending the opportunities as well as the capabilities of individuals and communities to look after themselves. It helps people to build stronger social networks, which supports wellbeing and makes communities more resilient.

Similar claims have been made in relation to the importance of co-production in research, wherein 'co-production is now also perceived as a solution to an argued 'relevance gap' in research and to the demands of 'impact" (Durose et al. 2011, p. 2), particularly in context of the significance of Impact to academic research for the Research Excellence Framework.

Additionally, according to Boyle and Harris (2009, p. 11), it is the lack of co-production which is at the core of increasing social needs, wherein:

> The fact that social needs continue to rise is not due to a failure to consult or conduct opinion research, or even a failure to find enough resources. It is due to a failure to ask people for their help and to use the skills they have. This is a key insight from the idea of co-production. Co-production theorists suggest that this is the forgotten engine of change that makes the difference between systems working and failing.

In relation to intrinsic benefits, the academic argument for co-production foregrounds two main arguments, as set out by Durose et al. (2011), the first being that research should not re-produce unequal power relations, but should be 'counter-hegemonic'. This means that research should be about enabling oppressed communities to challenge the dominance of more powerful interests and perspectives. This means that participation in knowledge creation and policy development through co-production should be seen as part of the wider citizenship rights accorded by society, including the right to social justice. Linked to this is the second argument that 'participation … is part of a more open and democratic process of knowledge production', as the 'legitimacy of decisions' based on research 'is undermined and weakened if the voice of affected people is absent in the making of those decisions' (Durose et al, 2011, p. 5). Boyle et al. (2010) have observed that co-production can also lead to a renewed emphasis on localism, wherein participants become more enthused to take responsibility for other services in their locality.

Instrumental and intrinsic benefits then illustrate some of the key understandings of co-production. However, such a clear division fails to recognise some of the common complexities within the process. Service users can also be carers and professionals; indeed, some of the authors within this book occupy two or even three roles. This intersectionality of lives and inherent assumptions about passivity of recipients fail to recognise the multiple roles which many people now inhabit.

▷   **Key Learning: Intersectionality** Intersectionality refers to the ways in which a person's social identities can overlap. The key point about intersectionality is that it highlights how individuals can experience oppression and/or discrimination in more than one of these identities, at the same time. So, for example, an individual can be characterised in numerous ways related to their gender, race, age, sexuality, marital status, class, religion and disability. These characterisations can overlap, meaning that it is possible to have more than one at the same time. Similarly, it is possible to experience discrimination which reflects this overlap, as, for example a disabled female may experience double discrimination both as a female and as a consequence of being disabled. A logical observation from this is that the more of these characteristics an individual or a group have, the more possible types of discrimination they are likely to experience. So, for example, a white, working-class, able-bodied male will very likely experience less discrimination than a black, working-class disabled male. This brings to our attention that discrimination can be experienced by individuals in multiple ways for some based on the multiple identities that they have.

What Are Some of the Challenges of Co-production?

There are a number of challenges that either limit the possibility of co-production or limit its potential benefits. According to Boyle et al. (2010), these can be grouped into four key themes:

- Funding and commissioning co-production activity.
- Generating evidence of value for people, professionals, funders and auditors.
- Taking successful approaches to scale.
- Developing the professional skills required to mainstream co-production approaches.

In terms of limiting the possibility, Durose et al. (2011, p. 4) have observed that at a most basic level, there is a question as to whether the timescales, pressures, politics and priorities of practitioners mean that while co-production may be an aim, its feasibility may not be as evident. Of particular relevance is the observation from Boyle et al. (2010) that co-production is often blocked because it poses a threat to the power of professionals. Linked to this is whether practitioners and professionals are truly committed to the notion of co-production or whether they see it as a hoop that has to be jumped through. This is particularly relevant when talking about co-production in research, where Durose et al. (2012, p. 4) question 'whether people can fully understand and estimate their own motivations and behaviour or can engage in analytical thinking on a topic merely on the basis of experience'. They also observe that co-production places significant changes and demands on individuals and communities, which calls into question both its viability and its true application in practice.

Additionally, Connor and Watts (2014) identify a number of 'barriers' which limit effective co-production in mental health, and these barriers could also be applied to other areas. They include issues such as:

- Stigma of service users—how other people perceive services and service user's low expectations for themselves.
- Money—not enough resources for service users to be involved in the planning and developing. (Often very small sums compared to the costs of providing services.)
- It is seen as time- and/or money-intensive, and there feels to be a lack of space and time to explore issues through co-production (system pressures).
- There is often a risk-averse culture within public sector organisations that is not conducive to co-production approaches.
- The current approach to commissioning and the culture of competition in public services.
- Lack of understanding that small and local solutions can be just as good (if not better) than large solutions.
- Many organisations do not have structures or systems designed to identify or make the most of the contribution different people could make if given the opportunity.
- Confusing/jargonistic language.
- The current culture of professional services is not conducive to effective co-production.
- There is no easy model of change to which co-production is seen to contribute.

Additionally, Morton and Paice (2016) identified the following characteristics in 'lay partners' as the most important:

- Lived experience as a patient and/or carer.
- Experience of working at a strategic level, in any field.
- Commitment to a shared vision—not single-issue champions.
- Willingness to challenge professionals.
- Ability to listen, weigh arguments and help reach a consensus.
- Diverse connections within the community.
- Time to read papers, attend meetings and communicate.

These are key characteristics which would be essential for effective co-production; however, this does require a range of skills, articulation and confidence in order for a service user to be fully engaged in co-production. Unless opportunities for training and personal development are offered to those people taking part, such involvement can be painful, ineffective and exclusionary.

Similarly, Sherwood (2013, p. 8) identified the three key barriers to co-production as staff culture, how services are measured and the value of them accounted for, and the challenge of commissioning (which refers to deciding who should provide services). Another issue relates to who can reasonably be expected to be involved in co-production, wherein the Equal Citizens Services (2011, p. 14) observes that:

without a collective critical mass, to guide, train and support, only the very able, white, middle-class had the personal resources to succeed. Organisations of disabled people in particular, in collaboration with all those engaged in the caring relationship, in my view, must be the critical mass at the heart of the personalisation agenda.

This is a point that has become more relevant in more recent years, as with the shift within successive Conservative-led governments to an emphasis on notions of 'freedom'… 'there is less emphasis on the wider, emancipatory aspects of personalisation, as the focus tightens to a more reactive, individualistic perspective' (Lymbery 2012, p. 786). Linked to this is the fact that it is sometimes not possible to square the emphasis on choice within co-production with the financial pressures on public expenditure to cut costs in social care, especially within the context of austerity (Hamilton et al. 2017).

Perhaps an important overarching point to make in relation to this is the observation that despite the emphasis within new legislation towards co-production noted at the beginning of the chapter, there is actually no legal requirement for organisations to co-produce (Pieroudis et al. 2019).

How Is Co-production Applied to This Book?

Having outlined the who, which, what, why and how of co-production in general, we now detail how co-production is applied to this book. As detailed in Chap. 1, the book originates from the writing of a previous book that has one chapter that is co-produced with a service user. This is a chapter in Sealey (2015) written by Simon Heng. We realised from the feedback provided on this chapter that there was a need for a broader sharing of service users and carer lived experiences.

The book is the outcome of this discussion which led to collaboration between the Universities of Worcester and Birmingham. Both of these Universities have established and recognised service user and carers groups which aim to integrate the voices of those with lived experience within an academic context and vice versa. These groups include carers, mental health survivors, people with long-term physical disabilities, care leavers, survivors of domestic violence and people with dementia. These service user and carer groups have a strong presence across teaching and learning, recruitment, selection, research and consultancy, to genuinely enhance the student learning experience and help bring about new cultures of care. Members have undergone in-house training and are well versed in protocols and research ethics while remaining true to their unique and passionate positions as service users and carers. We initially approached people within these groups who would be interested in involvement in the book. We also drew on service users and carers we knew personally.

Where service users and carers agreed to detail their lived experiences, the editors worked closely with them to enable them to do so, with the key focus being on enabling them to do so in their own way. This included discussions, reading of draft scripts and answering specific questions. Service users and carers were encouraged to detail their lived experiences in their own terms and in their words, with editors providing prompts and/or requesting clarification where necessary. Where necessary, accounts were edited by the authors, but this always occurred with the explicit consent and co-operation of service users and carers. Consequently, all of the chapters reflect the outcome of interaction over a period of months rather than a once-in-time meeting as per the usual academic process. This enabled the mutual exchange of lived experiences typical of co-production rather than a unidirectional research process. Additionally, this also meant that building relationships has been a key part of this process.

We have further tried to reflect the co-production nature of the book by naming the co-producers as authors of their chapters, which does not always happen in academic writing or research. The majority of co-producers were happy to do this, although this was not always possible for all chapters for reasons of confidentially and safety. Pseudonyms were again therefore discussed and mutually identified. We hope that this is one small but significant point that truly emphasises that this book, while not perfect, has been working with services users and carers in a co-production way at its heart and is stronger as a result.

Summary

In this chapter, we have discussed and analysed what the concept of co-production is, in order to explain how it relates to this book. We detailed the increasing trend towards co-production over the last 20 years, which highlights its contemporary relevance to policy and practice.

Following on from this the chapter then discussed when co-production could be used and noted that co-production benefits from a lack of specific definition to what it is, meaning that while it can be adapted and used as required, it is best suited to those types of services which are 'relational' in nature, which covers most social policy provision. The original roots of co-production reinforce the importance of non-professional voices to its functioning, as non-professionals can offer new types of evidence on which to base practice, thereby providing fresh insights from the inside and meaning that the resulting knowledge is less likely to be inaccurate, unreliable and distorted. This provides a clear rationale for the use of co-production in this book.

Finally, the chapter considered some of the some of the benefits and challenges that co-production presents. We identified that co-production presents the possibility for both instrumental and intrinsic benefits which can have outcomes beyond its stated aims. There are a number of challenges that either limit the possibility of co-production or limit the potential benefits, which are important to be aware of when working within the co-production framework.

References

H. Bown, T. Raines, *Co-production Involving and Led by Older People*, An Evidence and Practice Review (National Development Team for Inclusion, Bath, 2014)
D. Boyle, M. Harris, *The Challenge of Co-production* (New Economics Foundation, London, 2009)

D. Boyle, J. Slay, N. Stephens, *Public Services Inside Out* (New Economics Foundation, London, 2010)

K. Bunning, R. Alder, L. Proudman, et al., Co-production and pilot of a structured interview using Talking Mats® to survey the television viewing habits and preferences of adults and young people with learning disabilities. Br. J. Learn. Disabil. **45**, 1–11 (2017)

E. Cahn, *No More Throwaway People: The Co-production Imperative* (Essential Books, London, 2000)

C. Connor, R. Watts, Co-production and mental health – discussion in Scotland (2014). Available via http://www.gettingtheresds.com/wp-content/uploads/2014/07/MH-and-co-production-in-Scotland-1-July-.pdf. Accessed 23 June 2017

Department of Health, Care and support statutory guidance (2017). Available via https://www.gov.uk/government/publications/care-act-statutory-guidance/care-and-support-statutory-guidance. Accessed 23 June 2017

C. Durose, Y. Beebeejaun, J. Rees, et al., *Towards Co-production in Research with Communities* (AHRC, Swindon, 2011)

C. Durose, Y. Beebeejaun, J. Rees, J. Richardson, L. Richardson, *Towards Co-production in Research with Communities*. Swindon: AHRC (2012)

C. Durose, C. Needham, C. Mangan, J. Rees, Generating good enough evidence for co-production. Evidence and Policy **13**(1), 135–51 (2017)

Equal Citizen Services, Co-production: as easy as baking a cake! (2011). Available via http://www.equalcitizen.co.uk/documents/CAFco-productionMarch2011.pdf. Accessed 23 June 2017

J. Glasby, P. Beresford, Who knows best? Evidence-based practice and the service user contribution. Crit. Soc. Policy **26**(1), 268–284 (2006)

L. Hamilton, S. Mesa, E. Hayward, et al., There's a lot of places I'd like to go and things I'd like to do': the daily living experiences of adults with mild to moderate intellectual disabilities during a time of personalised social care reform in the United Kingdom. Disabil. Soc. **32**(3), 287–307 (2017). https://doi.org/10.1080/09687599.2017.1294049

K. Hatton, A critical examination of the knowledge contribution service user and carer involvement brings to social work education. Soc. Work Educ. (2016). https://doi.org/10.1080/02615479.2016.1254769

M. Horne, T. Shirley, *Co-production in Public Services: A New Partnership with Citizens* (Cabinet Office Strategy Unit, London, 2009)

M. Lymbery, Social work and personalisation. Br. J. Soc. Work **42**, 783–792 (2012)

R. Malby, *Co-producing health – a briefing* (University of Leeds: Centre for Innovation in Health Management, 2014). Available via http://www.cihm.leeds.ac.uk/wp-content/uploads/2014/03/Co-Producing-Health-Briefing-October-2014.pdf. Accessed 23 June 2017

M. Morton, E. Paice, Co-production at the strategic level: co-designing an integrated care system with Lay Partners in North West London, England. Int. J. Integr. Care **16**(2), 1–4 (2016)

National Co-production Critical Friends, National co-production critical friends' shared definition: January 2013 (2013). Available via http://api.ning.com/files/A1Qs8*3Ts4xAGEMdfQiEa21YSR8x1BKfFawmG5tQcDpcf2gBlmHBfL82ChkhblrDHzf3juE9cRk5LCFrxMfaM3LYxgOh4uUv/Shareddefinition.pdf. Accessed 23 June 2017

C. Needham, Personalization: from day centres to community hubs? Crit. Soc. Policy **34**(1), 90–108 (2013)

K. Oliver, A. Kothari, N. Mays, The dark side of co-production: do the costs outweigh the benefits for health research? Health Res. Policy Syst. **17**, 33 (2019)

E. Ostrum, R. Parks, G. Whitaker, et al., The public service process: a framework for analyzing police services, in *Evaluating Alternative Law Enforcement Policies*, ed. by R. Baker, A. Meyer, (DC Heath, Lexington, 1978), pp. 65–73

A. Paget, Pupil power. Every Child Journal 4.6 (2014). Available via www.Teachingtimes.com

K. Pieroudis, M. Turner, P. Fleischmann, *Breaking Down the Barriers to Co-production* (Social Care Institute for Excellence, London, 2019)

SCIE, *Co-production in Social Care: What It Is and How to Do It* (Social Care Institute for Excellence, London, 2015)

C. Sealey, *Social Policy Simplified* (Palgrave Macmillan, Basingstoke, 2015)

C. Sherwood, Co-production – involving citizens in government beyond the state, in *Beyond the State: Mobilising and Co-producing with Communities – Insights for Policy and Practice*, ed. by C. Durose, J. Justice, C. Skelcher, (Institute of Local Government Studies, University of Birmingham, 2013), pp. 7–8

Social Care Institute for Excellence, *Attitudes Towards Co-production. Findings from SCIE's Survey as Part of National Co-production Week 2019* (Social Care Institute for Excellence, London, 2019)

L. Stevens, *Joining the Dots: How All the System Elements Can Connect to Drive Personalisation and Co-production, Incorporating Individual Social and Community Capacity* (New Economics Foundation, London, 2010)

Experiences of Care Services in Childhood and Beyond

Francesca Crozier-Roche and Joy Fillingham

This chapter presents Francesca Crozier-Roche's personal experiences of having her child being made the subject of a care order, under the *Children Act 1989*. This outlines her experiences of having a child taken into compulsory care, negotiating with children's social care, encountering multiple assessments, the court process, challenging the decisions and eventually having the child returned from the care system. This is a lengthy and complex process and will relate Francesca's personal experiences and insights of how and why this occurred. The chapter will also consider the impacts that this has had on both the parent and child. It will conclude by outlining some possible improvements that could be undertaken when a local authority initiates and undertakes a care order.

The main aims of the chapter are to:

1. Outline the procedures employed within the care order process.
2. Consider the implications of the processes on a personal level.
3. Detail improvements which could be made to the care order process for parents and children.

Who Am I?

My name is Francesca Crozier-Roche, I am 31 years of age and currently reside on the outskirts of Birmingham with my two children. I am a qualified JNC Youth and Community Practitioner as well as a service user working with the University of

F. Crozier-Roche (✉)
Birmingham, UK

J. Fillingham
Department of Social Work and Social Care, University of Birmingham, Birmingham, UK
e-mail: j.fillingham@bham.ac.uk

C. Sealey et al. (eds.), *Social Policy, Service Users and Carers*,
https://doi.org/10.1007/978-3-030-69876-8_3

Birmingham. I am a single mother of two children of which I am a full-time carer as both children reside with me. My youngest is a 9-month-old daughter and oldest a 14-year-old son, who has additional emotional and behavioural needs, autism and attention deficit hyperactivity disorder (ADHD).

My son was made subject to a care order by the local authority (LA) from the age of five. This means that he was in their care until the age of 11 where he was returned to my full-time care on 1 August 2016. The LA became involved with our family due to a report being made to the school by my son that I had smacked him. The school acted upon their safeguarding procedures immediately and informed the LA, who removed my child from school for examinations to take place at the hospital, before informing myself. After investigations were made around the allegation, it was decided that my child could be returned to my care, if there was a working agreement in place to state that my partner at the time was not to reside at the property or visit the property. This was due to the significant domestic violence incidents and the injuries I sustained that had occurred the weekend prior to the report being made to the school by my son.

> **Key Learning: Care Order** A care order is a legal order a local authority can apply for under the *Children Act 1989* if they are concerned about the welfare of a child. The key principle of this *Act* is that the welfare of the child must always be the paramount consideration. The *Act* encourages partnership working with parents and seeks to keep children at home wherever possible. If staying at home with support is not safe for a child, then a care order will be applied for through the courts and, if successful, will mean that the LA has primary parental responsibility for the child, rather than the parent or previous primary carer. For example, when a care order has been made, it is the decision of the LA where the child will live. Parents and other designated people are entitled to a reasonable amount of contact. The child, the parent, the local authority or any person with parental responsibility can apply to 'discharge', i.e. cancel, the care order by demonstrating that there is a significant change in circumstances since the care order was granted. Children living under a care order are typically termed 'looked after children' (see Chap. 9).

Relevant Background Information

It is necessary and relevant to provide a bit of background building up to the event. Growing up me and my mother had a turbulent relationship and struggled with emotional warmth and communication. In my teenage years, I was a somewhat rebellious teenager and craved attention and affection. My biological father was not present throughout my life growing up, and my stepfather and I had a very damaging relationship. This included enforcing feelings of abandonment and rejection by telling me that 'I was not his daughter' and being verbally, emotionally and occasionally physically abusive towards me.

At the age of 15, I lived with my mother and sister in Derby, as my mother and stepfather had separated at this point. I followed the wrong crowds, and I engaged in underage drinking and drug-taking for acceptance from my peers, which quickly spiralled out of control into addiction using 'harder' drugs. Looking back on the younger me, I see now that the sense of rejection, abandonment and feeling of not being wanted by my mother and biological father led me to search for these feelings to be provided from my peers. I was engaging in physical and sexual contact with men that were a lot older than myself, and the life I led was completely separate from my home-life. As a young girl, I found it hard to manage both lives and would be abusive towards my mother when in the family home. My mother reached out to social services for support in managing my behaviour; however, due to us living in a nice home, my mother was turned away and offered nothing. I would not be able to say that this would have made any difference in either of our lives at the time, but without the offer of any intervention, the repercussions speak for themselves. Due to my behaviour at the time and my mother having another child to safeguard, I was asked to leave the family home. However, being 15 at the time, I was classed as 'a minor' and therefore I had to have a social worker assigned to myself, which leads me to question why the intervention was not offered in the first place. The only engagement I had with the social worker would be for an hour once a week; they would come and sign for my accommodation acting as my guarantor and take me food shopping.

The first property that I was ever housed in as a young girl was a warden-controlled hostel (shared accommodation), with staff present in office hours. There were several bedsits within the building that were occupied by residents who were of a wide range of ages, genders, race, religion, creed and so on. I believe this was a tipping point in my life around the age of 16; I became 'hard to reach', being missed by services due to lack of communication and time available and the intensity of their caseloads. Due to my breaking rules within the supported accommodation, I was required to move several times from the age of 15–18 making it hard for professionals to keep track of me. All the accommodation that I resided in during this period was supported, due to me being classed as a vulnerable young person and my needs at the time. I frequently visited services such as GP's, sexual health clinics, police/domestic violence officers and drug workers. However, due to the influences and pressures, my engagement was minimal and very sporadic.

▷   **Key Learning: Supported Accommodation/Housing** Supported accommodation/housing refers to housing that is provided with specialist support and/or care services as part of their tenancy agreement. This can include support and care with health needs, including mental health, drug and alcohol use, managing benefits and debt, developing daily living skills and accessing education, training and employment. The aim of supported accommodation is to give individuals the opportunity to live as independently as possible with help provided when needed. Arrangements can be long term as a way to enable people who need ongoing support to live independently or short term to help people develop the emotional and practical skills needed to move into unsupported accommodation/housing. Types of supported accommodation/housing can include hostels, sheltered accommodation, refuges and housing blocks.

Since leaving my mother's home I always had a relationship with a man. There was a pattern very evident to other people, that all the men were several years older than me. Growing up, reflecting over time and engaging in workshops, programmes and training courses has enabled me to identify the red flags and signs with these types of relationships. They have also helped me to identify that I was searching for a father figure, and by doing this I engaged in very manipulative, controlling and abusive relationships. From the age of 15, I entered into domestic abuse relationships.

The reason for me linking up with such men was that I yearned for the boundaries and discipline, and thought by being in these types of relationships that they were normal and that it was love. It just shows my level of understanding and immaturity at the time and the way I processed social interactions and relationships. My only sense of coping strategies for stress at these times was to self-harm in whatever way was available to me, including eating disorders, cutting, overdosing, sexual intercourse, drug-taking and drinking. When I did engage with services and highlight these challenges, there was little to no offer of help. I feel this is where barriers in communication arose, due to the lack of relationship built between myself and the professionals and that no clear lines of communication were established, which then contributed to a lack of trust.

At 17, I became pregnant with my son. Due to domestic violence between my son's father and myself, I moved into a women's and babies' refuge. Again, there were no red flags to me at this time of the abuse I had encountered, and I defined the behaviours as normal and caring. Therefore, I quickly fell back into the relationship as my child was due to be born. I moved into my son's father's mother's house after my son was born, but it became apparent that this relationship was turbulent, and again domestic violence began. Police were called to the property several times, but there were no further actions or follow-ups by social services at this time. I do feel that engagement at this time would have been beneficial as I had undiagnosed postnatal depression for 3 years after my son was born. There was no support in relation to this issue. This was not identified until moving to Birmingham much later due to no engagement from services and me being unaware of what it was. Derby City Council allocated my son and I a house a few months after my son was born and decided this would be a fresh start without my child's father.

There were a few serious domestic violent incidences at my property; however I acted appropriately and through the correct channels in order to end the repetitive cycles. Looking back, it is clear to me that this was another major turning point in my life. I was tired of the life I was leading, I was tired of the suffering, tired of not knowing what to do or where to go. I lacked knowledge, I lacked direction, and I lacked support. However, I was gaining self-awareness, hope and self-respect, and I wanted to engage. I reached out to local charities and support groups in the city at the time but again was offered a sign-up but no further support.

I became involved in another relationship, and my new partner, my son and I moved to Birmingham just before my son turned two. On the outside we led a somewhat 'normal' life; my partner worked a full-time job, and I worked three part-time jobs locally in the neighbourhood and attended college full-time doing an access to higher education course. In reality, we were both functioning addicts and the cracks began appearing. My partner was 20 years my senior. Again, I saw no red flags or warning signs, but 2 years into our relationship, the domestic violence began. This meant that I was experiencing <u>domestic abuse,</u> <u>mental ill health</u> and <u>substance misuse</u> at the same time. The incidences between myself and my partner were sporadic, although when they occurred, they were serious. Our names began being highlighted to services.

> **Key Learning: Domestic Abuse, Mental Ill Health and Substance Misuse—The 'Toxic Trio'** There has been an increasing recognition, particularly within social work, that issues of domestic abuse and or sexual violence, mental ill health and substance misuse can often be occurring concurrently within households. This is often termed the 'toxic trio', to illustrate that when these three things occur concurrently, the negative outcomes from each of these is intensified. For example, research shows that when the toxic trio occurs, children in such families are at greater risk of harm to their health, safety and well-being (Middleton and Hardy 2014). However, this notion of the toxic trio is not universally accepted, with some arguing that its use is stigmatising and can make it hard to discern what is the main problem within families suffering from these issues (Hardy 2018).

What Were the Specific Circumstances That Led to the Care Order?

In 2010, there was a serious domestic incident between myself and my partner one weekend. The injuries were becoming harder to hide to the school when taking and collecting my son. I make no excuses for the events that would unfold the Monday following this incident and take full accountability. The Monday following the incident, I was getting my son ready for school when he would not get ready. I made a choice to smack the bottom of his leg to encourage him to put on his shoes. I did not see this as abuse, nor did I use unnecessary force. However, my son arrived at school that morning and disclosed this had happened to a teacher. I was unaware of the disclosure until a social worker contacted me to inform me that my child had been taken out of school to a hospital for examination and that I was to attend the school for a meeting. This is when a number of services such as children's services, police, Women's Aid, family law courts, solicitors/barristers/judges, GP's, psychiatrists, psychologists, councillors, foster carers, drug charities, training groups and courses and *Narcotics Anonymous* became involved in our family, and the proceedings for my child to be permanently removed began. I felt that none of the professionals involved contributed to helping us, as my story demonstrates no interventions had been made throughout my whole life or my child's life until this point; then all of a sudden, they were all involved without warning. Professionals did not collaborate or share information with each other, so this process certainly did not help; it only made my journey to get my son back a lot harder. I had to meet with them all and seek to understand a complicated process, where no parts of the services appeared to relate to each other. Therefore, I also had to micro-manage all services and communicate information between the parties involved.

As well as the meeting with the school, I also had to attend the police station and be cautioned under interview about smacking my son's leg. I needed to be back to collect my child and therefore chose not to have a solicitor present in the interview. While under caution I admitted to smacking my son on the bottom of his leg without reasonable force, and they cautioned me for 'wilful assault on a minor'. I regret not having a solicitor present, and as I am now a JNC Youth and Community practitioner, this is something that will always be shown on my DBS. This therefore has a massive impact not only on me as an individual but on my child, my career, engagement with vulnerable children or adults and areas I am sure I am yet to encounter.

After a few months engaging with the LA, it was recommended that myself and my son were to enter a <u>mother and baby unit</u> in order for my parental engagement, skills and approaches to be assessed. I believe that this would have helped me and my son because then they would have been able to monitor my parenting. This could have resulted in vastly different experiences for us both, which would have been more beneficial to us all. We also would have been removed from a domestically abusive relationship and received the support that was required, rather than professionals coming into our home without offering any support. I also feel that my child's behaviour and emotional needs would have been picked up a lot quicker while in this placement, rather than being delayed and assumptions based on the opinion of one social worker, who was not qualified to have made this decision.

▶ **Key Learning: Mother and Baby Units** Mother and baby units exist to provide specialist care and treatment for mothers with their babies when they are encountering problems such as mental distress domestic violence and/or substance misuse. These units provide inpatient assessment and treatment for mothers and babies, enabling mothers to receive treatment they need without separating them from their babies or children. Outpatient assessments are also available within such facilities to ensure the women are able to effectively care for their children once the period within the unit has ended.

However, it quickly became apparent that the option of a mother and baby unit was not going to be possible due to the unavailability of these placements in 2010.

As there was no parallel plan in place, the LA decided the best course of action would be to permanently remove my son from our family home. From the time of the LA decision being made, to the process of it going to court and a final decision being made was no longer than 6 months. I felt this limited any possibility of our needs being met and was unrealistic to all involved, as the timescale of recommendations that were made for things that I needed to do to enable my child to remain with me were longer than the 6 months timescale of the legal process, and therefore were unachievable from the outset.

What Was My Experience of the Care Order Proceedings?

As a vulnerable 23-year-old young mother with no support networks, I quickly became overwhelmed with professionals and the processes and decisions being made for my child's and my future. The legal process I went through was a shambles. My solicitor from the outset was not prepared to advocate for me, and looking back now, I wish I had the knowledge I do now in order to represent myself. I did not know what was happening at the time, and I did not understand how it all happened and so quickly. I didn't understand their reasoning and also did not understand how they could constantly change the goal posts. From the outset of the legal proceedings there was never any option that children's services would not get the outcome they desired, even though I do not feel it was in the best interest of my child. To reach the outcome which we can see today, I have shown patience, commitment and professionalism even though I did not become a professional until 2018. I believe that the legal process is a shambles, and I can relate with so many other parents, carers, guardians and foster carers that agree the courts are set up to agree with children's services. The most frustrating thing was standing in court and hearing the judge make many inaccurate statements about my case and watching my solicitor not explore these or advocate on my behalf. It was a diminishing process and one I had to endure alone. I was not offered any support, representations or support networks. During hearings I was made to wait in the foyer with my abusive ex-partner and their current partner; it was intimidating and unpleasant to say the least. So, while taking me to court for not safeguarding myself or my child, the professionals were also not safeguarding me in any way.

I felt like the world was happening around me, but I had no control over anything or anyone. I had little to no support networks apart from a long-term relationship that was domestically violent. Regardless of the nature of this relationship, this man and my son were my only support network, as at the time I was estranged from my family. All these factors were used against myself in the final hearing. Looking back my life had spiralled out of control, and I could not see nor did I know a way out of the suffering that was happening. I lacked self-awareness, knowledge and confidence at this point in my life as I was oppressed by my situation and the systems that were supposed to support me, but instead were controlling me, and this impacted upon my trust and engagement with professionals.

The issues I had in these areas resulted in me being unable to pinpoint or identify risky behaviours that were around me and therefore around my child. This meant I was unable to safeguard myself or my child. At this point in my life, I was full of anger, as I didn't feel heard by professionals nor did I feel I was given the chance to keep my child in my full-time care, as previously mentioned the recommendations that were made were unattainable within the timescale required. I felt like a shadow in my own experience. It was required that there should be six supervised contacts per year, and this process was due to last 12 months; however it actually lasted 3 years as a result of constant changes in social workers.

What Were My Experiences of Living Under the Care Order?

When the LA became involved with our family it was recommended that I attend several courses such as pregnancy and parenting courses, baby to child development course, additional needs courses, self-awareness and anger management. At the time these courses were offered they were not beneficial to my healthcare needs, as they did not aid the process of having my child returned in any way. However, I do believe that these courses were beneficial to our care in the long run by equipping me with the awareness and ability to manage child/children appropriately and having almost a toolkit of techniques to help in any challenging situation.

There were additional financial pressures in order to attend these courses that were never considered by any professionals at the time. When your child is removed, your income goes to being a one person level of income which is around £62 a week. Not only was this to live on for the whole week, that is paying bills, food and so on, this also had to cover my travel costs to contact centres, training courses that I was recommended to go on and meetings which were never located in the town I lived, so therefore I had to travel. None of this was taken into consideration, and due to these commitments, I could not work. This process therefore put me under complete financial strain. Professionals do not consider these circumstances or costs to the parent, and they expect you to attend or they would say that you are not consistent and therefore are detrimental to a child's emotional needs. So again, the service user is being set up to fail.

I have also learnt that it is crucial to educate ourselves on what our rights are as parents and the responsibilities that we must undertake for the child's needs to be met, as before this happened to us as a family, I was completely unaware of the basics of the law and the *Children Act 1989* and our parental responsibilities. The courses that I have engaged in have taught me that keeping clear open lines of communication with your child/children is so important to their emotional and physical wellbeing.

▶   **Key Learning: Parental Responsibility**   Parental responsibility is a
defined legal term in the *Children Act 1989*. It identifies the right, duties
powers and responsibilities that the adult with parental responsibility
has towards the child rather than the adult's rights over their child.

In practice, this refers to the fact that certain major decisions about
the upbringing of the child cannot be taken without those with parental
responsibility having a say on the decision. This includes matters like
the child's schooling, religion, name, medical treatment, overseas
holidays and accessing medical records. Where agreement cannot be
reached on what should happen, the courts are required to make the
appropriate decision. The key point about specifically identifying these
as issues where agreement is required is to emphasise the importance of
these to the wellbeing of the child.

A mother automatically has parental responsibility, and where
parents are married at the time of the birth of the child, then the father
also automatically has parental responsibility. Where the parents are not
married, then the father must either be registered on the birth certificate
or apply to have parental responsibility. No one else has automatic
parental responsibility, but it can be applied for. Where a child is looked
after, parental responsibility can be shared between the parents or can
rest solely with the local authority.

My son was placed in long-term foster care when he was 5 with a view that he
would remain in long-term foster care and not be able to return home until over the
age of 18. My son was returned to my full-time care at the age of 11 after being in
full-time foster care for 6 years. I believe that this was because I never stopped
working towards getting my son back, and I educated myself on the policies and
procedures that were breached and not completed. I learnt the processes and made
sure I held professionals accountable, every time there was an injustice or a professional did not adhere to the requirements that had been placed upon them. I began
holding everyone accountable for their actions—I logged complaints, I reported to
managers, I plagued my independent reviewer, I attended everything they wanted
me to and so much more, so there could be no suggestion that I was not undertaking
every element required of me. I put the professionals under pressure like they had
done to me. I made them see my qualities and made them see the changes that had
occurred in my approach. I was commended by the judge when the care order was
revoked in 2018; she stated that in her entire service of over 28 years, she had never
witnessed such dedication, passion and commitment. Although my son returned
home to my full-time care in 2016, he remained on a Placement with Parents Plan
for another 2 years before the court revoked the care order in 2018; the delay in this

procedure was due to changes in social workers. Currently, there are no services or professionals involved with our family, although my son remains on an <u>Education, Health and Care Plan</u> at school due to his additional emotional and behavioural needs as previously mentioned.

▶   **Key Learning: Placement with Parents Plan** A Placement with Parents Plan is a legal requirement for local authorities to put a plan in place for children who are returned to their parent's care after being in local authority provisions arranged under a <u>care plan</u>. The aim of the plan is to monitor and support the parent for a period of time, lasting no more than 6 months, towards agreed improvements in care with the overall aim of fully withdrawing the care plan so that the child can fully return to the care of the parent. Where the improvements in care are not met, the local authority can take the child back into care.

How Did My Social Worker Relationship Impact on My Experiences?

Our lead social worker changed around seven times in a six-year period. That means that seven times an assessment or process had to begin again due to the lack in communication and 'handover', and meant that the present worker had to rely on the case notes from 2010 to set a scene, instead of identifying the current circumstances and recognising what changes had already been made. Seven times a mother and child had to endure being reminded of the failings, oppression and being assessed, all while being permanently removed from each other. Seven times a relationship had to be re-established between ourselves and the worker. All of this was expected to be completed alongside living a 'normal life'. Being a parent separated from their child can be a harrowing experience and highly emotional. Processes that are currently in place for families, parents and carers do not consider the parental emotional wellbeing as well as that of the child. Yet the expectation of services is that that family member, carer or parent is to be stable and emotionally available for the child through this process.

My child's behavioural needs were not explored until after he was placed in the full-time care of children's services. I believe that the judgement of a social worker who was not qualified in this area definitely contributed to the delay in this diagnosis. The social worker that intervened in the domestic violence incident, resulting in my partner and I separating, used the home environment as the explanation for my child's behaviour at the time. I do believe this contributed to him being removed and placed into care as children's services were trying to state that this behaviour was solely due to him witnessing domestic violence. However, when eventually explored by professionals in this field, he was diagnosed with <u>ADHD</u> and autism.

Following this diagnosis around the age of 6, professionals had the wish for him to be medicated as soon as he was diagnosed. This is something that I strongly disagreed with, due to undertaking research into the studies of the drugs used and recognising that both his father and I had had experiences of addiction. After a lengthy battle (around 12 months) advocating for my son not to be medicated, our views were considered, and it was decided that medication was not in the best interest for my child. I had to attend several meetings throughout this timescale and challenge professionals' opinions on this matter. I had to share studies that I was aware of and literally educate the professionals I was surrounded by at the time to widen their views on the matter. The kind of professionals that were involved in these meetings were social workers, independent reviewers, teachers from schools, family support workers, GP's, foster carers and so on. As a mother this felt ridiculous, not only was I fighting to change my life to get my son back full-time, I was now having to spend a lot of my time researching and educating others on facts surrounding the medications that are dispensed. I do not feel this was appropriate nor needed for myself or my son throughout this period. I do appreciate that these drugs do help with some children's conditions; however, it is imperative that equity is shown in these circumstances and all options are considered before prescribing drugs to an immature mind.

When my child was returned to my full-time care, it was stated that he should remain on the care order for another 6 months before returning to court to revoke the order. However, due to our social worker going on long-term sickness leave, this was delayed for 2 years until 2018, when we returned to court to revoke the care order. During these 2 years after my child had been returned home, we did not receive any mandatory spot visits and/or aftercare from social services.

After my son was returned to my full-time care in 2016 on a <u>Placement with Parents Plan</u>, it was said that the timescale for this was to be no longer than 6 months. Our social worker went on long-term leave sick, and the manager had also changed within the same period, so this process took just over 2 years. This is a prime example of how the instability for the child of these delays has massively contributed to the child's additional social, emotional and psychological needs. Even at this present moment in time after the final hearing, although social workers have not been involved for 7 months, they have still yet to give us any finalised paperwork, they have not handed over my son's identification (birth certificate, passport, savings accounts), and we have not had a closure meeting. Again, this highlights the frustrations in the current fractured services we are having to endure as a society.

Due to my son being on an <u>Education Health and Care plan</u>, I am in contact with the school on a weekly basis. My child's education is of paramount concern to myself—making sure he is offered the correct support to meet his needs while at school and being confident enough to advocate on his behalf, as a professional, carer and parent. Due to our past experiences, I feel confident enough to hold the school accountable should any matters arise, as it is now the responsibility of the parents/carers to oversee an education plan for their children.

What Have I Learnt from the Process?

Over time I have been able to recognise barriers in communication between myself and professionals. I believe the most resistance comes from me advocating for myself and the child and always equipping myself with the knowledge of mine or the child's rights. Whenever I have not/do not feel heard, then I act upon this by following procedures and holding those individuals that are responsible, accountable. This can be frustrating and time-consuming at times. I currently attend a health clinic for my daughter to be checked and weighed or seek any advice from healthcare professionals regarding her developmental stage needs. As previously mentioned, I liaise with the school frequently, but other than these services, I am not engaged with any healthcare services, nor do I foresee any changes to my healthcare needs within the future. Throughout my life I have been referred to numerous healthcare services, and while I did engage with some along the way, most of the interventions and services that were offered to me were at a time in my life when I was not stable and my life was unmanageable, limiting my engagement with the services and bringing about more challenges.

I feel over time I have become a more effective mother and have taken on board the issues raised by professionals. However, the level of scrutiny and years of assessment were seemingly based on the actions of the first ever case notes and never the current situation. There should have been the focus on the current situation due to the amount of change that took place over the eight-year period.

Whilst my initial actions throughout this process was not seeking the help and support of services or professionals which may have assisted me, for many years now I have been willing to engage with services and professionals to change my situation, but have experienced so much resistance and delays along the way. There are far too many incidences to mention that will have permanent and lasting impacts upon my son and myself and our relationship as a whole. We shall overcome these moments. However, you cannot help but sit and think that if this much change happened over 6 years, then was the permanent removal of the child really in the best interest of the child? In my opinion of our process as a parent and a professional, I would in certainty say NO, as the results speak for themselves.

The biggest lesson that I as a parent has had to endure in the process of being separated from my child is that regardless of how painful, we must apply Goffman's (1956) theory of presentation of self, meaning applying different masks in different settings. This helped me throughout the process. At the beginning of the process, I used to attend the meetings as a parent, and all the processes, criticisms, and scrutiny emotionally and physically broke my heart. Due to all this having such a massive impact on my emotional wellbeing, I was unable to advocate for myself or my child, and I struggled with communicating clearly and therefore was perceived as 'unstable'. When I learnt the theory of presentation of self, and I began attending the meetings as a professional, I completely detached myself from my emotions. I occasionally came across as cold. However due to my presentation and ability to adapt my language to meet other professionals, at this time I began being heard and others to take me seriously. Barriers can arise when new professionals are brought on board to work alongside yourself, as before meeting you in the first instance they would read your file which is based around the first encounters with yourself at the beginning of your journey. This means that progress or change is not the first thing noted, although it is actually the negative perceptions and assumptions based on the situation at its worst crisis point years ago, rather than assessing my actions and the welfare of my child(ren) now.

Regardless of the situations at hand, every individual should be treated with an element of humanitarianism. Even when reflecting on the situation now and taking accountability and fault for the situation, I still suffer from retriggering trauma of anger and frustration due to the lack of interventions offered before long-term care was decided. I also certainly still hold an element of injustice due to the fact that the only intervention that was offered was pulled away through no fault of our own. Even more so now because my child is back in my full-time care, which confirms to me that I always had the ability to look after my child; I just needed guidance and support to change certain oppressions that were present in my life at the time. The time that has passed cannot be given back to myself or my child, or the traumatic experiences that have occurred having permanent impacts upon us as individuals. My overall point of view on the services that are available to 'support families and children' is that they are severely fractured. Although the systems are damaged, this is what we as individuals, families and professionals must work with. We must equip ourselves with the knowledge of our rights and the procedures, and we must as individuals advocate for ourselves and hold professionals accountable when there are failings.

What Could Be Done to Improve Services?

Where do you even begin on this vast question? I believe that this country and services do have a lot to improve on. Partnership working, communication and collaboration between services and agencies are a must; it is unfair to expect parents, carers, grandparent and foster carers to facilitate such approaches while undergoing such stressful circumstances. I feel that, although we have mandatory review meetings to assess the situation of the children and the carers involved, we could adopt processes from the American care system in the UK and hold these within a court arena. I am aware all services are pressured, but to be honest I feel this is because multi-agency approaches are not working. I feel that if these review meetings happened in the court arena, then this would somewhat relieve the pressure placed on professionals while also holding them accountable. I find that throughout my situation this was the only way I got my child back in my full-time care. However, we have to question, was I the right individual in these circumstances to have had to do this and have these pressures on me while living without my child and without the professional qualifications? I feel that of course this served me well, because I do now have my child in my full-time care and am very educated in this arena, but was this really the correct way in order for me to learn this? The systems are failing so many children and are stating that any actions undertaken by the local authority are in the best interests of the child, but this cannot be true. Often paperwork and essential information relating to the child's wishes does not arrive until after the meeting has taken place. Decisions therefore have been made without reference to what the child wants and understands regarding the situation—these could not have been based upon the best interests of the child.

The child's welfare is of paramount concern, and I feel the services we are operating with now certainly need to go back to adopting their own espoused approaches. The ethics of the professions have changed in order to provide equality, but in doing this we are not taking into consideration the equity of the children involved.

Commentary

Francesca's individual experiences of having her child being made the subject of a care order and working to having this overturned, exemplify the immense barriers involved in the child protection system. This section provides an outline of key points that makes themselves apparent from Francesca's account. However, it is important to note that Francesca's account does highlight some key similarities with the accounts of other contributors to this book.

Firstly, Francesca outlined that she experienced a high turnover of social workers, which is something that is outlined by many contributors to this book, particularly in Chaps. 5, 7 and 9. It is interesting, though dispiriting, to note that although there are nearly 20 years between the two experiences, there are major similarities between Francesca experiences and Dionne and Dorothy's experiences in Chap. 9. In particular the lack of continuity in terms of workers and their approaches, and that monitoring, spot checks and aftercare were not offered to either family. Francesca outlines that this was highly significant in extending the duration of her child's care order. In other words, had there not been such a high turnover of social workers, her child could have been returned to her much earlier. This is also similar to the account of Charles English-Peach in Chap. 5, who outlines how the constant changes in social workers limited the possibilities available to him while in care. Another key similarity between these two chapters is Francesca's account of a perceived willingness on the part of professionals to medicate children in care who display behaviours deemed to be problematic. This is also evident in Charles English-Peach's account and suggests a specific problem.

Francesca had to advocate for herself. A complete lack of aftercare was demonstrated and extensive examples of professionals failing to adhere to their own policies and procedures. The fact that this process in itself required great skill and endeavour on Francesca's part, which many service users would not have been able to undertake, must be acknowledged. The stress of the process and complexities of the system, in particular the lack of 'joined up' thinking between agencies, are evident within this account.

In relation to differences, the attitudes which Francesca encountered and assumptions about her capacity to care are evident here. In particular, she illustrates that ongoing processes appeared to relate to a single assessment of her capacity to parent on an occasion in 2010, rather than professionals basing their approach on her current capacity and circumstances. This suggests that professionals' approach towards Francesca focused more on the risk factors and deficits attributed to her, rather than giving attention to her strengths and positive parenting approaches (Yoo and Abiera 2020). It should be noted the Munro Review (2011) identified that such a preoccupation with risk, 'has unintended and wholly undesirable repercussions on the total service offered to families in difficulties' (Munro 2011, p. 117). In contrast, research has shown that:

> creating room for 'strengths discussions' in practice would help service providers to conduct more balanced assessments of parents' capabilities and risk factors…[wherein] sensing that their service providers perceive them as more than their 'problems', parents may find it easier to let their guard down and more willingly engage in the services provided (Yoo and Abiera 2020, pp. 131–133).

In other words, the deficit-based risk approach may be counterproductive in its outcomes compared to the strengths-based approach, that 'it is time to recalibrate the balance in child welfare policy and practice between investigation of risk and supportive, needs-focused interventions' (Kemp et al. 2014, p. 33).

Regular changes in professional staff involved in Francesca's case, including long-term sickness and high turnovers, repeatedly resulted in delays which impacted negatively on both Francesca and her son. It is evident that the lack of continuity, or at least contiguous processes, was not in the interests of anyone involved. From a practitioner's perspective, there is little opportunity to recognise the complexities and hurdles, brought about by having to begin the process again. Forrester et al. (2019, p. 2164) have observed that there is 'a relatively strong relationship between 'relationship-building' skills and the self-reported engagement of parents'. As relationship building can occur only over a period of time, Francesca's experiences of having have to start again on seven occasions with different social workers, suggest that this was a significant limiting factor in her case.

Francesca's experiences identify several opportunities where the earlier involvement of professionals could have made a significant difference to the outcomes she experienced. These include when she was 15 and placed in hostel accommodation, when she became pregnant at 17 and was subjected to domestic violence and abuse, and when she was offered a place in a mother and baby unit, then having the opportunity withdrawn, owing to cuts in services. This follows on from the emphasis in Munro's Review (2011), which specifically stated that early intervention was a key to good outcomes for children. However, it is important to distinguish specifically what is meant by early intervention and which types of intervention could be the most beneficial. Featherstone et al. (2020, p. 1736) distinguish between early support and early intervention as respectively 'meaningful, hands-on, practical support … [versus] a seeming preference for telling the parents what they [need] to do' and argue that the focus should be on early support, rather than early intervention. The important distinction here is that a focus on intervention 'suggests practices delivered to families rather than practices with families' (Featherstone et al. 2020, p. 1740). The difference is on risk aversion rather than meeting needs (Axford et al. 2019). Such a difference also emphasises that intervention tends to focus on a short-term action which is focused on making the child safe, while the support needed is often more long term and encompassing of the whole family. It is clear in Francesca's case that the focus was on intervention, when a focus on support for her, and other people in similar situations, may have the most beneficial outcomes. To clarify what this difference would have meant in Francesca's case, a focus on early intervention could have meant her child may have been taken into care at a much earlier stage, while early support could have meant that she was able to take up the place at the mother and baby unit and given the opportunity to build and demonstrate her capacity to care.

Indeed, this is supported in Francesca's account which details that she received a lack of support from professionals throughout the time of their involvement. In effect, she felt that she was having to deal with issues on her own, with no help from professionals, which caused her considerable distress and may have also prolonged the time that her child spent in care. Such a lack of support has been shown to have important negative outcomes in terms of increasing the stress and anxiety that parents experience, especially the anxiety of not having any support in times of crisis, which in turn increases the likelihood of negative outcomes for the child (Corwin et al. 2020). Conversely, a key benefit of having relevant support during the child protection process is the buffer that is provided during a time of stress, which can function as a protective factor for the child and the family (ibid.). The importance of providing relevant support during involvement with professionals is something that needs to be considered for future practice. Beyond the extensive negative impacts which this experience has had on both the service user and her son, the financial costs of providing 6 years of foster care and innumerable assessments and court appearances are substantial. While the initial involvement of social services may have been required, it appears from this example that once a person has a label of unfit to care for their child, that position does not change from the perspective of the professionals, regardless of the current circumstances and what may have changed within that time.

Francesca's experiences also indicate that, within the child protection system, the expectations and requirements of what a person with a child under child protection should undertake to keep their child(ren) safe appear to be to a higher standard than those applied to the local authority. For instance, the lack of aftercare or the frequency with which welfare visits took place by professionals was not seen as significant by professionals, despite these being statutory requirements. However when Francesca outlined that when she missed an appointment or did something that was seen as contradictory to what was expected of her, she was penalised. This perspective is supported by Axford and Berry's assertion (2019, p. 258) that 'early intervention has been hijacked in some quarters to support an agenda whereby marginalised families must quickly prove themselves adequate carers or lose their children to forced adoptions'. That a parent can be held to a higher standard of scrutiny than the system which oversees them appears to lead, as in Francesca's case, to situations where children may be held in care longer than they need to be. Part of the problem is the persistent and chronic underfunding of children's services, particularly during a time of austerity (Grootegoed and Smith 2018), which is undoubtedly having an impact on service provision. However, as Horwath (2016) observes, where the actions of the system or individual social workers equates to them 'talking the talk' but not 'walking the walk', this can lead to the parent becoming demotivated and/or lacking engagement, which impacts the outcomes for the child. So, the expectations of both the parent and the system and/or individual social worker need to be upheld and maintained throughout the process.

Specific improvements to the systems can and should be made to minimise the poor practice and inadequate systems demonstrated in this chapter. From Francesca's commentary it is clear that these need to include the following:

1. A clear system of accountability in terms of local authorities' need to adhere to the time frames specified for certain actions, for instance, a named manager being required to submit an accessible written report explaining the reasons for the delay and what is being done to rectify the situation. If this was required to be sent to all related professionals, the service users and courts involved in the case, there would be much greater clarity as to the how the processes and delays impacted upon the cases.
2. That any assessments are required to outline the current situation and to specifically refer to what changes have occurred, rather than solely focusing on the initial incident(s).
3. That multi-agency working places clear responsibilities for relaying information to all other relevant parties, and that such engagement and partnership working be outlined in documents distributed to all concerned.
4. That the changing expectations and requirements that professionals may make upon a person who has children within the care system, such as attending courses, training and far-flung contact centres, are recognised as significant. Francesca identified how the financial implications of undertaking all training which was asked of her were never taken into account or acknowledged.

The guidance in Working Together to Safeguard Children (HM Government 2018) sought to provide a clearer statutory framework upon which to safeguard and promote the welfare of children. Much of the emphasis of the framework relates around agencies working together in the interests of the child or young person, a process which has been recognised as previously lacking cohesion. Francesca's story suggests that there is a long way to go before guidance and frameworks truly position the welfare of the child as paramount.

Reflective Questions

1. At what stages were Francesca's child's best interests considered, and at what points were these not paramount?
2. How might social policy better ensure that parents demonstrating change have their voices heard in cases like Francesca's?
3. To what degree was a strengths-based or a deficit-based approach from professionals evident?
4. What social policies could be enacted that might better guarantee that key agencies work together with a common goal?
5. What are the impacts of a demonstrably fractured system for those negotiating with child protection services?

References

N. Axford, V. Berry, J. Lloyd, *How Can Schools Support Parents' Engagement in Their Children's Learning? Evidence from Research and Practice* (Education Endowment Foundation, London, 2019). https://educationendowmentfoundation.org.uk/evidence-summaries/evidencereviews/parental-engagement/

T.W. Corwin, E.J. Maher, L. Merkel-Holguin, et al., Increasing social support for child welfare-involved families through family group conferencing. Br. J. Soc. Work **50**(1), 137–156 (2020). https://doi-org.apollo.worc.ac.uk/10.1093/bjsw/bcz036

B. Featherstone, A. Gupta, K. Morris, et al., Protecting children: a social model. J. Soc. Work **20**(4), 523–527 (2020). https://doi.org/10.1177/1468017320907483

D. Forrester, D. Westlake, M. Killian, et al., What is the relationship between worker skills and outcomes for families in child and family social work? Br. J. Soc. Work **49**(8), 2148–2167 (2019). https://doi.org/10.1093/bjsw/bcy126

E. Goffman, *The Presentation of Self in Everyday Life*, Monograph No.2 (University of Edinburgh. Social Sciences Research Centre, Edinburgh, 1956). https://monoskop.org/images/1/19/Goffman_Erving_The_Presentation_of_Self_in_Everyday_Life.pdf

E. Grootegoed, M. Smith, The emotional labour of austerity: how social workers reflect and work on their feelings towards reducing support to needy children and families. Br. J. Soc. Work **48**(7), 1929–1947 (2018). https://doi.org/10.1093/bjsw/bcx151

J. Hardy, Parental incarceration's effect on family: effects on mothers, fathers, marriage, children, and socioeconomic status. Canadian J. Family Youth/Le Journal Canadien de Famille et de la Jeunesse **10**(1), 119–140 (2018). https://doi.org/10.29173/cjfy29345

HM Government, Working together to safeguard children (2018). https://www.gov.uk/government/publications/working-together-to-safeguard-children%2D%2D2

J. Horwath, The toxic duo: the neglected practitioner and a parent who fails to meet the needs of their child. Br. J. Soc. Work **46**(6), 1602–1616 (2016). https://doi.org/10.1093/bjsw/bcv086

S.P. Kemp, M.O. Marcenko, S.J. Lyons, et al., Strength-based practice and parental engagement in child welfare services: an empirical examination. Child. Youth Serv. Rev. **47**, 27–35 (2014). https://doi.org/10.1016/j.childyouth.2013.11.001

C. Middleton, J. Hardy, Vulnerability and the 'toxic trio': the role of health visiting: this article explores the association between domestic violence, maternal mental health and alcohol substance misuse, and how when they are combined, the risk of significant harm is made more probable. Community Practitioner **87**(12), 38–45 (2014) PMID: 25626292

E. Munro, *The Munro Review of Child Protection: Final Report, a Child-Centred System*, vol. 8062 (Department for Education. The Stationery Office, London, 2011). https://lx.iriss.org.uk/sites/default/files/resources/cm_8062.pdf

H. Yoo, K. Abiera, Stories less told: parenting strengths and family-of-origin experiences amongst parents involved with child protective services. Br. J. Soc. Work **50**(1), 119–136 (2020). https://doi-org.apollo.worc.ac.uk/10.1093/bjsw/bcz107

Improving Transitions for Independence to Adulthood for Care Leavers

4

Charles Mark English-Peach and Clive Sealey

In this chapter, Charles English-Peach presents his experiences of the transition from leaving care into independent adult life. While the transition into independent adult life is typically fraught with difficulties and complexities for most young people anyway, for those in care these difficulties and complexities can be compounded for a number of specific reasons that occur from being in care. For example, their transition to independent living tends to occur much earlier than non-care leavers, and while this can be empowering, the research suggests that this earlier transition is more problematic than empowering in a number of ways. There have been numerous recent policy initiatives and changes to the system of support for care leavers which acknowledges the problematic nature of this transition into independence. However, the evidence suggests that despite these changes, the system is not working effectively, particularly in relation to the number of care leavers not in employment, education and training (NEET) (National Audit Office, (NAO) 2015). Negative outcomes like these have significant financial costs to society, at close to a quarter of a billion pounds (National Audit Office 2015). And as the number of people entering the care system has been rising since 2010 (NSPCC 2019), so the cost of this failure will also increase. This chapter provides Charles' first-hand account of the impact and outcomes of the main policies that exist for care leavers and changes that could be made to improve the process of transition to adulthood.

The main aims of the chapter are to:

1. Provide a first-hand account of the transition from leaving care to independence.

C. M. English-Peach (✉)
Redditch, England

C. Sealey
School of Allied Health and Community, Worcester, UK
e-mail: c.sealey@worc.ac.uk

C. Sealey et al. (eds.), *Social Policy, Service Users and Carers*,
https://doi.org/10.1007/978-3-030-69876-8_4

2. Highlight key strengths and limitations of the current system.
3. Present suggestions for improvements to the current system.

Who Am I?

I am aged 21, and I live with my nan and have done so since the age of one, when I was fostered by her. I am currently at college studying IT and Computer Systems. I visit my Mum lots more than I did previously and have a good relationship with her. I also see my sisters a lot, since they live close to my Mum. I visit them on the train.

I was two years old when I was first taken into care. This was because of an abusive father. The decision was made by social services to intervene. I was too young to remember what actually happened, but I do remember conversations about why I was living there. Shortly thereafter the decision was made to put me into care. I was in short-term foster care for about six months with a view to returning me to the family home. However, when it became apparent that this would not be possible, my nan made a quick decision to foster me and my sisters through kinship care; this was in order to keep us together as in the foster care system we would likely have been separated due to age differences. This happened to a friend of mine and she still misses her siblings. This means that kinship care was used as a care arrangement, and I was treated as being in care.

▶ **Key Learning: Kinship Care** Kinship care, sometimes also called family and friends care, refers to where family and friends other than the biological parents take responsibility for the upbringing of children. This can include siblings, grandparents, godparents and close family friends who are caring for children. It should be noted that there is a legal requirement for local authorities to consider kinship care first before other possibilities. There are no definitive statistics on the number of kinship carers, as kinship care arrangements can be both formal and informal. A key point is that most kinship carers are not foster parents, and the arrangement for this can be both informal and legal. According to Grandparents Plus (2019), the vast majority of children who cannot be raised by their parents are looked after by kinship carers, with around half of all kinship carers being grandparents. Some kinship carers do receive payment, but there is no national minimum financial allowance for kinship carers, and so payment is typically less than what foster carers receive. However, kinship care is less costly in comparison to both foster care and local authority care.

I had ongoing supervised contact with my parents when I went into kinship care, but this was initially limited to half an hour four times a year and was gradually increased in the case of my mother. One thing I do remember about these contacts was the social worker making notes and judging throughout the contact, which I thought was uncomfortable. I have seen my mom continuously since then, but I maintained contact with my dad only until I was nine.

What Impact Has Being in Care Had on You?

I was diagnosed with attention deficit/hyperactive disorder (ADHD) at either four or five years and higher-level autism at seven to eight years. I was given Ritalin for my ADHD and antipsychotic drugs, and as a consequence I cannot really remember much about this time. I am not on any medication now and have not been so since the age of ten. The intense symptoms that I was experiencing from taking the Ritalin required me to convince the social workers that it was an unsuitable prescription. Once they saw that my symptoms were not as bad as when I was on the medication, they agreed. I do feel my ADHD diagnosis was used as a catch-all diagnosis, in terms of a way to explain something they did not understand. It is said that this happens with a lot of children with 'behavioural difficulties' at early ages. I did have issues at school related to my circumstances. I was confused and angry; treated as an outsider, as not wanting to do work, and also had behavioural issues. I was provided with a support worker which helped but also had the effect of making me feel different from other people. I feel that one of the reasons for this is that I was not provided with help to make my awareness of my situation easier, when I should have been.

> **Key Learning: Attention Deficit/Hyperactivity Disorder (ADHD)** ADHD is a mental health disorder for which the main symptoms are an ongoing pattern of inattention and/or hyperactivity or impulsive behaviour that interferes with functioning or development. This can include being easily distracted, not paying attention and making careless mistakes, not staying seated, always being on the move, not able to wait in turn and interrupting others. It mainly affects children and teenagers but can continue into adulthood. It is more commonly diagnosed in boys than girls (Willis et al., 2017).

For about a third of my time spent in primary and secondary education, I went to a special school. It is tricky to say if this was the right decision, as I did not have learning difficulties, but at a same time I was clearly not fitting in at the school I was at and being picked on. So, changing schools helped me to avoid that, but it did not help me academically. I felt that they had lower expectations at this school. A special school will naturally have lower expectations, but perhaps I could have been treated as an exceptional case. This is definitely something that I was up against, not just at school but throughout the time that I have been in care. Despite this, I left with the highest qualification possible, which was an ASDAN vocational qualification which is just below a GCSE. My teachers at school really pushed me and said that I could go further educationally.

It is important to understand that I was not asked whether I wanted to go to this school. The decision was made through a crisis review meeting, where the decision was made that the school I was at was not the right one. This kind of exemplifies the point that the thread running through this period was that things were always just done to me; I was never consulted on the things that happened. The decision to send me to a special school may have been a different decision with a completely different set of professionals if they had actually asked me what I wanted.

I think the fact that I went to a special school worked against me and I was labelled due to this. I feel that in fact, it slowed me down, and because of effectively having to catch up educationally due to the school I went to, I have been at college for five years instead of two years. I do feel that this means that I have been at college longer that I would have been had I not been in care. This means that I have had to work harder just to catch up, due to the education I received earlier. At the first college I went to, I did well enough to progress but was not told this. I feel that I was deliberately held back, even though I was student of the year. I then went to another college and passed easily and progressed. I could have progressed earlier on but I feel that being in care has held me back. My overall experiences of attending college are really good; I have made friends and been able to develop educationally.

Through being in care I had lots of different experiences with social workers; I would say that some were better than others and that there was a wide range between the good ones and bad ones. The better social workers had a more personal connection and spent more than the allotted time getting to get to know me, for example stopping at a service station service station to have coffee and a chat. However, these social workers were the exceptions, as generally they were more concerned with ensuring that boxes were ticked and their career as a social worker, not in getting to know me. I cannot remember how many social workers I have had but it has been quite a few, with some lasting longer than others. I would generally see my social worker a few times a year, some more often than this. However, I only saw some just before review meetings to sort out paperwork and then at the actual review meeting itself, and this made it very difficult to build up a rapport with them. My social workers provided varied levels of support, although in the early days it felt more like I was being inspected, rather than being offered support. This was because our conversations were like interrogations, as they were asking mainly about school, home and meals. I would have preferred more of a conversation on things not necessarily directly related to my care.

What Happened in the Process of Leaving Care?

My transition overall to leaving care was relatively smooth, but this could have been because of the fact that I was fostered by a family member. It would have been good if when I was younger, I had been integrated more into the local authority care community. By this I mean I would have like to meet more people in local authority care, as I had a lot more in common with people in care so it would have been good to interact more with them. They also had a group that would have been useful for me to go to. However, as I lived with my nan, my social workers and others did not consider that this would help me, so it did not happen.

Conversations about leaving care began when I was about 16–17. My social worker came to see me with a <u>Personal Advisor (PA),</u> and they gave me a talk about how things were going to change, although they did stress that it was up to my nan whether I would be able to stay where I was.

▷ **Key Learning: Personal Advisor (PA)** When a looked after person reaches the age of 18 and/or they are no longer looked after by the local authority, the local authority is not legally required to provide them with a social worker. Instead, the local authority is required to appoint an individualised Personal Advisor (PA) to support them until they reach the age of 21 or non-individualised PA support up to the age of 25. PAs have the responsibility for coordinating services provided to support care leavers. This includes advice and support, coordination, reviewing and liaising in the implementation of the <u>Pathway Plan</u>. It should be noted that there is no mandatory professional or occupational qualification for a PA.

We worked on what would happen in the future and they did a <u>Pathway Plan</u> with me, and I also worked loosely on what would happen. We also made a plan for going to university. I understood up to a point what was happening as I was coming to an age where I would no longer be living in care. The closer it got to the deadline, the more that it was explained to me. Part of me was relieved about this as I felt it meant that I could be normal and no longer in care. When I was young, I did not know that I would ever leave care, so I was actually relieved when I knew it would end as this is what you want to hear when you are young. Generally, I felt that this was explained well to me. However, I do feel that they could have started the conversation earlier. My Pathway Plan covered what it needed to, and it set the scene for first couple of years and was relevant up to a point.

▷ **Key Learning: Pathway Plan** Local authorities are legally required to provide support to care leavers until they are aged 25. The level of support provided depends on the status of the care leaver. Care leavers who turn 16 in care and former care leavers up to the age of 21 not in full-time education or up to age 25 in full-time education are entitled to have their current or former local authority carry out an assessment to find out what advice and support they need to help them to plan their future. This includes preparing a Pathway Plan to prepare for leaving care to enable them to make a successful transition to the responsibilities of adulthood. The Pathway Plan must include planning for health needs, identity self-development, continuing education where relevant and/or training and employment, family and social relationships, emotional and behavioural development and financial needs and capabilities. The Pathway Plan is required to state what support the care leaver will get in relation to each of these and be amended as necessary as it functions as a 'live' document'.

When I left care there was a change from having a social worker to having a PA. Luckily, I got on with my PA. Since then, I have had lots of different PAs, but I know that the average for most care leavers is higher than for me. I feel that 16 is too early to have to leave care. As I left care officially when I turned 21, this means that I no longer have an allocated PA but can still get access to one on an as required basis.

It felt that unofficially I had left care at the age of 18. This is because I was put on <u>Staying Put</u> arrangements, which meant that my nan lost her <u>Carer's Allowance</u> entitlement, and I had to pay rent to my nan as lodger. This was done through Housing Benefit. This made us as a family less financially stable. While the arrangements put in place from Staying Put did help with my transition, I was told that support would be provided if I wanted to go to university but not if I left education. I don't think that this is fair as this is not what happens with other families; there is an expectation of financial support from the family regardless of whether they stay in education continuously. I am aware that lots of other young people in care have to move out at the age of 18, due sometimes to financial issues, and I think that they could be supported to remain for longer.

▶   **Key Learning: Staying Put** From the age of 18 young people are no longer legally 'in care' and young people can decide where they live. Staying Put, which was introduced in 2014, relates to where a young person in care chooses to continue to live with their foster carer after their 18th birthday, with the emphasis being on the young person making this choice. It is important to note that under a Staying Put arrangement, legally the young person is no longer in care but is a care leaver, and their foster carer becomes their 'former foster carer'. In effect, under Staying Put, young people become lodgers in the household, which means that they are paying rent to live there, and this has implications for recipients of means-tested benefits who suddenly find themselves as landlords. The rationale for the introduction of Staying Put is so that a young person in care can continue to experience the security and stability of familial relationships which non-looked after children typically experience.

The financial support I have had since leaving care is good—I have had grants, a bursary, Housing Benefit and Income Support. However, while the bursary that I get from college is enough for me as I am still living at home, it would not be enough if I was not living at home. For my future, I would like to go to university and then on to a local government career, in order to give back what I have been given. I am optimistic, but I do need a push for encouragement. This is what I feel is missing from young care leavers; many of them are not told that they can achieve, and this should be a specific responsibly of the <u>corporate parent</u>.

▶   **Key Learning: Corporate Parenting** Local authorities have a legal responsibility to a child as a corporate parent. This means that they take on the responsibility of ensuring that they provide the best possible care and outcomes for the child. The word 'corporate' emphasises that this responsibility does not reside with one individual in local authorities (such as the child's social worker) but is a collective responsibility that resides with every individual within that local authority. In practice, this means that they are expected to carry out many of the roles a parent would do, such as ensuring that the child is in good health, safe and happy, does well at school and enjoys good relationships with their peers. Furthermore, they are required to ensure that the child transitions to adulthood either through higher education or through work, preparing them to lead a life as a financially secure independent adult.

What Are Your Positive Experiences of Your Transition from Leaving Care?

I think being in long-term care has probably put me on a different path to what I would be on if I hadn't been in long-term care. The reason for this is because it is now part of my identity and part of how I see myself. It has set me apart from others not in long-term care. One of the good things that have come out of this is that I am now in a position to advocate for others. It has also changed me emotionally, as at times I feel as an outsider from being in care.

I was 13 when I started to be actively involved in understanding and advocating about being in care, so it would have been good if I could have learnt and started this at an earlier age. I particularly wish that I had started advocating for others during the first half of my time being in care.

I have found college very useful, especially as it has given me the opportunity to get what most people have in terms of qualifications, which was not the case at the school that I went to. I have been at college for five years, and it has made me more confident, intelligent and aware of what I can do, made me more capable and also made me more confident to take chances. The tutors have been aware of my care leaver background, which I think has meant that they have helped me more than others. I have improved personally, by building relationships and becoming more outgoing. I don't think there is anything more that could have been provided; I have just got by. I have an Education, Health and Care (EHC) plan, and it means that I can apply for extra time for assessments. I have been provided with a bursary, but I have had money issues in the time between going to colleges and term times. This has meant that I have had no money and have had to borrow money from my nan. In relation to my mental health, the *Youth Help Team* have been particularly helpful in providing me with practical help such as emotional support and a shoulder to cry on.

▶   **Key Learning: Education, Health and Care (EHC) Plan** Education Health and Care (EHC) plan is a legal plan for children and young people attending mainstream education settings (such as nursery, school or college) who have been assessed with special educational needs and who require more help than would normally be provided in their educational settings. The EHC plan describes the extra support that will be provided to meet the extra needs of the individual. This extra support can include equipment, resources, specialist services, particular activities or one-to-one support. The plan also includes the outcomes which the child or young person wants to achieve. EHC plans can start from birth and can continue up to the age of 25 years. It is funded by local authorities. There has, however, been recognition of the limitations of the effectiveness of this policy (Adams et al. 2018).

I think that Staying Put has come along a lot recently compared to what it was like five to ten years ago, because the age of care leavers leaving home is going up and up, which is a good thing, compared to the situation previously where care leavers would leave care before they were ready. People were just leaving care and being put into supported housing. Care leavers should build towards independence while living with in care. It should start when people are young, not just thrown at them between the ages 16 and 18.

An example of good practice that I experienced is the *Youth Voice* team, which is service for care leavers and is run by the county council. They have been a source of constant support to me over the last five years, especially when I have had major changes. Another service that has been important has been *Rees*, which is a charity that supports care leavers. They provide loans, equipment and housing support, work experience, free meals and a free safe space for care leavers. They have helped to fill some of the gaps I identified as present in my transition.

I learnt most about leaving care from the *Care Leavers' Council*. I started attending 13 and would have been in the dark about leaving care if I had not been provided with information by them. I was first of all part of *Who Cares We Care*, which is part of *Care Leavers' Council* and is for those still living in care. This involved going to meetings and speaking to people about experiences in care. As a consequence of the *Care Leavers' Council*, I do feel that some things have changed such as contact arrangements and the language used. For example, the term siblings is no longer used, or 'LAC' for looked after children, as we pointed out that we are not lacking in anything. Also, the previous sleepover policy meant that a decision on whether we as a child in care could attend a sleepover could take up to six months, which was far too long. Now, the policy is that it is up to the carer's discretion.

At 21 I became a member of *Speak Out*, which is also a part of the *Care Leavers' Council* for Worcestershire. It provides signposting to other services. I feel that all care leavers should be made aware of this service, as it provides valuable information. This could be done by going into schools, colleges and youth clubs.

I have also helped in the development *Mind of My Own*, which is an app for children in care and care leavers. The local authority decided to try to use technology to engage care leavers following a bad OFSTED report. I became an ambassador and wrote an article for them. The app allows you to raise issues, say how you feel and ask for help. You can also get in touch with a variety of professionals such as a PA, teacher or social worker. The key point about the app is that it is monitored, so if a young person raises an issue and it is not picked up by a relevant professional, then it is sent to higher-up professionals and has to be picked up or sent higher. I think the use of technology for young people is an interesting development.

What Are Your Negative Experiences of Your Transition from Leaving Care?

There should be financial support for fostering after 16. I think that young people should be given more responsibility and autonomy, such as for rent, less review meetings and more contact should be maintained.

When I turned 18, it was apparent that the level of concern for me dropped off compared to when I was under 18. I did have four PAs who came to see me at the colleges I went to. I think because I tended to muddle through and was probably reluctant to ask for help, this contributed to this drop off. However, I know that there are people who need much more support than I needed when I turned 18, and if the level of support that I received is the same as they received, then it would not be adequate. Overall, the drop off is probably too steep; it needs more individualised support.

I would highlight my experiences with social workers as something that particularly needs to change. In the early days my social workers were too cold and detached especially during contact, which did not make me feel like I was part of a wider extended family. I would also have like to have been part of the conversation and decisions that social workers made about my schooling and medication. I do feel that things were done on me rather that with me, as I didn't have a choice about most things; I was just told that there was a deadline and the deadline had to be met. I wasn't given the choice to say no to a lot of things that happened to me, which would have been good.

I had lots of different social workers while in care. I am aware that a reason for this is that lots of social workers struggle with the system, such as paperwork and workload, and so are not able to be amazing social workers. The high turnover of social workers is a real problem. There obviously needs to be more of them, and they should also have less cases, as this would allow them the time to build relationships with the people they are working with. As kids, we do not want to talk to strangers about intimate details, and it gets harder if there is a strange face every time. You can only understand what care leavers want, find out what their interests are and build contacts with other organisations that can help them if you spend time with them. This normally doesn't happen because of costs but the benefits of this would be huge for everyone. Also, with many of my social workers, it felt as if I was being inspected by them as they would come along and write things down. This was especially the case during contact sessions with my family; then taking notes during these sessions made me feel very uncomfortable.

I am aware that PAs have different skills, but sometimes young people are given the wrong one for their needs. There should be better mapping of the skills of PAs to the needs of the young people they work with. For example, there could be PAs who specialise in certain fields, such as mental health or pastoral care. I needed someone who understood the process of getting me to college and university. Unless your PA has this skill, then you have to talk to someone you don't know. Better mapping to the needs of the young people with the PA skills would overcome the issues of not knowing people and being passed around from person to person for guidance. The PA that I got on with let me come and visit him in the office, we talked about things, he came with me to interviews; he understood my goals and worked along me. Other PAs have been more hands off, which may have made sense to them as I may have come across as very independent. I appreciate that there are lots of other care leavers in a worse off position, and so as I seemed to be doing OK, then leaving me alone may have seemed appropriate. However, I would have appreciated more from them like what this PA provided to me. There perhaps needs to be more workers to help those who may seem independent, but still need help and support.

What Are the Specific Improvements That Could Be Made for Care Leavers in the Transition to Becoming an Independent Adult?

I do feel that the preparation for me leaving care was adequate, but only because the level of care leavers support was explained to me. They sat down with me several times and planned with me. They also spoke to school, so it did seem that like everyone was working together at that time. However, I do feel that there needs to be earlier conversations about this, particularly in relation to introducing to care leavers what their place in the world is. By this, I mean that when you are in care, your sense of identity and the path that you are going to be on in life is not made clear. There is no philosophical conversation about your place in the world, in terms of who you are and what that means. Rather the conversation is fact based, focused on 'this is what we are going to do'. There needs to be more emphasis on the emotional side of leaving, such as your identity. The need for this is perhaps not apparent as many people dealing with care leavers do not come from a care leaver's background, but this is very important. People generally don't know what a care leaver is, and not all people understand what being in care involves, such as the issues around it that need to be dealt with. The need for this kind of philosophical conversation needs to be something that people should be made more aware of. I was not able to access this kind of provision and support through my PA, but luckily, I have been able to access this through other services.

I would have assumed that I would have my own PA until 25, but this is only until 21. I feel that care leavers need support from a PA until the age of 25, as even though it may seem they do not need support, there's always something that may come up. Young people should not be completely cut off as a lot can happen between the ages 20 and 25, and not everyone is lucky to find their role in life by 20. At 21, if I needed a PA, I was referred to the duty team rather than having my own PA. I think that if I feel like this in my position of being relatively independent, then it is very likely that those in a worse position than me will definitely need this kind of help.

It should be statutory for LAs to ensure that care leavers are given the opportunity to go to university. One of the reasons why it is harder for care leavers to go to university is because they are on their own. As an example of this, while non-care leavers will have their families with them to go to open days, this is less so with care leavers. Instead, care leavers are expected to step out on their own. And as some of them come from children's homes, they really cannot be expected to go back to their 'home' for help when needed. Again, this emphasises the importance of corporate parenting responsibility, which could include working more closely with local universities. Care leavers are funded to go to university up to a point, but not extensively enough. As an example of this, if I wanted to take a gap year before going to university, then I would no longer be funded to go to university, I have to go straight through to university. However, this is possible for children not in care, an issue which corporate parenting should address.

Care leavers often suffer from emotional and mental health issues. They are entitled to Child and Adolescent Mental Health Service (CAMHS) until the age of 18, but then have to go onto adult mental health services. However, stigma is one reason why care leavers do not access this. They should be provided with a counsellor by default as every person in care needs help.

Up to the age of 25, there should be groups and activities for care leavers to talk to each other, as this provides important support. As an example of this, I went on a boat trip recently with other care leavers, and I got to hear their stories, share experiences and build some good relationships. It's not normal to build relationships like that and that was only through knowing people for a long time. This was organised by the *Youth Voice Team*, who I have known for eight years and they were good. Relating this back to social workers, it was often the case that I would know them for less than a year, and working with someone for such a short period so doesn't lend itself to building relationships.

I think that there are too many services, duplication of services and a lack of coordination between services. There is a lot of duplication of services, and this is not good. Service providers need to talk to each other more and ensure that what they are doing is justified in terms of its difference from other services. They need to be more aware of how what they do fits into the overall puzzle and links together.

Supported housing is there for people that need it, but it's quite 'hands off', and it can be a tricky place to live. If anything, supported housing should be short-term, with a specific progress plan which provides a pathway for people to leave; otherwise people can be there for a long time. I have not been in supported housing, but I have spoken to people who have, and there are lots of bad experiences of it. For this reason, I don't think that I would enjoy it.

Overall, there needs to be better balance between care and support; the two should be married. My positive experiences with the *Youth Voice Team* shows what can be achieved if people are allowed to be more caring. I think for a lot of people working with care leavers, it has all became a bit of a business. This means that things are not looked at on a case-by-case basis; people are acting like robots. The consequence of this is that people are not allowed to be the best versions of themselves, and this provides a very negative outcome for all.

Commentary

The account above from Charles presents a detailed and vivid account of his experiences of his ongoing transition from care to independent adult life. His account identifies some clear ways in which the system of support put in place had both positive and negative outcomes for his transition, and he identifies some clear ways in which policy and practice can be improved. This section analyses some of the key issues that Charles identified, which are evident for care leavers in their transition to becoming independent adults and suggests improvements for the future.

As outlined in the introduction to this chapter, a key issue for care leavers is the low level of educational and employment achievement compared to non-care leavers, and Charles' account provides concrete evidence of this. His account presents an explanation for this in terms of the low expectations that occurred from being put in a special school. It should be noted that Charles' experiences of being in a special school matches those of other participants such as Julia Smith in Chap. 7 and Mark Lynes in Chap. 8, in terms of the low expectations of people attending special schools, and so points to a systemic issue within such schools. However, as Charles makes it clear, the key word here is 'put', as that this was not something that was discussed with him. This is also reinforced when he talks about the medication he was put on following his diagnosis of ADHD. Charles' observation that the diagnosis of ADHD was most probably based on a misunderstanding of the complex effects of early childhood trauma by the medical professionals is supported by the research of Willis et al. (2017), which observed a tendency of medical professionals to misdiagnose any inattention or impulsivity as indicative of ADHD, rather than being an expression of attachment or other issues. This presents a wider debate about whether the cause of such negative outcomes occurs from low expectations or whether it occurs from the voice of those is care is not really listened, to as set out in Baker (2017). However, it should be noted that by attending college and having aspirations to go to university, Charles' educational outcomes are much better than most care leavers, as the proportion going to university is well below that of those young people not in care (NAO 2015).

A key point of debate is the age at which the transition to independent living should occur, and this aspect is clear in Charles' account. The earliest age that young people can leave care is 16, but they are able to stay until the age of 18 or longer if in a Staying Put arrangement. However, it should be noted that in general, care leavers' transition to independent living is earlier than when most non-care leavers leave home, and Charles' account suggests that can be problematic for a number of reasons. Research has detailed that the transition from youth to adulthood is a period characterised by instability and chaos which needs to be mediated by extra support and guidance from supportive adults (Marion and Paulsen 2019). However, for those in care, the possibility of such mediation is not always possible.

As an example of this, financially Charles is reliant on his income being supplemented from a number of sources, most notably family members. Whilst this is not unusual for people his age, it is worth noting that people living in care often do not have family members to rely on. Furthermore, a particular point of note from Charles' experiences is the needs he had beyond material needs, such as emotional support related to his developing identity and guidance. Current policy details that guidance is provided by PAs, but as Charles makes clear, this is guidance focused specially on concrete outcomes, not related to emotional needs. This is something that has also been identified as an issue specifically for care leavers by Baker (2017). For looked after children in general, Nelson et al. (2020) make the specific observation of a focus from professionals on material possessions in contrast with looked after children's focus on connections with the past, as evident in Charles' account.

From Charles' account, the case could be made for raising the initial age for leaving care from 16 to 18. This would reinforce the requirement identified by Charles that a significant area for improvement relates to local authorities functioning as the corporate parents of care leavers. The legislation specifies that 'as corporate parents, responsible authorities should provide support to care leavers in the same way that reasonable parents provide support for their own children' (Department for Education 2014, p. 21), and corporate parenting applied in this way would more accurately reflect the parenting that occurs for non-care leavers.

One of the reasons outlined by Charles why developing his sense of identity has been problematic has related to the inability to build relationships with professionals who have responsibility for his welfare. This relates to PAs in part, but most acutely to social workers. Charles' account of multiple social workers reflects the experiences of other contributors to this book and is identified by him as making it hard to build relationships and therefore relate intimate details necessary to construct an identity. In addition, he identified the impersonal and functional manner in which social workers treated him, and this is related to the point above of not being listened to. This is supported in Dugmore's (2019) observation that social workers often seem to overlook, ignore or distance themselves from some of the emotional experiences shared and communicated by the children and young people they meet. The second of these issues is perhaps easier to solve, in terms of training social workers to be more personal and empathetic towards care leavers. The recruitment and retention of social workers is something that is discussed in more detail in the Conclusion chapter.

It should be noted that Charles has had some significant achievements in relation to his involvement with other organisations, which has enabled him to use his experiences of being in care to try to improve services for others. Charles is also clear that he has benefited personally from his involvement with these organisations and is certain that there is a need for such organisations to facilitate the transition to independence. These organisations were particularly relevant in terms of enabling him to build an identity. Charles is clear that in preparing him for leaving care, one of the things that he struggled with was his sense of identity and his place in the world. As the charity *Become* (2019) explains, whilst those living with their birth parents are able discuss their past and family history with people who can help them to understand where they have come from, this is more problematic for children in care. This limits the opportunity to understand how their life has come to be as it is which can lead them to not only blame themselves for having been placed in care but also to lack a sense of identity at the critical time of identity formation.

Charles is optimistic about some of the recent changes that have been made to the system of support for care leavers. In particular, he views Staying Put as having had a beneficial outcome for him. The current statistics on Staying Put in terms of the numbers of care leavers who have successfully used it is not clear (Roberts et al. 2019). One reason for this may be that the level of funding provided for it is insufficient and the relatively low payment paid to Staying Put landlords (Armitage 2017). However, Charles' account suggests that Staying Put can, and does, have a positive impact, and so more funding and provision could be made available to engender these positive outcomes.

There have been a number of recent policy initiatives for care leavers. These include the following:

- The introduction of payment by results Social Impact Bond-backed projects for care leavers.
- A new Care Leavers' Apprenticeship Bursary of £1000.
- The introduction of Staying Close to enable to children living in care homes to move to independent accommodation close to their children's home.
- The Care Leavers Covenant to improve the employment outcomes of care leavers (Roberts et al. 2019).

It is too early to assess the outcomes form these policies. However, one thing that is missing is a policy that would improve the opportunities for care leavers to go to university, which Charles identified as a pressing need. This is clearly one policy innovation which would improve the outcomes for care leavers in their transition to being an independent adult.

Reflective Questions

1. Why is developing a sense of identity important to care leavers in their transition to adulthood?
2. Which social policies are needed to better ensure extra support is provided for care leavers in their transition to adulthood and independence?
3. How could mental health policies better help the transition to independence journey for care leavers?
4. Looking at the list of recent policies that have been put in place for care leavers, are there any gaps or limitations that need to be addressed?

References

L. Adams, A. Basran, S. Dobie, D. Thompson, D. Robinson, G. Codina, Education, Health and Care Plans: A qualitative investigation into services user experiences of the planning process. London: Department for Education (2018)

S. Armitage, *Key Issues in Fostering: Capacity, Working Conditions, and Fostering Agencies*, Briefing Paper Number 7998 (House of Commons Library, London, 2017)

C. Baker, *Care Leavers' Views on Their Transition to Adulthood: A Rapid Review of the Evidence* (Coram Voice, London, 2017)

Become, A system that cares: a manifesto for care experienced children and young people (2019). Available via https://becomecharity.org.uk/media/2090/a-system-that-cares.pdf. Accessed 2 Dec 2019

Department for Education, *The Children Act 1989 Guidance and Regulations Volume 3: Planning Transition to Adulthood for Care Leavers* (Department for Education, London, 2014)

P. Dugmore, *Acknowledging and Bearing Emotions: A Study into Child and Family Social Work Practice*, Doctoral Thesis (DSW) (University of Sussex, 2019)

Grandparents Plus, Kinship care state of the nation 2019 (2019). Available via https://www.grand-parentsplus.org.uk/state-of-the-nation-2019-survey-report. Accessed 6 Mar 2020

E. Marion, V. Paulsen, The Transition to Adulthood from Care, in *Leaving Care and the Transition to Adulthood: International Contributions to Theory, Research, and Practice*, ed. by R. Mann-Feder, M. Goyette, (OUP, Oxford, 2019) Chapter 6

National Audit Office, *Care Leavers' Transition to Adulthood*, HC 269 Session 2015–16 17 July 2015 (Department for Education, London, 2015)

P. Nelson, C. Homer, R. Martin, What makes a looked after child unhappy. Adopt. Foster. **44**(1), 20–36 (2020)

NSPCC, *Statistics Briefing: Looked After Children* (NSPCC, London, 2019)

N. Roberts, T. Powell, S. Kennedy, et al., *Support for Care Leavers*, Briefing Paper Number 08429 (House of Commons Library, London, 2019)

R. Willis, S. Dhagras, S. Cortese, Attention-Deficit/Hyperactivity Disorder in Looked-After Children: a Systematic Review of the Literature. Curr Dev Disord Rep **4**, 78–84 (2017)

The Realities of Fostering in a Flawed System

Vivienne Tongue and Joy Fillingham

This chapter presents Vivienne Tongue's experiences of <u>fostering and foster care</u>. Vivienne's account provides some detail on the training she underwent to become a foster carer, and the pressures and expectations encountered when doing so. Her account provides detail on some of the practical and emotional issues relevant to fostering and considers whether the processes she underwent were in the best interests of the child concerned.

> **Key Learning: Fostering and Foster Care** Fostering is the process by which a child or children unable to live with their birth parents or other carers because of their own wellbeing or safety live with other families who have been approved for these roles. The key distinctions between fostering and adoption is that fostering is typically a short-term arrangement until a permanent solution is found either though adoption or returning to birth families, while adoption is a long-term solution. There is rarely any long-term payment for adoptive parents, but fostering does typically entail the payment of fees.

According to the OFSTED (2020) up to end of March 2019, there were almost 55,000 children and young people placed with foster carers in England. Perhaps most significantly, this was an 3% increase on the previous year, and these numbers have been increasing for the last decade (see Chap. 9 for more information on this issue). However, the number of spaces available in foster care and people accepted

V. Tongue (✉)
Birmingham, UK

J. Fillingham
Department of Social Work and Social Care, University of Birmingham, Birmingham, UK
e-mail: j.fillingham@bham.ac.uk

© The Author(s), under exclusive license to Springer Nature Switzerland AG 2021
C. Sealey et al. (eds.), *Social Policy, Service Users and Carers*,
https://doi.org/10.1007/978-3-030-69876-8_5

67

as becoming foster carers continue to decline, despite prominent advertising campaigns suggesting 'anyone can foster' as detailed in Vivienne's account below.

The main aims of the chapter are to:

1. Explore the lived experiences of becoming and continuing to be a foster carer.
2. Analyse the appropriateness of the training and processes related to becoming a foster carer.
3. Discuss the relevance of the process to the 'best interests' of children.

Who Am I?

In late 2008, along with my husband of 20 years, I began the journey of fostering which we had planned in an organised and detailed way. I had suffered a very difficult past, which had seen my childhood marred by sexual and emotional abuse. As a middle-aged woman now, I had taken the perpetrator to court, and a conviction had been secured. After many decades of counselling and huge difficulties in my life, I felt ready to offer what I knew as a skill in dealing with the invisible pain of broken childhoods. In many ways I knew from my own experiences that emotionally, the child(ren) we would have placed with us would be pushing against any positive and mainstream philosophies we tried to place. In a way that was what attracted me, as I felt that I knew the children to some degree, even though I had not even met them.

Assessing the Foster Care Agency

The foster agency was lovely and welcoming with smiley-faced workers, even if it was a little corporate in appearance, everything neat and tidy but no sign of children. All of the social workers I met were interested, motivated and very friendly, and overall, I rated the agency highly. In my inexperienced mind, I thought I would find a building in which toys and posters and pictures drawn by children were on the wall. I found instead a very lovely clean magnolia-walled office suite with reception and a posh coffee machine. Although there was no sign of children in the building, I felt they were genuinely at the centre of their organisation.

The agency supplied an eight-day training course over four weekends. Descriptions of past difficult placements were described to weed out the easily upset at the beginning of the process, and it did certainly eliminate a number of potential foster carers. After the first weekend we both felt we liked the agency; there was a feeling that was very well communicated—that this was going to be a team that supports each other. We were told continually that we could call out-of-hours for help if it were needed, that we would be kindly enveloped and supported by an experienced social worker who would be allocated to our family and that the agency had legal and administrative experts at hand. While training for foster care I wondered would any children show me the same kindnesses should the 'challenging behaviour' situation arise; I hoped so.

Evaluating the Foster Care Training I Received

The training for foster carers was broken down into compulsory required training and that which the agency felt would be of use to us. First aid, 'managing challenging behaviour' and 'equality and diversity training' are but a few of the compulsory trainings. The first aid was children and baby focused, and I think everyone in the group could understand the need for such a training, along with the hope we would never need it.

The 'managing challenging behaviour' was a little nerve-wracking in that we were taught restraint and avoidance. This brought home the realisation that there was an expectation on me to at least manage such situations. The first person I was partnered with in training was a gentleman who was many times bigger than myself. The purpose was to restrain him and to me; it seemed ludicrous—how on earth was I going to restrain this huge man? Then I remembered, I'm 5 feet 1 inch, and virtually all children of 13 or 14 years of age would be bigger than me. With this in mind I gathered myself and committed to trying to hold him down confidently. I have to say it was embarrassing because the man could clearly have overwhelmed me; but I think he was being kind. Again, I realised that damaged and confused children could not be expected to show me the same courtesy should the situation arise.

The diversity training, I felt, was interesting and relevant; it encouraged foster carers to be accepting of the individuals they were supporting. Children are only likely to be able to be comfortable in their own skin, if they feel accepted by their carers, be they birth parents or foster families. Confidence building, anger and recognition of our own preconceived ideas about disability, amongst other thought processes, were challenged during role play in this training session: I loved this. Role play bought situations to life and allowed for an insight into the feelings that can be ignited by ignorance and bias.

However, it was never going to prepare me for the complexities of fostering or the ongoing twists and turns in which you find your life channelled when you are dealing with children who feel little value of their precious selves. Stories I heard from other foster carers ranged from children who smeared faeces on the bathroom wall to foster carers being threatened with weapons. The social worker visits helped to put context around such behaviour, as I learned about smearing and it being used as a communication tool by children who feel unable to express their thoughts and difficult pasts. It was possible I learnt to turn very negative events that occurred in my home into opportunities for helping the young person to unpick their thoughts and begin to find healthy ways to express themselves.

By the time the young person had arrived with me, I had achieved a number of certificates. Every talk or training at the agency generated a certificate, and certainly this gave a feeling of achieving something relevant. Honestly though, the discussions during training opened up dialogues that were to become very useful in recognising and dealing with children's problems. The certificates themselves for me felt like they were satisfying a process rather than meeting the needs of the children and foster carers.

Meeting the other foster carers was invaluable and took place at the agency office during training sessions; it was at this office that we were able to discuss with other children who were placed with foster carers. Suddenly our own issues seemed less urgent when we heard of the problems encountered by some of our foster care colleagues.

Predominantly, these informal chats took place during coffee breaks and the lunchtime. I wanted the clock to stop when we had these breaks, because the experiences, drama and challenges that some foster carers were managing were very powerful. More 'middle ground' conversations were heard when standing by the coffee machine during the training breaks. There were repeated accounts of children bedwetting and becoming regressed in their behaviour when it was time to see Mom and Dad at contact visits. Often children arrived at the contact centre to find no Mom or Dad had arrived or were in fact ever intending to visit their child.

We could learn a lot through such experiences, but often we were called back to training and never learnt how people had resolved such issues. Have you heard the saying 'it takes a village to bring up a child?' Foster carers meeting together to discuss these challenges is our special kind of village, a hive of information and experiences, and would, I feel, be an incredibly helpful approach. Collectively, with the support of a social worker, we could have brainstormed and maybe found direction and solutions. This type of specific work was not done, perhaps dismissed because it could not be 'certificated'. This does not recognise the years of insight and experience some foster carers have and how these could be shared. Overall though I realised a good quality and range of training was offered, and we took every opportunity given.

I heard from other foster carers that some children had learned that the only way they could express themselves was through violence and intimidation towards others. I had heard of a couple who as foster carers had the placement of an 11-year-old boy who held a knife to the neck of the female foster carer. This resulted in police intervention and the breakdown of the placement. I heard that lots of reflection took place between these foster carers ranging from 'I wish we could have done things differently' to contemplating if a boy so damaged should ever have been placed in a family situation when he so clearly needs specialist care.

This was a very difficult situation for the foster carers to come back from and where the fostering agency came into its own. I thanked God I wasn't this foster carer and that although I had complexities to deal with, they didn't include violence. Imagining the scenario, I put myself in the knife situation and the foster carers' position and asked how would I cope. Would I carry on after such an event—I was awash with questions and few answers. I felt less confident after hearing about this lady and the knife.

An open dialogue was made available with the social worker with whom I discussed my fears; this I felt was essential contact. Without it I'm not so sure I would have audited the other fosters carers' situations, in a way that took into account my own abilities to manage. I think I would have just focused on the dramatic situation and got 'stuck' in fear which would lead to me concluding that I could not manage such a challenge.

The foster carers who had endured the knife threat were afforded high levels of support and visits from the social worker. This culminated in a visit from the foster carers to see the child in his new residential home. The purpose was to bring about a closure for the foster carers and the boy, which led to the continuation of fostering for these resilient foster carers. All these insights I heard, reflected upon and absorbed to build my understanding of how to care for and support the child I fostered.

Regular agency social worker visits always involved discussion on further training; I often felt a more tailored personalised training would have been useful. I imagined a situation in which regular meetings with other more experienced foster carers, where we could discuss issues in an open forum. On reflection, I can see that there is no amount of training that can prepare you for the actual placement of foster children. Having the agency contact is a protective factor in managing the local authorities' demands for paperwork and legalities. The skilled approach of an experienced and empathic person-centred social worker in the beginning part of a placement is invaluable in pre-empting and giving context to the behaviours you may encounter.

Can Anyone Foster?

I recall driving to a training session and getting behind a bus that proudly boasted a huge poster saying 'Anyone can foster all you need is a spare room'. Really that's all you need?! That was not my experience and certainly not the experience of any one I knew. The skills needed include patience aligned with a recognition that the young people will not be comfortable or fall neatly in line with your family values. By the time you have them, their views on life are often already entrenched.

The pain you see in such children is raw; they blame themselves for their parents' perceived loss of commitment and care. I sometimes felt that at the risk of sounding like a Mills and Boon novel, that the only thing that could possibly help was love. This love would need to be resilient to all that was thrown at it, never breaking in its commitment, because these children were looking and waiting to be thrown away and let down again.

Fostering is a function that has a <u>foster carers wage</u> attached to it and an attempt from social service authorities to make it a professional position. My concern was that such advertisements would attract some people who would see it only as a money pursuit. Where is the recognition of the complexities and the tireless work which is carried out by foster carers? Foster carers are people who jump into the world of pain and loss and chaos of these children, so that they can walk together with them and help them find avenues not yet explored.

▶ **Key Learning: Foster Carers' Wage** Technically, foster carers are not paid a
wage but are paid an allowance to meet the general household costs of the
child (food, clothing, transport, etc.) and a fee for the carer. There is no
nationally set rate for foster carers' wages, and this means that rates can vary
between local authorities and private agencies. Generally, local authorities
tend to pay the lowest rates and private agencies the higher rates, and the
private agencies' rate can be double that paid by local authorities. The rates
vary depending on the age of the child and their specific needs. The Fostering
Network provides detail on current rates at https://simplyfostering.co.uk/
how-to-be-a-foster-carer/fostering-allowance/

Fostered children are damaged by the very fact they are not able to be with their
parents. Our human psychology means we need to feel attached, safe and loved, and
this process has been broken by separation. Foster carers re-parent and skilfully
build the <u>attachments</u> that the child's adult life will depend on. Advertising for foster
carers in such flippant ways devalues both child and carer.

▶ **Key Learning: Attachment Theory** Attachment theory is a psychological
theory based on the work of John Bowlby (1995 [1952]). It outlines the
importance of a secure and trusting bond or attachment between an
infant and their primary caregiver, usually the mother, and the negative
impact that neglect or other types of deprivation can have on a child.
The essence of the attachment theory is that different types of attachment
will take place depending upon the quality of the relationship between
the child and their primary caregiver in early childhood and that these
attachments that are made in early childhood are likely to impact on an
individual for the rest of their lives.

Day to day, we the foster carers are fixing fractured souls, wanting to be loved
and yet pushing against it when it was offered. They will of course grow into adults.
It is a sobering thought that we often determine the ingredients that will enable a
child to be able to conform, commit and be part of a world they can enjoy. If these
children ever had a chance to achieve adult lives that were emotionally regulated
and balanced, they would need to learn to trust. For children to allow themselves to
be loved, and to give love, is the titanic work on which foster carers and the children
embark. The level of damage you encounter mentally, emotionally and sometimes
physically can only be understood by those heavily involved with these children.
Teaching children that they can take the risk to love and be loved is a very difficult
process that relies on foster carers' continuity of love and boundaries. I see it as an
end goal for the child or young person to be enabled to experience love and loss in
a way that is acceptable to our society. This equalises the situation and puts cared
for child(ren) into a position of power and control over their adult life.

We, the new foster carers, were like deer in the headlights at some of the descriptions of children we may look after—those who start fires and children who had

been unsustainable in previous foster placements and were on last chances (we would be the last chance!). There was discussion of some foster children that were just unable to behave in a socially acceptable ways and were only able to be cared for in the private sector of the foster system. The reason: the local authority had exhausted all avenues of the care that they offered.

The Form F Assessment Process

The process through which a child will go to a particular carer is made by social workers, the choice being made from a database of available foster carers. The Form F assessment is an extensive detailed write up of the family, their work, life experiences and childhoods—it can take up to a year to collate. I didn't mind that the process took so long as I felt that I wanted the authorities and the agency to know everything about me to help make a decision right for the children and my family. My difficult and complex past needed time to write and explain; it also allowed further reflection about how far I had come. It became clear through discussion and reflection that when confronted with reminders of past traumas, some foster carers could overidentify with the child issues, and that is not healthy for anyone concerned. I learned that those who had not made peace with their past could be triggered by children in this forum, so it is essential the carer is ready for this potential dynamic.

▷   **Key Learning: Form F Assessment** As part of the assessment process to becoming a foster carer, prospective foster cares are required to complete a Prospective Foster Carer Report Form assessment, typically referred to as a Form F assessment. The Form F assessment is essentially used to determine whether applicants for foster care are suitable and can be approved as foster carers and to rule out those carers who are unsuitable. This information is also used by fostering panels to help them make their decisions on which kind of fostering their applicant is suitable for and to outline any specific terms required for approval. The Form F is also aimed to ensure that applicants have thoroughly considered all relevant implications of fostering. The Form F assessment is a detailed process which can typically take from six months to a year to complete.

We learned about paperwork and the absolute need for recording for self-protection and the very real threat of allegations. Daily and weekly forms would be needed to be filled out, along with all incidents recorded and each medication, even a paracetamol, documented in the large folder we were presented with. All terrifying and all relevant, we walked away shell-shocked but resolved in our commitment. The truth is the training was a taster course. It certainly helped with the understanding of why so much paperwork was required and how the recording could be essential in the event, for example, of an allegation. But it did not and could not help with the realities of the foster care system.

Because we were new foster carers, it appeared on paper that my husband and I had little to offer these complex and deserving children because of lack of experience in care. I am sure there are very able potential foster carers who hold back their desire to care because they take the commitment very seriously; they feel they may not have enough to offer. The 'enough' in this case is an open and very changeable character that at times requires skills you don't even know you possess.

Our First Placement

I could not help thinking 'don't people realise I can do this'. I felt this was because I had no relevant daily work experience with children. I was told by the agency that it could take a considerable time to find the first placement. I didn't want to be a 'bus poster' carer whereby just anyone can be a carer, but no one knew what I had to offer so no authorities were interested, which meant we waited three months for a call we thought would never come.

'Vivienne, we have a placement for you, we don't know too much but if you are interested, we will go ahead'. 'Yes, just go ahead'—and after three hours of waiting, a lovely young person arrived, and I just couldn't believe it; he was here, a new part of our family.

My husband and I had decorated the spare room; I recall how I lay on the bed of new quilt covers and pillows and looked at the freshly painted walls. I tried to imagine how a child may feel lying in his new bed looking at these walls in a completely strange house full of people he did not know. I panicked, the sheets felt too new, the walls were too sterile, and we had been told by the fostering agency not to stamp our mark on the room, as the young person should do this.

The new family member was a mystery; I didn't really know how much I was entitled to know about their past. This was probably good because as it turned out, I was to be told very little indeed. The age 14 years, the name, and that there may be an intellectual disability. Much later along the line, I was told that providing minimal information is not unusual, especially with emergency placements.

I was very reliant on the agency at the beginning in terms of protocol and processes. Forms to fill in, documents to record every single thing and suddenly in my panic I couldn't recall any of the training relating to forms. The agency was very supportive and helped a great deal with this, and along with regular supervision, I soon got into the flow of things.

It would be fair to say this child presented with complex learning difficulties. The agency had educational specialists, so I was guided by the agency social worker to ask for assistance. News came from the placing authority that we should not look for a school. I was very confused by this decision while the child looked out of our lounge window watching schoolchildren walk by for months, and he asked me, 'When will I go to school? When do I get a uniform like those kids?' I had no answer and I had no idea where this child could go to school and what school might accept him.

Unexpectedly and heart wrenchingly, we were informed by the local authority that the child needed to return to the local authority borough he came from and not be out of borough any longer. We were distraught; how could any faceless departmental manager make this decision? I am certain many discussions were had at authority level, but my family was never part of those. My understanding was the placing authority has the right to place children in or out of a borough and move them as wished—there was no consultation or child-focused approach.

They didn't know how the foster child had started to tell us about their life and had put posters on the wall in their previously sterile room. Our dogs had a new friend in this boy; he fed the dogs and helped walk them, and this child was quickly becoming established in the family; he was hungry for attachment. I was starting to see a wish from him to be included in trips to the shop or cinema, and he was less suspicious of us. At first, I had noticed that any attempt to cuddle or to hold his hand was met with panic, but that was beginning to fade now with him sometimes coming for a hug. I felt a real sense of progress socially and emotionally as the child began to invest in his new life. I also knew that if he realised the insecurity that really existed in his basic right to know where he would be living, if he knew how uncertain his life with us was, he may never want to invest in his life again. The training did not address any issues relating to physical contact, beyond safeguarding, which did make us fearful of expressing physical affection for the child, despite the fact he clearly needed such attention.

I was told by the agency to contact an advocacy agency, who could provide the child with an independent voice to try to help him stay within the borough with his new family. It was quickly established he really did want to stay and be part of a family he had previously been denied. He told the advocate how frightened he was to return to the previous borough, and the area the child later identified as dangerous for him.

I breathed again, relief, because no one could send a child back to danger. I was wrong, they would, and indeed they tried. I was informed that no school would be available in the out-of-borough area, and I was forbidden to attempt to enrol the child, as it would commit the authority to keeping the new address as an out-of-borough placement, which is expensive.

There were many tears shed by me to the agency social workers who shared the disbelief we felt. This awful situation was affecting my health, I was in shock, and I just couldn't shake the thought—social services will do anything to help a child, won't they? I forgot to eat as I dealt with the uncertainty of the safety and the hopes of a normal life for this vulnerable child. I felt it was a juggling process as to how much information to tell the child; do I prepare them to leave when this might or might not occur—no one knew or could suggest a way forward. We, the family, felt the huge burden of injustice that was being visited upon this child. I had so many questions and I noticed that I was the only one surprised by this situation. Professionals involved in this case seemed to be quite familiar with this problem.

Challenging Professionals

The social workers connected to my young man's case were very experienced and appeared almost dissociated from the potential of disaster for this boy. I could see it was not that they didn't care; it was that they didn't dare care. To do so when change seemed inevitable risked their burnout, and some social workers in the local authority had told me this. I heard about workers who argued with their managers about cases and were not listened to. I also heard about social workers who had so big a case load that any possible means of reducing the amount was welcomed regardless of how. I explained to workers how hopeless and helpless I felt in securing this boy's future with us; I threatened to go to the press.

I was naive, I had made enemies now, and instead of protecting the child, I had unwittingly done the opposite. I felt the tide change towards me by the local authority, and a determined effort by them to get the child back in borough ensued. It felt lonely and frightening as if we were on our own fighting a huge infrastructure that I had initially thought was on the same side as me—the side of children and of safety, choice and best interests.

▶   **Key Learning: Best Interests** 'Best interests' is a concept originating from the *United Nations Convention on the Rights of the Child (UNCRC)*. The aim of this document is to set out key civil, political, economic, social, health and cultural rights for children. Article 3 of this document refers to the 'best interest of the child'. This means that it requires the focus of all involvement with the child to be mindful of what is in the child's best interests including their happiness, security, mental health and emotional development. Also, if the child is of an age or capacity to understand, their views are required to be taken into consideration. The UK has ratified the UNCRC, but has not incorporated it into law, meaning that an individual cannot go to the courts to complain of a breach of their treaty rights, unlike the *Human Rights Act 1998*.

Through a formal complaint made by the child and facilitated by the advocate, to and about the local authority, a call eventually came that stated the child could go to a school and remain with us for now.

The Impact on the Child

Throughout the years with our family, our foster child has continued to feel the tumultuous waves of threat of the placement not being funded. Opportunity and love have been heaped upon the child, and the one thing that has been apparent is the need for him to feel permanent without risk to his future in what he calls 'his new life'.

Periods of relative calm where stress has been less have always been in relation to large gaps in visits from the social workers from the local authority. The child has become fearful of the social workers and their searching questions which trigger bad memories and has led to a reluctance in the wish to speak to them. The need to be 'normal like other kids' cannot be ignored, and visits from social workers are a great reminder of how different his life is compared to his friends. Social worker visits are often undertaken by workers who have changed since the last visit. This wasn't lost on the child who consistently voiced that they were not being listened to when asking if he could be excluded from talking to them.

My husband and I could genuinely see the difficulty of social services supervising a placement with a child who refuses to be part of the process. Inevitably though it all returns to the need to serve the child and provide a service that is personalised. Secure and promised settlement where they can grow and progress shouldn't surely be a hope: it should be a promise.

I wondered sometimes who are we, the foster carers, are actually serving—the local authority, the social workers, the fostering agency or the child? It had actually become a question that relied on quiet reflection in order to clarify in our minds. Best practice should promote policies from a local authority that works in conjunction to the unique nature of the child they are working with.

It became necessary for me to be an advocate for fairness and to be helpful to the social workers. This had to done with explanations that from the beginning the child had suffered the inexcusable threat of returning back to a geographical area of which they were frightened. The thought of leaving a home they had grown to love, along with the long delay for a school, had all impacted their view of social services. Social services were no longer to him people who help; instead they were part of the threat that his difficult past had already entrenched in his mind. Could things have been done differently to facilitate a different result?

I wish the paper I write on would scream because YES it could have, and the whole entire life of this child would then have the opportunity to be different. For example, a child cannot invest in their own lives when they didn't know where they will be living in a month's time. If the home, school and friendship groups can be terminated at any time—there is nothing but uncertainty. I'm not surprised that children in these circumstances often hold back their emotional states and teach themselves not to trust.

When the services see a child prosper and begin to take on the values of a family, surely the services would do what it takes to allow and maintain self-esteem and hope for the child to grow. The concern for me is that during his adulthood, this child may well exclude any proposed assistance from social workers as a result of the earlier mistakes of others. The vulnerabilities he has will then be experienced without support, so the consequences become his burden as a result.

What Could Be Done Differently?

Social services and foster agencies have such a huge privilege in being able to care for these children's lives. I feel policy such as the one that was pushing the child I looked after out of his new and prospering life should not be the problem it is. Surely, simplifying a system that will put the child's wishes and needs first is ethical and justified, as well as a legal requirement.

However, I witness a greed over the funding for each authority that doesn't even consider a child in the process. This child was placed in a geographical area that an authority later regretted because it costs more. The consideration should be focusing on the child not the cost.

I could never be so calculating—this is a life that hopefully will have many more years to be on this earth; we must help these lives thrive. By the time a child is in foster care, damage has been done, and surely the governments' social funding shouldn't go to worsening that damage. So just stop. Stop what you're doing and remember who social services are working for—the children you're paid to look after.

Agencies fight between themselves in the attempt to eliminate their area of support financially. There are issues such as 'should the local authority pay for this or the NHS', and so the battle commences, with each protecting its funding. All of this is done with assessments to enable and benefit the agency concerned to be able to fiscally justify their decision-making process that in little way addresses the needs of the client. Social services regularly remind cared for children entering adulthood that they will have a voice and absolutely will be listened to. In reality, the focus is on the limited resources the funding provides and the actual funding that is available.

The need to maintain control by authorities is seen in its assessment process, which relies on pre-written questions that put answers in a certain category. The price of its limitations falls straight on the doorstep of the families who are left feeling powerless and dismissed by processes they feel unable to challenge.

We know, we really understand the people we look after, and we are the ones who listen to their hopes, fears and dreams. We are not people to be suspicious of or presume a self-centred interest in the person we look after. Indeed, we are paid just as the social worker is, and our profession is to care every single day; we don't clock off at 5:30 pm, and we give something priceless: love.

Commentary

Vivienne's account provides some very useful insights into the whole fostering process, from the training required at the start of the process through to the trial and tribulations of having a foster child. She is generally positive about the training process she underwent. Vivienne's details reflect Davies et al.'s (2015) observation that effective training can lead to good outcomes for children. In general, though, there is very little research on the perspectives of foster carers themselves in relation to the training they receive (Kaasbøll et al. 2019).

As the title of the chapter suggests, Vivienne's account details that there are specific flaws in the system which make themselves apparent. In this respect, it is important to note that an important limitation within Vivienne's experiences and the experiences of other service users and carers in this book is related to social workers and the negative impact that the high turnover of social workers had for her foster child in particular. Another similarity is the lack of promotion of the child's voice by professionals.

To analyse the specific flaws in the system identified by Vivienne, it is first necessary to consider the context within fosters carers operate. As discussed above, foster caring is typically an emergency or short-term placement for children who cannot be cared for by their own family. Reasons for this are often neglect or abuse. This means that, on the one hand, prior to fostering the child is living in an environment which is not meeting their needs, and on the other hand, fostering involves a dislocation for the child from their normal environment. It is into this context that foster carers are pitched, with the expectation that they will provide a stable, mainstream environment for the child that is not only stimulating but also nurturing, sensitive and promotes attachment security (Meetoo et al. 2020). It is also important to consider the fact the that children in foster care are among the most disadvantaged, with many having complex trauma as well as higher developmental delay and a range of social, psychological, behavioural and emotional needs compared to the general population (Wretham and Woolgar 2017). It is a highly fraught and complex context in which foster carers are typically expected to operate.

This makes relevant Vivienne's frustration at adverts suggesting that 'anyone can foster', as this demonstrates that such approaches may negatively impact on both children in the care system and prospective foster carers. For example, Meetoo et al. (2020) detailed how the everyday practices of foster carers orient them as 'experts' in meeting the highly complex needs of the children that they look after. Taking into consideration this context, it perhaps could be expected that foster carers would be operating in a framework which provides them with the resources and skills which mirror the evident complexity of their work when dealing with vulnerable children and young people, who may have challenging behaviour. However, Vivienne's account suggests that this is not the case for a number of reasons.

Firstly, while Vivienne was generally positive about the training that she received, she does outline the assessment process as somewhat rigid, lacking flexibility and is process driven, which is reflected in Sebba's (2016) outline of complaints about paperwork by foster carer applicants during the application process. This suggests that there needs to be a streamline of the assessment process in terms of making it less rigid and process driven.

A clear concern that Vivienne highlighted in particular relates to the inadequacy of training for dealing with 'difficult' children, which is supported by Adams et al. (2018) in their outlining a need for more training for foster carers in dealing with disruptive behaviours. Vivienne identifies that a possible way to overcome this limitation in training is drawing more on the experiences of current and former foster carers during the training process. It is apparent from Vivienne's account that one of the most valuable elements of the training was the practical knowledge and insights of experienced foster carers she met during breaks. However, this was never part of the formal training process. Rather, there appeared to be a focus upon certification of training, rather than tailoring this to the needs of the carer.

The skills of long-term foster carers who have worked closely with vulnerable and damaged children and young people need to be recognised and utilised. Rather than professionals being perceived as the only people able to have an insight into what it is like to foster and to work with young people and children in the care system, working with and valuing experienced foster carers in the training process offers the inclusion of an alternative and essential perspective. It is also cognisant with Onions' (2018) observation that a key to retaining high-quality foster carers is embedding of reflective practice into the foster care role, through enabling current foster carers to reflect on their experiences. This is a suggestion which on the one hand provides a practical solution to a live issue and on the other hand reinforces this book's focus on the importance of the lived experiences of service users and carers to improving policy and practice. Over the longer term, this may begin to alter and explore the power disparity between professionals and foster carers and allow recognition of the abilities and commitment of all concerned.

Secondly, Vivienne's account illustrated enduring disagreements regarding permanence of the placement, which seemed to predominate over any child-focused approach. In particular, from Vivienne's account, it would appear that these decisions made were different from the wishes and views of the child, which is contrary to Standard One of the *Fostering Services: National Minimum Standards* set out by the Department for Education (2011). Standard One relates that the child's wishes and feelings and the views of those significant to them should be significant to any decision. These fights over responsibilities are also contrary to the general direction of policy and practice over the last 20 years or so and its emphasis on achieving permanency in foster placements (Baginsky et al. 2017), as evident through the introduction of Staying Put (HM Government, 2013). Staying Put is discussed in detail in Chap. 5. Furthermore, Adams et al. (2018) observe that dealing with such disagreements is a cause of stress for foster carers and hence why they leave.

Thirdly, it is clear that the main underpinning of the disagreements which Vivienne outlined was funding or more specifically dealing with a lack of funding. Vivienne is clear that the main reason why the local authority wanted to terminate the placement was to try to save money, and this also impacted on what she could do in relation to meeting the educational needs of the child. The underfunding of foster care has been an ongoing issue and has been compounded by both the growth of private equity and venture capital Independent Foster Agencies (IFAs), and the emphasis on austerity measures since 2010. These developments have combined to increase the costs of private fostering placements, while local authority funding in general has been significantly reduced (Baginsky et al. 2017). At the same time, the demand for foster placements has also been increasing. This meant that local authorities have been expected to provide more services with less money in a context of increasing costs. So perhaps it is understandable that local authorities keep a keen eye on costs, even when this may contradict their legal requirements as set out above. There is no doubt that overstretched services are seeking to minimise their costs at any opportunity, where possible moving looked after children across different regions and local authorities to avoid liability for the costs of their care. It is challenging work in an underfunded area, and as demonstrated above, fostered children and their carers can get lost in the process (Barrow 2016).

The UK signed up to the *United Nations Convention on the Rights of the Child* in 1991, which has as a key aim making decisions which are in the best interests of the child. This emphasised the rights of children to be heard and have a voice, particularly in relation to children involved in the care system. However, Vivienne's account suggests that this is not always the case, as decisions were made without any reference to the best interest of the child. The negative attitudinal responses that Vivienne encountered when she tried to challenge such decisions were damaging to the child and appeared to negatively impact on the foster placement. The attitudes of professionals to foster carers challenging their practice can be variable, but this is a recognised barrier to effective working with service users and carers (Fillingham 2013). However, this has been recognised as an area which also causes practitioners extreme frustration, in that many professionals lack the capacity to engage as fully as they wish with children and young people (Caldwell et al. 2019).

It should be noted that the *Adoption and Children Act 2002* introduced Independent Reviewing Officers (IROs) in 2004 to protect children's interests throughout the care planning process. The aim of the IRO is to provide a voice for the child in care through being empowered to act on their behalf and challenge local authority decisions where necessary. In Vivienne's account, the ability of the IRO to do this is unclear, and this is supported by other research which challenges the effectiveness of IROs to undertake the role they are supposed to (Jelicic et al. 2014), suggesting a need to strengthen their role. Vivienne's account supports the idea such a measure is required to be used to ensure that when decisions about foster children's care are made, that foster carers and fostered children alike can be confident that these decisions are truly in the best interests of the child.

Reflective Questions

1. How might social policy better support foster carers who face the types of problem illuminated by Vivienne's situation?
2. How can attitudinal barriers impact upon fostering arrangements?
3. In what ways can both policy and practice impact upon the young people concerned?
4. How best could the experiences and related knowledge of existing foster carers be used to inform future policy regarding foster care training?
5. Is there a place in social policy for a hybrid role of foster carer/social worker?
6. How can the voices of the child(ren) be heard in the development and review of social policy?

References

E. Adams, A.R. Hassett, V. Lumsden, What do we know about the impact of stress on foster carers and contributing factors? Adopt. Foster. **42**(4), 338–353 (2018)

M. Baginsky, S. Gorin, C. Sands, *The Fostering System in England: Evidence Review*, Research Report, July 2017 (Quest Research and Evaluation Limited, 2017)

M. Barrow, Is the government neglecting the dedication of foster parents? (2016). https://www.newstatesman.com/politics/uk/2016/01/government-neglecting-dedication-foster-parents

J. Bowlby, Maternal care and mental health (1995 [1952])

J. Caldwell, V. McConvey, M. Collins, et al., Voice of the child – raising the volume of the voices of children and young people in care. Child Care Pract. **25**(1), 1–5 (2019). https://doi.org/10.1080/13575279.2019.1552447

P. Davies, M. Webber, J.A. Briskman, et al., Evaluation of a training programme for foster carers in an independent fostering agency. Practice **27**(1), 35–49 (2015). https://doi.org/10.1080/09503153.2014.983434

J. Fillingham, *Changing Needs and Challenging Perceptions of Disabled People with Acquired Impairments*, Doctoral Dissertation (University of Birmingham, 2013)

GOV.UK, Fostering national minimum standards. https://www.gov.uk/government/publications/fostering-services-national-minimum-standards

HM Government, Staying put: arrangements for care leavers aged 18 years and above (2013). https://www.gov.uk/government/publications/staying-put-arrangements-for-care-leavers-aged-18-years-and-above

H. Jelicic, I. La Valle, D. Hart, *The Role of Independent Reviewing Officers (IROs) in England: Final Report* (National Children's Bureau, London, 2014). https://www.ncb.org.uk/sites/default/files/uploads/documents/Research_reports/role_of_independent_reviewing_officers_in_england_final_report.pdf

J. Kaasbøll, E. Lassemo, V. Paulsen, Foster parents' needs, perceptions and satisfaction with foster parent training: A systematic literature review. Child. Youth Serv. Rev. **10**, 33–41 (2019). https://doi.org/10.1016/j.childyouth.2019.03.041

V. Meetoo, C. Cameron, A. Clarke, et al., Complex 'everyday' lives meet multiple networks: the social and educational lives of young children in foster care and their foster carers. Adopt. Foster. **44**(1), 37–55 (2020). https://doi.org/10.1177/0308575919900661

OFSTED, Fostering in England 1/4/2018–1/3/2019 (2020). https://www.gov.uk/government/publications/fostering-in-england-1-april-2018-to-31-march-2019/fostering-in-england-2018-to-2019-main-findings

C. Onions, Retaining foster carers during challenging times: the benefits of embedding reflective practice into the foster care role. Adopt. Foster. **42**(3), 249–265 (2018). https://doi.org/10.1177/0308575918790433

J. Sebba, Recruiting and supporting foster carers. Masterclass Presentation to the Association of Child Welfare Agencies Annual Conference, Sydney Australia, 17 August 2016 (2016)

The Fostering Network, Fostering legislation in England (2020). https://www.thefosteringnetwork.org.uk/policy-practice/policies/fostering-legislation-in-england

A.E. Wretham, M. Woolgar, Do children adopted from British foster care show difficulties in executive functioning and social communication? Adopt. Foster. **41**(4), 331–345 (2017). https://doi.org/10.1177/0308575917730295

Negotiating the Strictures and Structures of Being a Service User and Carer

Benefits and Employment Support for Vulnerable and Disabled People

Joanne*, Becki Meakin, Jon Andrew Powton, and Peter Unwin

This chapter will discuss key recent policies which are designed to help vulnerable and disabled people get into work and off the benefits system. Getting people off benefits and into paid employment has been a goal of all governments since the early days of the welfare state, work being seen as the route out of poverty as well as a source of personal and social development (Department for Work and Pensions 2010; Newman 2011; Wiggan 2012). These policies will be critiqued from Joanne's*, Becki's and Jon's lived experiences of such policies and make recommendations improving the welfare to work employment opportunities of vulnerable disabled individuals and groups.

The main aims of the chapter are:

1. To detail the lived experiences of benefit and employment support for vulnerable and disabled people.
2. To explore the particular issues faced by vulnerable and disabled people in relation to work and welfare to work policies.
3. To make recommendations to improve contemporary work and welfare to work policies.

Joanne* (✉) • J. A. Powton
Worcester, UK

B. Meakin
London, UK
e-mail: becki@shapingourlives.org.uk

P. Unwin
School of Allied Health and Community, University of Worcester, Worcester, UK
e-mail: p.unwin@worc.ac.uk

C. Sealey et al. (eds.), *Social Policy, Service Users and Carers*, https://doi.org/10.1007/978-3-030-69876-8_6

Joanne's* Story

I am a single parent of two young children, and I have just completed my professional qualifying social work course and secured my first qualified post. My specific story is about my experiences of the benefit systems I encountered for the first time in my life while waiting for the necessary clearances prior to starting work.

It is said that you can judge a society by the way it treats its most vulnerable citizens. For me a fair society treats all its citizens with dignity and respect, and recognises all human beings have inherent value and worth. A fair society also recognises how diverse and intricate the human experience can be. For me being a human being is valued on more than being in employment and during difficult times having the right to be treated fairly and supported to explore options to thrive. My worth is based on more than what I do and how much I earn.

When I reflect on my personal experience over the past few months, sadly, my experience is contradictory to what my expectations of a fair and equal society would look like. I would go so far to say that instead of going forwards, society has moved backwards at the cost of its most vulnerable members who are dehumanised, diminished and stereotyped, trapped in a system that no longer values all human beings. At times I have felt nothing short of living back in Victorian Britain. Whilst there are no workhouses or slums in sight, poverty lurks everywhere. This poverty looks a little different from its historic ancestor and wears a deceitful mask to divide in order to conquer and gain control. This poverty is brought on by a system and an ideology that is governed by self-interest that values the economy more than it values human beings, and then masks itself in the belief that somehow these human beings are different from the rest of society because they are unemployed and have brought their situation on by their poor life choices. For the family that had to go to the food bank this week for their weekly shop, to the teenager who wants to take their own life as they do not meet the criteria for support from a crumbling, undersourced and underfunded mental health service; I am appalled that this is happening in Britain in 2019.

My First Experience of the Benefit System

Reflecting over the past few months, having found myself in a position over the summer of having to claim Universal Credit as my only recourse to support two small children and myself, I was shocked at what unfolded. To be sarcastically asked by a Work Coach if I have ever worked at all in my life was the most degrading and humiliating experience. I am extremely curious regarding what prejudices, personal bias and performance targets drive the thought processes of the benefits systems' employees. I was fortunate to find a couple of empathic work coaches, and after sharing my personal journey with them, of being a survivor of trauma, I was suddenly viewed as a human being. If the government wants people to return to work, I do not believe this to be the best approach. Neither can I understand how people with no money can pay childcare fees upfront and then be reimbursed by universal credit. This is illogical and a barrier for parents to return to work especially with childcare costs being so high.

▷ **Key Learning: Universal Credit**   Universal Credit (UC) is a means-tested income benefit first introduced by the 2010 coalition government in 2013. The government's primary rationale for its introduction is to increase the incentives for working to make it much more attractive to work than to be on benefits, and to simplify the benefit system to make it easier to claim and receive benefits. Universal Credit is both an in-work and out-of-work benefit, meaning that people who are working and not working receive it, at different amounts. Universal Credit replaces the following six legacy benefits into one single benefit:

- Jobseeker's Allowance
- Housing Benefit
- Working Tax Credit
- Child Tax Credit
- Employment and Support Allowance
- Income Support

This means that rather than receiving separate payments for each of these benefits, those on Universal Credit receive one single payment. Government estimates claim that this will make claimants about £16 a month better off than with the previous separate benefits. It is important to note that Universal Credit is not universal but is means-tested, meaning that it changes with income and circumstances. This means that some people will be worse off under the Universal Credit than under the previous system, such as those with complex needs and disabilities. Universal Credit recipients are required to sign a contract with their <u>Work Coach</u> which sets out the responsibilities that they must meet in order to received Universal Credit. Universal Credit is also primarily an online benefit, meaning that having Internet access is typically necessary to receive Universal Credit.

Challenging the System

Having just finished my social work training I was experiencing hardship and having difficulties finding affordable childcare for the summer break to embark on my career as a newly qualified social worker. After challenging the system, and several complaints later, help was sourced. I am deeply concerned for individuals who are not confident to challenge or who are so worn down and accept what they are told, alongside powerlessly being at the mercy of employees who are clearly trained to make the system as difficult as possible to navigate. I feel that it is unacceptable that people are told they can be forced to find paid work, when many of the individuals claiming benefits are doing the very best they can with what they have got. Is this not a dictatorship? We do find it acceptable to condone spending billions of pounds on Brexit. If the government wants to help families out of debt, how is this achieved through a disjointed system that is encouraging individuals to accrue more debt? A system that tells you previous entitlements to other benefits payments automatically stop, only to establish you have accrued an overpayment that is termed a 'debt'. On trying to arrange a payment plan to ensure as a family you do not face too much financial hardship, you are passed between Child Tax Credits and Universal Credit, neither of which takes accountability. When you enquire as to what policies are in place to enforce certain rules and are told you will receive a swift response, yet months of chasing go by before any such response appears. Is this a deliberate policy to avoid paying benefits and to force people to rely on short-term loans or endure desperation and hunger? It appears that nobody within the government takes responsibility; neither are they accountable for the decisions that they make that potentially adds to the adversity that people are already facing.

Stereotypes of Claimants

How disgraceful that the media and the social elite are willing to pathologise and blame individuals for their own circumstances. Failing to consider the detrimental effects of globalisation, technical development and business process re-engineering, alongside the high increase in the cost of living that is not subsidised by the wages, to me is a total injustice to society. I can understand that the powerful elite have enjoyed generous pay rises, bonuses and expenses in times of austerity and therefore have yet to experience how oppression and inequality feels. Alongside brushing under the carpet the billions it costs to bail out the rich bankers who were responsible for the crash in the global economy—are these not crimes against humanity? Apparently not. The British public are led to believe that the 'workless' class are choosing their circumstances by not going to work and somehow are responsible for their situation and the ills within society. Or even more insulting, families that are trying their best to work and provide for their family are not trying hard enough, by not earning enough money. This is social injustice at its core, and we, the British public, are playing along with this. We believe the lies that are portrayed in the media, and we grow to believe the stereotypes that divide and segregate us, stereotypes driven by the demeaning and prejudicial policies of austerity. If we continue to support this ideology and condone a system that puts money above justice and self-interest above humanity, we will all fall victim eventually to a morally corrupt society based on distorted truths that make the gap in equality bigger.

> **Key Learning: Stereotypes and Stereotyping** Stereotyping is where the general characteristics of a particular group of people are oversimplified to make specific generalisations about their personalities, behaviours and appearances. These stereotypes mean that all members of that particular group are seen to have the oversimplified generalisation. For example, common stereotypes are that all Italians are good cooks, all

teenagers are rebels and that all women like the colour pink. As can be seen from these examples, a stereotype makes the assumption that what may be the case for some members of a group is the case for all members of the group. While some stereotypes may be positive, for example the stereotype above that all Italians are good cooks, most stereotypes are negative and have a negative impact on individuals and groups. Stereotyping often leads to <u>discrimination</u>.

Resilience in the Face of Oppression

For me, there is light at the end of the tunnel as I embark on a professional career with a salary and pension, yet I leave many of my fellow citizens behind, battling in the trenches. I will continue to fight for them and for social justice and bring the truth to the front line. I did not choose to be workless. Neither did I choose the life that I have as a lone parent. I thought I had my life mapped and beautifully planned until four years ago when my dreams were cruelly snatched from me and I was left with no other option but to be a lone parent. I have paid my taxes and have previously given my own time to serve the community in which I lived as a special constable, and am absolutely horrified and baffled as to how society thinks that it is ok to adopt mindsets that discriminate against the most vulnerable members of society. Have we been brainwashed and lost our compassion for all human beings?

What I have witnessed is a system that lacks accountability and responsibility. A system that dictates to people and places <u>benefit sanctions</u> on people, directly affecting their income and livelihoods without having to explain themselves.

▷   **Key Learning: Benefit Sanctions** For recipients of Universal Credits, they are required to sign a Claimant Commitment contract with their <u>Work Coach</u> which states the specific requirements that they need to meet in order to continue to receive Universal Credit. Where these requirements are not met, the Work Coach can apply a benefit sanction to the recipient. The sanction can be in the form of a reduction in the amount of benefit for a period of time or the complete ending of their benefit. The level of sanctions is graded from low to high, and the length of time can vary from seven days to three years. It should be noted that while benefit sanctions existed before Universal Credit, under Universal Credit both the scope and lengths of sanctions have increased.

Some would say we are already entering the realms of dictatorship. It appears the disenfranchised class must account for everything in order to receive miniscule payments that they can barely survive on, as the gap between rich and poor ever widens. You are constantly viewed with suspicion and instructed to comply with an endless series of measures designed to avoid benefit fraud. When you are told by your <u>Work Coach</u> that they want to help you and then find out, following your initial complaint and a couple of other work coaches later, that what you were promised has not been fulfilled, it is very upsetting. I have had to take a four-year-old and a five-year-old into the job centre and expect them to sit in a chair for up to half an hour whilst you try and complete the necessary process. You are looked upon as someone who is unable to control their children by panicky security guards, who clearly have no idea that the environment is not child-friendly and provides little space to respect confidentiality.

▶   **Key Learning: Work Coach** People receiving Universal Credit are
    assigned a Work Coach. The stated aim of the Work Coach is to provide
    support and advice to make the recipient work ready, through identifying
    relevant training and activities to facilitate this, for example making a
    certain number of job searches per day. This is done through the
    Claimant Commitment contract which the Work Coach draws up for the
    claimant to sign before receiving Universal Credit. Where a recipient
    does not meet their contract requirements, the Work Coach applies a
    benefit sanction to the recipient.

This whole experience of being jobless, albeit only for a temporary period, has taught me that when facing adversity, it takes superhuman qualities to overcome and be resilient. I think we would all fare well if we remember all our circumstances are uncertain and could change in a short space of time. Rather than judging people, let's try to look at the world from the other person's perspective. There is a challenge for us all to stop just accepting 'this is just the way it is' and looking the other way—we all have human rights, and one of those is a right to financial assistance when facing hardship. This is a given right and not one that we should have to fight for when the chips are down.

On a positive note, my lived experience of the benefits system has given me an invaluable insight into the oppression experienced by some of the families I will be working with as a social worker. I will make it my mission to challenge all such oppression and will challenge all fellow professionals who display discriminatory views about those who are stuck in the above dehumanising maze.

Becki's Story

I am a disabled person who became blind in my adult years. I have been a single parent for most of my son's life, having successfully raised him through to adulthood. I work as General Manager for *Shaping Our Lives National Network of Service Users and Disabled People*. Disabled people experience difficulties in finding employment, and a disproportionate number of disabled people are unemployed (The Office for National Statistics, Labour Force Survey 2018) compared to non-disabled people. My story below highlights the dilemmas in declaring one's disability in a work setting and the complications and difficulties in negotiating systems.

As a person who was working full-time in a London high-flying marketing agency, being diagnosed with a sight disease likely to make me blind in two years meant that my life changed in many ways very rapidly. I assumed my job was a constant, and while struggling with the shock of a serious diagnosis and a period of operations and recuperation, I clung to the one constant factor, my work. My employer behaved in several strange ways. Firstly, they promoted me to a manager, and my line manager visited me in the hospital after my first eye operation to announce the promotion and present keys for my new Golf GTI, a red one I had always wanted. I never drove my company car. After the eye operation and promotion, my eye consultant informed the Drivers and Vehicle Licensing Agency that I could no longer drive, and my licence was revoked immediately. After four operations, and a six-week period of sick leave, I returned to work to find all my client accounts had been given to someone else, meaning that my initial confidence that work would be my fallback began to decline. I had been 're-deployed' to the least popular client account and the least popular manager. Things went rapidly wrong, and eventually, I resigned because I missed my old job so much, and I had somehow become a second-class employee. I cried when I resigned even though I had a new job to go to, but my line manager assured me that it was for the best and that I would feel happier working in the voluntary sector earning less money and doing a fundraising job. I did not, even after I had adjusted to my health situation.

Some years later, when I had gained confidence and my sight loss was not so severe that I needed any mobility aids, I decided I wanted to return to the marketing sector. I got offered a senior job in a small private agency, where the hours were long, but the team was very supportive of each other. I bluffed my way through the company car offer and explained I had a perspective problem with my sight that could not be corrected by glasses. Looking back on it I doubt anyone believed me and I am sure I made many mistakes that seemed odd. Probably the worst moment was when I had to choose a national campaign for a well-known brand, and the designer arrived with initial concepts drawn in pencil. I could not see any of the design concepts and chose something that I am still not sure was appropriate! At the time I was partly very happy to be back in the marketing agency business, but I was also living a double life which was stressful and tiring. Eventually, my eyesight deteriorated so much that I could not do the job and I made excuses and left. I never declared my sight loss.

After this I was faced with the decision of whether to disclose my sight loss in a job application or not. For many years and applications, I did not disclose my sight loss until I had been to at least the first interview. My sight loss was such that I could present as a non-disabled person and believed this gave me the best chance of being employed. In reality, it would have been better for me to disclose in my application. The employers who would not consider employing a disabled person would not bother to ask me to interview, and I would not need to bother turning up for a process that I would fail just because I was disabled. However, to accept this, and confront my disability in this way, I had to grieve, accept and manage my sight loss, and this took many years. This is very common for many people who develop an impairment in adult life; many try to deny and hide it because they have not been able to work through normal coping stages. The pressure of carrying on can lead to further health problems and mental health distress, potentially leading to worklessness.

Lived Experience of 'Enabling' Policies

Ironically, employment policies for disabled people have not necessarily made the challenge of getting work any easier. The *Two Ticks* standard, *Investors in People* and more recently the Department for Work and Pensions (DWP) *Disability Confident* system can both be an enabler and a barrier to meeting your potential in work. Although these systems and diversity policies encourage a disabled person to apply, it also creates the non-disabled candidate vs the disabled candidate syndrome. Candidates end up in silos, and feelings that you are only there because you are disabled can reduce your confidence.

Reasonable Adjustments?

In theory, recruiters should not have access to diversity data, but I have had to telephone the line manager in advance to discuss the content of the job and what aspects I would need to arrange <u>reasonable adjustments</u> for. In addition to this, requesting a large print or other accessible application form normally needs to be done by special request, immediately breaking the equal playing field basis you should be able to compete on. Someone who is shortlisting applications is going to notice an accessible application alongside the standard format, and despite best attempts to create an equal system, unconscious and conscious bias will start to take a role.

▶ **Key Learning: Reasonable Adjustments** Under the *Equality Act 2010*, employers, businesses and services are legally required to make reasonable adjustments to remove or reduce the effect of the disability that a person has. This legal requirement applies when a disabled person applies to a job and when they are employed. The reasonable adjustments that can be made could be to the physical workplace (e.g., installing a ramp at the entrance to a building), the way things are done (e.g., changing an employee's shift pattern) and/or getting someone to help the employee to do their job (e.g., providing dyslexic support tutoring for employees). It is employers' legal responsibility to make reasonable adjustments either when they know or expect someone has a disability or when an employee requests them to do so. However, requests for adjustments have to be reasonable and can be refused by an employer for not being reasonable.

   Underemployment of disabled people is a common problem. Employers often make the mistake of making a reasonable adjustment by removing what they believe to be the difficult aspects of the job for a disabled person. A reasonable adjustment actually means that support should be provided so a disabled person can work equally alongside non-disabled colleagues. This should mean providing support and equipment to allow this to happen. However, employers and people often assume it would be 'kinder' or 'easier' if some perceived barriers or tasks are removed. All this achieves is that the new disabled employee feels less important and capable than their non-disabled colleagues.

Reasonable adjustments can also be flexible working patterns, for example to allow someone to work without travelling in rush hour. Unfortunately, fellow employees can quickly feel envious of special conditions and become antagonistic towards the disabled colleague. Managers and organisations need to consider employment policies carefully and make similar adjustments possible for everyone in the appropriate circumstances.

I once phoned a manager to discuss a job at my local authority. I was qualified for the job, but it stated I needed to be able to drive; I telephoned to discuss this aspect and establish if a support worker driver could meet this aspect of the job. The recruiting manager asked me how I would get to the office. I replied I would travel by train and walk from the rail station. He replied that he thought I would not manage this on my own, even though it was only a 5-minute walk. I have since worked with this local authority as part of my current job and have walked to the office even though my sight loss is more advanced now. Most surprising is that I just accepted this at the time.

Access to Work Scheme

The Access to Work Scheme is designed to support disabled people into work, provided by the DWP. It offers a sliding scale of financial support depending on the size of the employer. It can be used for specialist access equipment, for support workers and travel in and to work.

▷   **Key Learning: Access to Work Scheme**   Access to Work is an employment
         support scheme which aims to help people living with a disability or a
         long-term health condition to start or stay in work. It is provided as a
         grant, which means that it does not have to be paid back and does not
         affect other benefits. It can be used for things such as extra travel costs
         getting to work or a job interview, an interpreter, adapting equipment
         and buying equipment. It can also be used to start up a business. There
         is no set grant amount; this depends on each specific case.

However, the system is difficult to navigate and impossible to put in place without the support of your new employer. My own experience (even in the disability Voluntary and Community Services sector) is that the employer expects you to negotiate and arrange the support on your own. You have to be able to arrange the support as quickly as possible as it takes six weeks or more for the DWP to approve and put in place your support. This means that many people must either start a new job without support for several weeks or delay their start date. Both actions discriminate against a disabled person and often lead to early failure in work (most commonly disabled people fail in a new job within three months). My own experience was that I negotiated a rate of hourly pay for two self-employed support workers. Once I began work the employer then decided they needed to employ the support workers and in order to meet the add-on costs of employing extra staff wanted an additional £4 per hour in pay. It took me many weeks to re-negotiate this with Access to Work, and I had to work without a support worker in the interim as the employer's insurance did not cover my support workers as self-employed people. More recently, after claiming Access to Work for more than ten years, the DWP failed to renew my contract for support in time before my current contract expired. This meant I had to take the liability of the costs of my support workers personally or let them all go and re-recruit once the contract was renewed. It is essential that disabled people have someone in their new workplace who is knowledgeable about the Access to Work programme and is a single point of contact for all enquiries.

I know someone who had an accident and needed to use a wheelchair. He applied for a job and was delighted to be successful and secured an Access to Work Scheme grant for a specialist chair and some access equipment to assist with using a computer. On his first day, his new manager apologetically explained that they could not fit his chair and equipment at the desk in the main office, so they had created a working space in a basement room with no windows and no colleagues. There was an accessible lift, but to use this meant transferring into his wheelchair which took considerable effort. He left the job a couple of months later with mental health distress and health problems relating to not getting enough natural light. He has never worked since.

Making Policies Work

Employment policies for people with learning disabilities have been particularly disempowering over the last couple of decades. A young female person with learning disabilities was forced to wash up in a hotel kitchen to get work-related benefits. She hated the job and did not utilise any of her skills. She is now a successful member of a user-led organisation, has written a book and is working on a project to enable other people with learning disabilities to take part in mainstream social and leisure activities, none of which have required washing-up skills.

Environmental infrastructure is very important for disabled people to have successful working careers. Provisions such as the assistance service on national rail providers and the London Underground are vital to allow disabled people to travel independently and to work. I would only be able to work with these types of support systems.

On a positive note, there are environments where disabled people can thrive. Traditionally, these used to be inclusive workplaces such as local authorities and voluntary sector organisations. Although austerity policies have led to fewer opportunities, disabled people may find long-term work in these more inclusive environments. Those employers who can embrace disabled people in their workforce are rewarded with more loyal employees, who are proven to take less time off work, work longer hours and stay longer at companies. For the disabled person, there is a possible conflict in work-life balance, but many disabled people will make this compromise in order to take part in society.

Jon's Story

I am a married man in my 40s who has enjoyed a career as <u>foster carer</u> for the past 11 years. Prior to this, I was an engineer, a job I also loved but which I had to leave due to its physical demands not suiting my muscular dystrophy. My story below reflects on wider attitudes within the workplace, and I hope it will provide some inspiration at a time when so many disabled people are needlessly unemployed.

I became disabled slowly over time in an ever-decreasing spiral of capacity. I trained to be an engineer, and I worked in industry for as long as my condition would allow, until I was eventually turfed out on my ear because I was disabled. I then spent several years trying to get back into work and failing because I have a disability, as I was often the best candidate in the interview until I mentioned my condition. Funny how things change.

This was perhaps my first taste of disability adversity, the way employers run away from it and don't see beyond the heightened insurance risk or the possible slightly lower productivity. I have become gradually aware over time to how these new kinds of adversities creep up on you. For a disabled person, adversity isn't something that stands alone; it comes with a whole host of other issues that pile weight onto it. <u>Discrimination</u>, bigotry, bullying and exclusion also play a part in day-to-day life. This can present itself in many ways—some are obviously cruel and intentional, like being laughed at and called names because you walk differently or look differently, not being given equal opportunities and so on. Some are unintentional, such as when events don't have disabled access or toilets or parking.

▶ **Key Learning: Discrimination** Discrimination refers to where a group or individual is denied equal treatment or are disadvantaged based solely on their evident or perceived characteristics. Examples might be where an older person is denied treatment because of their age, a woman is paid less because of her sex or a person from a certain country is denied employment because of their ethnicity. The key point about discrimination is that a person is treated unequally to another person not based on their capacity or aptitude but based on a prejudgement about the person. Discrimination can make itself apparent in a complete lack of access to services, a lower level of services and/or a lower quality of service. There are two main types of discrimination, direct discrimination (where a person is treated less favourably specifically because of their characteristics) and indirect discrimination (where a rule or condition negatively affects one group over another).

Society itself has a lot to answer for in the way people with disabilities are treated, especially considering that 1 in 5 people have a disability of some kind. Most people only see disability that is either extreme or obvious—most of us don't look like Stephen Hawking—and, because of their own discomfort around serious disability, form a negative opinion about it that they apply to the word in all circumstances. Most disability is hidden, for example diabetes, or hearing or visual impairment. I can't tell you how many times I've been told to get out of a disabled parking space because I don't 'look' disabled.

I personally know what it is like to apply for dozens of jobs and be the lead candidate right up to the point I mention my disability, I know how it feels to be laughed at on the street, and I know what it's like to not be able to attend events because it's on the third floor with no lift. This has given me the ability and the right to speak out about it from my firsthand experience.

Society doesn't engage with disability because historically, all the way back to antiquity, a person's value is judged on their productivity. Even now, how many companies have a 'piece work' production mentality, where the more you do, the more you earn? It's called the pay packet society. This ethos is carried to this day into the mainstream; perhaps in many it's a subconscious thing, but in my experience often it's not; it filters down through generations where disabled in real terms becomes a label that seems to mean lesser than abled. This is the reason employers don't want us, this combined with the obvious insurance factors, the health and safety aspects or the provision of support they need to put in place to facilitate disabled people in the workplace. Great word is 'facilitate'—great in hyperbole, not so good in reality. I see very little facilitating in the wider world at a pace that meets the needs of a disabled person. Let's face it; as an employer why give yourself the hassle of employing Mike, when you can employ Bob who doesn't have a disability? Well, perhaps with a little more insight into disability, employers would see the hidden skill sets that disabled people possess, their constant ability to adapt, their drive to overcome challenges, their determination to prove themselves equal, their compassion for others, their pride at being valued and productive plus the loyalty they show to the companies who give them equal opportunities.

Ending on a positive note, my wife and I decided to pursue a career in foster care, expecting that such organisations would genuinely model equality of opportunity. However, because of my being disabled, we were turned down by two agencies without even being assessed, suggesting that discrimination and ignorance about disabled people is alive and well, even within 'caring' organisations. The third agency I approached, the *National Fostering Agency*, took a completely different approach, recognised the strengths and insights of having lived with disability and saw these as strengths, not weaknesses. Working from home suits my wife and I, and we have proved ourselves to be effective foster carers for the past 11 years. We have been flexible and adaptable, and so have our fostering employer—there are hundreds of foster agencies across the UK, yet hardly any disabled people are working as foster carers. This is not a financial or risk issue—it is an issue of institutional discrimination which must be challenged by disabled people and professionals alike.

Commentary

The accounts of Joanne, Becki and Jon above provide a varied and illuminating account of navigating the benefits and employment spheres as a vulnerable or disabled individual. Due to the similarity of their experiences, their combined accounts provide validity, clarity and significance to the proposal for changes, as detailed below. However, before discussing these, it is also important to outline the similarity of their accounts with other service users and carers in this book.

A key point that emerges is the importance of legislation to improving, albeit in limited ways, the lived experiences of individuals, as also evident in Julia Smith's account in Chap. 7. Prior to the Industrial Revolution, disabled people worked in low paid and menial jobs in the agrarian economy, and the subsequent industrialised economy employed disabled people in similarly low paid jobs. Social opinion began to bring about changes from 1900 onwards. The harsh regimes of workhouses (originally created by the *Poor Law Act 1645*) were gradually replaced by more caring regimes, and pensions and benefits begun to be paid to certain marginalised groups who were unable to work. Sheltered workshops where training and rehabilitation were promoted grew from the post-war years up until the *Employment Act 1980*. Despite this *Act* having stated that employers with 20 or more employees must have a minimum of 3% of disabled people represented, such high aspirations have never been met, even by the government as an employer. Such potentially transformative quotas were subsequently quietly dropped, and as Jon's narrative indicates, there are hundreds of foster agencies who do not employ any disabled people as foster carers.

More recently, The *Disability Discrimination Act 1995* promised a new world wherein diversity would be genuinely embraced across all walks of life, including the workplace. *The Equality Act 2010* was a significant milestone for disabled people in that it brought a range of previous measures together and introduced statutory categorisation of people's 'protected characteristics' (age, disability, gender reassignment, marriage and civil partnership, pregnancy and maternity, race, religion or belief, sex, sexual orientation), which must be respected by employers who now fall under an obligation to make 'reasonable adjustments' to the workplace to accommodate the diverse needs of marginalised groups. This latter piece of legislation has done much to bring about more diverse workplaces, but as evidenced by the narratives above and by the many cases brought to industrial tribunals, there is still a long way to go to accommodate diversity across the wider economy. The Papworth Trust (2018) found many disabled people still experienced discrimination in the workplace, particularly regarding being given lesser levels of responsibility, not being promoted and being unsuccessful when seeking a new job. Becki's example of the very skilled young woman with learning difficulties having been given a washing-up job is an example of such practices. The changing nature of contemporary jobs and advances in new technology theoretically mean that disabled people, for example, should have wider work opportunities available to them. However, today's low-paid jobs often involve zero-hours contracts, poor pension provisions and flexible working patterns, all of which primarily serve the employer, not the worker. Some people on benefits choose to stay on benefit rather than risk entering a precarious workplace with no security and no guarantee of returning to a level of benefits which may have been built up over some years.

The lived experience narratives above highlight the enduring battles within welfare policy for poor and disabled people seeking work, battles which are eloquently described also by Ryan (2019) in a wide-ranging critique by service users of the contemporary state of welfare in the UK. The introduction of welfare benefits in westernised societies is based on two main rationales—the moral good of providing 'safety net' levels of income for those members of society unable to work either due to disability or because of structural unemployment, and also the need for governments to keep their citizens clothed, housed and fed to a sufficient extent that social unrest (at its extreme leading to governments being overthrown) is avoided. Some governments, however, deny the structural reasons for unemployment and perpetuate the line that the fault for unemployment lies with the individual. Perhaps the most famous example of this ideology is found in the words of then Conservative Minister, Norman Tebbit, who told an audience about being brought up in the 1930s by his father who had become unemployed; his father 'didn't riot – he got on his bike and looked for work' (Tebbit 1981). This blaming of individuals for their unemployed status has remained in western culture, and a war on 'benefits scroungers' has been waged by right-wing governments ever since, while the tax avoidance and evasion of corporations remains largely unchecked (Ryan 2019). Joanne was certainly made to feel like she was 'undeserving' in her first encounter with the benefits system, and Jon's narrative above also shows that such attitudes still exist, and it is of concern that these are both articulate people, well able to self-advocate and aware of their rights.

Jon's testimony states that an avenue to using his skills was to become a foster carer, and he has since been a champion of disabled people as foster carers. Foster care (see Chaps. 4 and 5) is a very interesting area of social policy, but the problems disabled people face even in such a caring field are considerable. A study into the absence of disabled foster carers in the workforce found that fear of losing benefits was a significant barrier to disabled people applying to be foster carers, especially in an age when disabled people have been demonised as 'scroungers' (Unwin et al. 2020). Joanne was certainly made to feel like she was 'undeserving' in her first encounter with the benefits system. Policies regarding benefits and foster care fees/allowances were found to be very confusing at government and local levels, compounded by the fact that most foster agencies were not contemporary in their understanding of benefits systems for disabled people. The project produced some guidelines to help clarify the situation, guidelines which essentially state that any benefits relating to an individual's disability, for example Personal Independence Payments, would be retained in a fostering situation and that other potential sources of income such as Access to Work would be assessed on a case-by-case basis.

The recent introduction of Universal Credit by the 2010 coalition government was partly intended to streamline a complex series of benefits but was also to make it 'worthwhile' to come off a reliance on benefits and take up employment. However, early indications are that this initiative is proving to be a cost-cutting exercise which has been roundly condemned by disabled people's movements (Ryan 2019). Universal Credit is still being rolled out by a Conservative government at the time of writing, and almost all critique received to date suggests it has failed to achieve this goal, leaving many in poverty and even driving others to suicide (Pring 2018).

Other measures such as <u>Disability Living Allowance</u>, introduced in 1992, were designed to accommodate the extra costs of being a disabled person and, being non-means-tested, were initially welcomed by disabled people's organisations. However, its replacement with Personal Independence Payments (PIP) in 2013 has attracted a lot of criticism for being overly intrusive and geared to deny claims rather than support claims. Assessors are employed by a private agency and not specifically expert in the areas of disability they are assessing. Some 70% of PIP appeals are successful (Disability Rights UK 2018), which indicates a core problem with the system.

McLoughlin (2019) discusses attitudes towards claimants of benefits in a reflection entitled *Stop Treating Disabled People as Criminals* and laments the fact that assessors are working to targets which reward a drop in successful claims. Joanne's suggestion in her testimony is that the personnel she met in benefits offices were working to a 'results' culture, results in this scenario meaning denying benefits, rather than encouragement of take-up. Access to Work provision was a discretional grant introduced in 1994 and was a scheme intended to accommodate disabled peoples' extra costs incurred through being employed (travel/transcribers/British Sign Language interpreters/support workers). Various reforms have been made to 'Access to Work', but significant problems, misinterpretations and local interpretations by civil servants remain key barriers to the fuller take-up of this scheme.

The above lived experiences and commentary would suggest that all areas of employment are affected by a complex and unfair system which traps many marginalised people in low paid jobs or forces them to remain on benefits. No government since the second world war has managed to find the balance between providing a decent income safety net for its citizens unable to work and making work a worthwhile enterprise for those who might otherwise stay on benefits.

Reflective Questions

Joanne's Story

1. How might her experience have been different had she not had English as her first language or if she had, say, a cognitive disability?
2. What would you suggest a training course for benefits centre staff should cover regarding interpersonal skills?
3. Could social policy regarding benefits systems incorporate a user voice in its development and review?

Becki's Story

1. What do you think are the benefits and disadvantages of declaring a disability at the point of application/interview or after you have started a job?
2. Do you work for or have contact with an organisation which has the *Disability Confident* award? What does this policy mean in practice at that organisation, for staff and customers?
3. What might a simpler policy regarding 'Access to Work' look like?

Jon's Story

1. With reference to Jon's testimony above, how might you explain the differences in employment between disabled and non-disabled people?
2. Why do you think there are so few disabled foster carers employed by fostering agencies?
3. What could be done in terms of social policies to encourage more disabled people into workplaces such as foster care?

References

Department for Work and Pensions, *Universal Credit: Welfare That Works*, Cm 7957 (The Stationery Office Ltd., 2010). www.dwp.gov.uk/universal-credit. Accessed 12 June 2020

Disability Rights UK, 4 out of 10 PIP claimants do not appeal. It would be too stressful (2018). https://www.disabilityrightsuk.org/news/2018/september/4-out-10-pip-claimants-do-not-appeal-it-would-be-too-stressful. Accessed 02 Jan 2020

J. McLoughlin, *Stop Treating Disabled People Like Criminals. Professional Social Work* (British Association of Social Workers, Birmingham, 2019), p. 33

I. Newman, Work as a route out of poverty: a critical evaluation of the UK welfare to work policy. Policy Stud. **32**(2), 91–108 (2011). https://doi.org/10.1080/01442872.2010.533510

Office for National Statistics, Labour force survey (2018). https://www.ons.gov.uk/employmentandlabourmarket/peopleinwork/employmentandemployeetypes/methodologies/labourforcesurveyperformanceandqualitymonitoringreports/labourforcesurveyperformanceandqualitymonitoringreportoctobertodecember2018. Accessed 10 June 2020

Papworth Trust, Facts and figures. Disability in the United Kingdom (2018). http://online.flip-builder.com/afjd/uvad/mobile/index.html. Accessed 02 Dec 2019

J. Pring, DWP's secret benefit deaths reviews: universal credit death linked to claimant commitment 'threats (2018). https://www.disabilitynewsservice.com/dwps-secret-benefit-deaths-reviews-universal-credit-death-linked-to-claimant-commitment-threats/. Accessed 01 June 2020

F. Ryan, *Crippled. Austerity and the Demonization of Disabled People* (Verso, London, 2019)

N. Tebbit, Norman Tebbit Interview | Conservative Party | Afternoon plus (1981). https://www.youtube.com/watch?v=kBe-nyb1e7c. Accessed 12 Dec 2019

P. Unwin, B. Meakin, A. Jones, *Disabled Foster Carers*, Practice Note 73 (CoramBAAF, London, 2020). https://corambaaf.org.uk/bookshop/practice-notes. Accessed on 24 June 2020

J. Wiggan, Telling stories of 21st century welfare: the UK Coalition government and the neo-liberal discourse of worklessness and dependency. Crit. Soc. Policy **32**(3), 383–405 (2012). https://doi.org/10.1177/0261018312444413

Living with Long-Term Disability and Care: A Perspective on the Adequacy of Provision and Areas for Improvements

7

Julia Louise Therese Smith and Clive Sealey

This chapter is by Julia Smith who has personally lived with an acquired physical impairment for close to four decades. The focus is on Julia's experiences of long-term care provided by a wide-ranging group of professionals and service providers working within the National Health Service and local authority social services. Over this extensive length of time, there have been many changes which Julia has experienced and witnessed, with many having been personally significant in terms of the care and support received or not received. In particular, there have been marked changes in the structure of the social care sector and organisations which have affected the roles of the people working within them and which in turn have impacted to varying degrees the care and support Julia received.

The main aims of the chapter are to:

1. Detail the lived experience of living with a long-term disability and receiving long-term care.
2. Chronicle key policy and societal changes that have occurred in relation to living with a long-term disability and receiving long-term care.
3. Outline possible improvements in policy and practice in relation to living with a long-term disability and receiving long-term care.

J. L. T. Smith (✉)
Birmingham, UK
e-mail: smith.j422@talk1.com

C. Sealey
School of Allied Health and Community, University of Worcester, Worcester, UK
e-mail: c.sealey@worc.ac.uk

© The Author(s), under exclusive license to Springer Nature Switzerland AG 2021
C. Sealey et al. (eds.), *Social Policy, Service Users and Carers*,
https://doi.org/10.1007/978-3-030-69876-8_7

103

Who Am I?

My name is Julia Smith, and at the time of writing this, I am 50 years old. I experienced a happy childhood growing up in the early 1970s within a large family of ten siblings and loving parents. As I approached my teenage years, I began to find myself with tiring legs as I climbed flights of stairs at school and trailed behind classmates in school cross country runs which I easily attributed to a general dislike of sports on cold days. However, as I progressively dropped schoolbooks on a daily basis and cutlery fell from my hands in the school canteen, a visit to the then 'family GP' was followed soon after by a consultation with a hospital paediatrician. Despite numerous medical procedures and investigations and finding myself thrown into an alien world, doctors continued to be baffled by my symptoms, with a suggestion that my symptoms were being caused by delayed shock and grief following the premature passing of my mum three months previously. A rapid deterioration ensued, and within a three-month period, I had shifted from being a fully mobile young teenager to one who was paralysed from the neck downwards, unable even to lift a finger. I underwent a further gamut of in-depth investigations undertaken within the setting of a children's hospital ward, which subsequently went on to become 'my home' for close to four years. It was some years later I learned that doctors had met with my newly widowed dad and informed him of a grave prognosis with a suggested life expectancy of six months, something which was not then shared with me given my young age and my then time of grieving. Somewhat baffled, the medical profession offered with reluctance, given my age of just 13, a diagnosis of multiple sclerosis, and much time was spent travelling to hospitals UK wide in seeking to find a definitive diagnosis. It was three years later before doctors reached this milestone when an extensive spinal tumour was discovered, and so began a new point in my journey to which I shall return.

The chapter will discuss a number of areas that have impacted on my life in a variety of ways, such as adapting to life as a disabled person in the early 1980s. This was a time when society and public spaces/buildings overall were for the large part only accessible to people who were able-bodied and able to mobilise independently and when people with any form of physical difference were predominantly invisible within local communities. It will examine how NHS and social care provision has changed for people living with a physical impairment over the past three decades and will discuss the impact and the effect of pieces of disability legislation on areas such as employment and housing. In addition, it will discuss, from my personal perspective, the changes that are perceived to have taken place across society overall with regard to improved disability awareness, changed attitudes towards disability and an increased acceptance of disabled people generally in the early twenty-first century. For most people living with a long-term physical impairment in the UK, their personal circumstances will often be determined to a significant degree by receipt of social policy provision that impacts on most aspects of their lives. This includes the level of financial support available, access to suitable accommodation and care and support received. I will outline how my experiences of such social policy provision have often determined many aspects of daily living and continue to do so.

In enabling me to begin writing of my experiences of long-term care, some knowledge of and background to 'my story' is required which is where I shall begin.

My Transition to Being 'Disabled': Early Experiences

On New Year's Day in 1980, aged 13, I was admitted to the children's ward of my local hospital, following the abrupt, unexplained and scary onset of sudden paralysis. There, I found myself thrown into an alien environment of crying babies, 6 am lights on and a dependence on an array of nursing staff for absolutely everything. Days were spent in the company of doctors, porters, physiotherapists and nursing staff, with the reality of family members only permitted to visit one hour a day. Visiting school friends were unsure how to react to my altered physical status, but did their best to lift spirits with talk of returning to school and sharing the latest school news. These visits were tolerated in the belief that this was a temporary condition. However, as weeks became months and I observed other patients come onto the ward and return home, I found myself a permanent fixture on the ward with any hope of discharge a distant dream. With no improvement in my condition, I unwittingly heard whispers of assessments for a permanent wheelchair and the possibility of attending a <u>special school</u>.

▷ **Key Learning: Special Schools** A special school is a school that is specifically designed to meet the specialist medical, social or welfare needs of children and young people. These needs will usually be stated in an <u>Education, Health and Care plan</u> (EHC), although having a EHC plan does not guarantee entry to a special school. Special schools teach children with specialist needs together, rather than with other children without such needs. Special schools teach the national curriculum and follow the same assessment processes as mainstream schools. The main advantage of a special school is that class sizes are usually much smaller, meaning that there is greater attention to the individual needs of the child. The main disadvantage is that it can lead to the segregation of children away from other mainstream schooling and other individuals (Norwich 2008).

Attempts to spend short periods of time at home soon brought the realisation that the family home where I had grown up was no longer somewhere I could mobilise. Additionally, with any venture into the outside world now requiring a wheelchair, I was faced with adjusting to the possibility that I may now be permanently disabled and that what lay ahead was a future of many unknowns. In local communities, I encountered totally inaccessible environments with steps or narrow doorways into shops or public buildings the norm. This meant that I had to be 'parked' outside on my own whilst passers-by would stare, wear expressions of sympathy on their faces or even throw money in my lap, thus providing a stark reminder of my 'difference' within an able-bodied world which I was to discover and was to prove slow to change.

After 18 months of steadily outgrowing the children's ward, where stimulation and meaningful education were non-existent, I resumed my education at a local special school. However, this provided further confirmation of my disabled status in several ways. Firstly, each day I would be manually lifted into a taxi by an escort, with a wheelchair and a smiling carer awaiting at the school doors and the process reversed some six hours later. Secondly, welcome though the change of environment was, special school was yet another alien environment in which I found myself alongside pupils with a range of physical impairments, none of which I either had awareness of or had come into contact with during my previous able-bodied life. All too soon it became apparent that my previous expectation of resuming the ten subjects I was studying for at my private girl's school was not going to be possible. Rather, the school had low academic expectations of its pupils, with the maximum available for pupils to study being the then CSE's in English, maths and biology. Whilst 'special' arrangements were made for a French tutor to come into school so I could continue to learn a language at which I had previously excelled, frustratingly lesson times were often interrupted by physiotherapy or hydrotherapy sessions. Disappointingly, little encouragement was given to work hard as there pervaded an air of expectation that upon leaving school the prospect of entering into employment was unlikely. This was because typically, many pupils upon leaving the school attended local day care or training centres, so there was perceived to be no need to encourage pupils to set their aims higher. Having attended the special school for three years, I subsequently left with the equivalent of four O levels (CSE Grade 1), which was to coincide with a new chapter on my journey through long-term care.

Accepting a New Physical Identity

The discovery in 1983 that the central cause of my paralysis was a spinal tumour led to its removal followed by a six-month admission to a spinal rehabilitation unit far from home. This is where I came to realise that my dream of resuming full movement of all limbs would not be fulfilled. Such was the level of damage to the spinal cord that the mid-1980s became a time of accepting that this was my new life, my 'new identity'. Throughout this time a gamut of professionals descended into my life, whose roles and purpose I often struggled to understand at a time when I had so many 'problems' to sort out, so many questions to which I was seeking answers. With the belief that their job was done, I was discharged from rehabilitation to the children ward, which remained 'home'. However, as I approached my later teens, this was no longer somewhere I wished to consider 'home', yet equally the prospect of living within a nursing home with people much older than me filled me with dread. Likewise, the family home (which many of my siblings felt was no longer 'home' following the death of our mum at such a young age) was wholly impractical to adapt. By chance, within my local area the local authority was constructing a purpose-built residential home, Hollybank, for younger adults with a physical disability, which they would run. The opening of this new facility was attracting interest for its pioneering aim to offer care that was predominantly 'resident led'. Whilst the prospect of residential care concerned me, fuelled by a worry I could possibly spend the rest of my days invisible behind closed doors, in reality this was my only option, and thus Hollybank became my new 'home'.

To live within the residential care setting of Hollybank, I had to learn about the world of disability benefits and an associated constant cycle of form filling. 'My social worker' (a term which now rarely exists), assisted in applying for 'Mobility Allowance', an allowance paid as part of Disability Living Allowance to severely disabled people subject to criteria and paid by the then Department of Social Security. This, along with Income Support (more form filling), enabled me to pay for 'B&B lodgings', with an allowance of approximately £15 per week able to be retained for 'pocket money expenses', such as toiletries and personal items.

▷   **Key Learning: Disability Living Allowance/Mobility Allowance** Until very recently, the main benefit for people living with a disability was Disability Living Allowance (DLA). This is a non-means-tested cash benefit that provides for the personal care needs and/or the mobility needs of the individual. The mobility component of DLA is called Mobility Allowance. The benefit is paid dependent on the needs of the person, meaning the higher the care and mobility needs a person has, the higher the amount of benefit received. It is also possible to exchange Mobility Allowance entitlement for the lease of a car. Since 2012, DLA has been gradually replaced by Personal Independence Payment (PIP), with the intention that DLA will be totally phased out.

Within the home, all aspects of care were provided by care staff with daily routines determined mostly by each resident. For example, whilst all meals were provided, having the space of a personal bedroom and bathroom not only felt like a luxury after dormitory hospital wards and large shared bathrooms but also promoted independence skills amongst residents. As one of many agencies now seemingly involved in my long-term care planning, the local wheelchair service provided a powered wheelchair which, despite being cumbersome, ugly and grey, enabled me for the first time in four years to move independently and unaccompanied throughout the purpose-built building. Whilst not representing the outcome I had either anticipated or hoped for when admitted to hospital four years previously, this environment nevertheless brought a new sense of freedom and somewhere I could call 'home'.

However, whilst suggestions of attending day care centres and disability social clubs were regularly raised at placement reviews, the absence of proper education and mental stimulation over a four-year period remained something which my brain craved for. Whilst the change in my physical being could not be argued, I held a strong belief that this should not be justification for the mind being permitted to become non-functioning also.

New Opportunities, New Horizons

With the encouragement of an innovative, forward-thinking home manager, whom I would later go on to work alongside, I moved to a residential college for students with physical disabilities, where two years were spent studying for A levels whilst living alongside 100 other students. Here I became exposed to a whole new world of disability in which I was gradually becoming more comfortable being a part of. This contrasted with a feeling in earlier times of being nervous of entering an alien world and facing the reality of a non-return to my able-bodied status. Thus, my focus shifted beyond that of A level study and daring to dream of potentially a university education.

During the mid to late 1980s across the UK, it was becoming apparent that there was occurring a slow shift towards making the outside world more structurally accessible to disabled people, arguably to some degree resulting from the first International Year of Disabled People in 1981. For example, the residential college I attended allowed students to use the adapted minibus to make trips to the city centre at weekends and outings to concerts at local concert venues which were beginning to accommodate wheelchair users. Likewise, shopping areas were very slowly starting to consider the needs of disabled people with wider and level access doorways, whilst local councils in some areas began to provide allocated parking for disabled people. Furthermore, there became a growing recognition that disabled adults of various ages wanted to be able to learn to drive given the appropriate adaptations to vehicles. Thus, after two years spent at residential college, I emerged with three A levels and a full driving licence neither of which, just a few years previously, would I (nor others) have considered to be achievable or possible. Whilst historically over many centuries both perceptions of and attitudes towards physical disability were overwhelmingly negative ones, there emerged in the late 1980s a slow but definite feeling that positive shifts were beginning to take place. The voices of disabled people, for so long unheard or ignored, were slowly emerging with a voice both locally and nationally.

During the latter years of the 1980s, a small group of forward-looking UK universities emerged who sought to cater for the needs of disabled people wishing to pursue higher education. One university was exemplary in this shift, and thus the following three years were spent at the University of Nottingham studying for an undergraduate degree. Whilst challenges arose and obstacles had to be overcome, a campus university was beneficial practically, and the provision of an adapted minibus with an employed driver enabled disabled students to move around between lectures and campus generally. In addition, *Community Service Volunteers* who were provided with university accommodation alongside the student they were working alongside provided care and support to disabled students requiring help with aspects of daily living. Assistance with any health issues was provided by the onsite nursing team working at the campus-based health centre, and together things were made to work successfully. Finding myself as the sole disabled student in a hall of residence with 200 students was initially overwhelming and provided a stark reminder of my previous able-bodied status and feelings of what 'might have been'.

However, gradually friendships were built, my physical difference seemingly accepted, and without exception, I found people across campus willing to help with any tasks that required a helping hand. Thus 1990 saw proud family members watch on as I graduated with an undergraduate degree alongside friends who, three decades later, I feel privileged to have continued close friendships with.

Challenging Perceptions: Personally and Professionally

I had now lived away from 'home' for five years, during which time I had become more independent. Now I yearned to move into my own home despite the inevitable fears of whether it could work given the 'obstacles' involved, intertwined with a fear of becoming institutionalised if I didn't at least try. Having been awarded compensation for the delay in diagnosis which was shown to have resulted from medical negligence, during my final year at university, this enabled the purchase of a bungalow in the area where I had spent my childhood. Post-graduation, the bungalow became my new 'home' with the required adaptations carried out and with care support in place from a local care agency funded through Disability Living Allowance until more comprehensive assessments could be undertaken. Evident among the health and social care professionals with whom I maintained involvement (among whom there were a number whose overlap in roles began to frustrate me), there remained many scratched heads concerning my expressed wish to continue with further study. While social workers were happy to offer day care provision where I could mix with others while learning crafts and doing puzzles, they had no idea how I could continue my studies, indeed my knowledge proving greater than theirs. Whilst not wishing to deny the role that such establishments have played in the lives of many disabled people (though increasingly less so in recent years as budget cuts have led to closures or restrictions on who can attend), it was apparent that these professionals seemed unable to comprehend my wish to expand horizons. Coming from a family who had all achieved academically, worked hard and enjoyed their chosen occupations, this was a possibility that I wished to explore despite my different circumstances, and an interest in studying for a social work career was expressed.

To the surprise of many 'professionals', I was accepted onto a master's degree course in social work at Birmingham University, having shown I met the same entry criteria as other candidates, whilst my life experiences were also considered by the interview panel to be relevant to my intended area of study. Two years of hard work ensued both from the demands of the course and negotiating a campus that, like Nottingham was beginning to recognise and cater for the needs of students with mobility issues but by the nature of many buildings' structures, was a slow process. Additionally, this period brought renewed physical challenges and extended spells of hospitalisation due to a recurrence of tumour growths, but with unending support and encouragement from staff and fellow students alike, I graduated in the early 1990s with a combined master's degree and a social worker qualification.

Having qualified and now keen to find employment, I remained under no illusion that I represented to many people the 'very sort of person' a social worker would have on their caseload and not vice versa. Furthermore, given the often-challenging nature of a social worker's role and the physical and mental demands that such a job could entail, there would be a question of whether I was physically strong enough to cope. However, my medical team supported me in my efforts, whilst realistically highlighting that a front-line role may prove physically challenging. With a sense of amazement, I was offered employment within an adult services team where I had spent a three-month placement. In this role, I was continually learning week by week and overcoming challenges along the way. From both a professional and a personal perspective, sadly to a large degree, these challenges were mainly from older members of social work staff who had traditionally 'taken care of' people with disabilities and now had to question both their attitudes towards and awareness of disability. Regrettably, I experienced further health complications including the removal of further tumour growths and recurring chest infections which often necessitated hospital stays long distances from home. This led to a decision after five years to reduce my working hours to part-time in wishing to be fair to both work colleagues and clients I was working alongside, in addition to acknowledging the need to maintain my overall well-being as best as possible.

During the latter years of the 1990s I worked within a neighbouring local authority in a post that, whilst physically and mentally challenging, was enjoyable and through which I gained a wealth of knowledge that was to be invaluable in later years. Regrettably as time passed, the physical challenges and noticeable changes in what had become classed as a progressive condition began to be visible to all. Thus, with the support of the Occupational Health department, a difficult decision was made to retire from work on medical grounds. Whilst personally saddened by the somewhat inevitable outcome, likewise I was heartened at having left front-line social work with a sense that disability awareness was heading in a much improved and positive direction. Shortly before my departure, I met with the Head of Adult Social Care and was heartened by her telling me of how through being in post I had changed staff members' perceptions of disabled people. Likewise, she believed that awareness and understanding of disability had improved across the organisation in a way that could not be taught within training days or lecture room walls. For me, this was felt to be a fitting end to a decade or so spent in front-line social work. In departing, I felt that a considerable amount had been achieved throughout the 1990s from the perspective of disabled people who were service users and with a hope that such foundations could be built upon. The reality of this or otherwise will be explored later within the chapter.

Towards More Flexible Care

From a personal viewpoint, I believe that a slow but gradual shift within society of improved awareness and understanding of disability was to a certain extent determined by the introduction of disability legislation including the *NHS & Community*

Care Act 1990 and the *Disability Discrimination Act 1995*. As this chapter (indeed the book) has as its focus service user experiences, I shall not comment here in any detail on these two *Acts* as much has been written elsewhere across a range of literature.

However, from my perspective (and indeed for many disabled people who required a level of care and support to live independently or within family units in the community), the *Community Care (Direct Payments) Act 1996* was a significant piece of legislation. The *Act* allowed for the first time for a disabled person aged 65 or under to be offered greater involvement in their care and support needs and how they would be met, through direct payments, following an assessment by a social worker to assess their individual needs. The choice to be in control of an allocated budget from the local authority based on assessment of need meant individuals who so wished could now choose their own carers/PAs, the care agencies they wished to use and the hours and times at which they wished for support and assistance to be provided.

> **Key Learning: Direct Payments** Where an individual has been assessed
> as needing social services support, for example for shopping or personal
> care, the assessment will also provide a budget for how much this
> support will cost. This is known as a personal budget. The assessed
> individual can then be given the option of giving social services, the
> responsibility for arranging and paying for the support that they need, or
> they can be given the option of taking on the responsibility for arranging
> and paying for that support themselves. If the latter option is chosen,
> then the personal budget is paid directly to the individual, and this is
> known as a direct payment arrangement.

My physical health changes (and more latterly emotional and psychological ones) in the years following paid employment slowly felt like they were becoming all enveloping, reluctantly finding myself back as time progressed on the other side of a fence as a service user. This led to a feeling of drowning in multi-disciplinary assessments, with red tape and long waits following referrals to various agencies increasingly becoming the norm. Furthermore, the unpredictable progression of my condition and ever-changing care needs led to extended episodes of paralysis with each change frustratingly requiring renewed assessments and meetings.

For some time, I relied financially on the receipt of direct payments into a bank account and used to purchase the care which had been decided by a social worker I needed on a weekly basis. Whilst direct payments have been widely welcomed and proved popular overall amongst disabled people for the greater control or say it has enabled in their own care and support needs, issues do remain. From a personal perspective, fatigue and frustration would often result from continual searches for decent, hardworking carers who understood the values of respect and dignity and acknowledged that they were guests within my home. Likewise, hard to fathom health and safety rules could often prevent the most basic tasks/requests from being carried out. Additionally, in the early years of the millennium, there seemed to be a revolving door of health and social care professionals all seemingly responsible for a different element of your impairment and all seemingly keen to move into new jobs in management. This added to my exasperation in searching for consistency and continuity of care. At a time when 'joint working' and 'seamless health and social care services' were talked of constantly, this only served to add to ever constant frustrations.

Continually, I had to remind myself of being fortunate to have family members nearby who, from the point of onset of illness, had remained supportive at every turn despite their own need to adjust to circumstances which affected family members in different ways. I know categorically that I would not have been able to continue living 'independently with support' in my local community without this support on a number of levels, a level of support which all too often health and care professionals, I consider, can take for granted.

With the passing of time and given the nature of a progressive impairment, my needs reached a point that were beyond the 'ceiling' of what the local authority would fund, and my needs were now a mix of personal care needs and 'health' needs which fell outside the remit of social care department (so much for the holistic approach). The assessment of my need was now the responsibility of the NHS and thus followed more assessments and more decision-making as to determine the criteria were met for a personal budget. Thankfully (I use the term lightly), I learnt some four years ago that I met the criteria for a <u>personal health budget</u>. A consideration of my health needs meant I had the autonomy to use an allocated budget for treatments or activities considered to be beneficial to health yet not available by virtue of my impairment on the NHS.

▷   **Key Learning: Personal Health Budgets** Personal health budgets are relatively new and not as well-known as social care personal budgets. As with a social care personal budget, there is a calculation of the costs of meeting the assessed needs that the person has. The difference is that the money is solely to support a person's health and well-being needs, not social care needs. A personal health budget may be used for a range of things to meet agreed health and well-being outcomes. This can include therapies, personal care and equipment. However, there are some restrictions in how the budget can be spent.

For the most part, the positives of a personal health budget have for me outweighed any negatives with the benefits having been felt on a number of levels. For example, I have been able to fund physiotherapy treatment on a weekly basis which has enabled me to retain a level of mobility needed to maintain a degree of independence whilst also assisting to alleviate pain caused by muscle spasms. A personal budget has additionally enabled me to maintain a small team of regular carers to whom I can pay a wage that reflects the quality of care they provide and with their work schedules agreed solely between them and me. Furthermore, care arrangements made allow for fluidity, determined by any week's commitments or appointments, thus enabling a level of spontaneity that is taken for granted by able-bodied individuals. The award of a personal health budget has likewise enabled a greatly increased level of control not only relating to my care need but to everyday life overall with minimal involvement from health and social care professionals. This represents, in my opinion, a significant advance in how social care for people with physical impairments is, or can be, provided in the early twenty-first century in comparison with the narrow approaches to care provision during latter decades of the twentieth century.

A Contrast in Care

As a consequence of recurring tumours in body organs where they had previously not occurred and thus resulting in renewed paralysis, I have spent long periods of time in hospital over a number of years. On many occasions, complex surgery has been required followed by long spells of rehabilitation, though now with less frequency as my condition has progressed and surgical intervention has not been an option. For close to three decades, I was fortunate to have received mostly exemplary care for my rare condition from a specialist London hospital. Additionally, I was fortunate through much of that time to have been under the care of one neurologist with whom I forged a long-term professional rapport which helped considerably in providing continuity of care. However, in later years as my condition progressed and symptoms became more complex, it became increasingly evident that choices of treatment were gradually diminishing. Any form of surgical intervention became too high a risk to carry out at a number of levels, including anaesthetic difficulties such as a risk of total body paralysis or indeed the real risk of not surviving surgery.

Having muddled through for over two decades, often battling the odds or benefitting from advances in medical science, inevitably such news came as a huge blow both physically and psychologically and understandably took its toll. For a period of time, I found myself in what I could best describe as living in a darkened tunnel with any glimmer of light hard to see. Having learned some years previously that my condition was progressive in nature but with the rate of decline a total unknown, to arrive at what felt like a huge change in life direction took considerable time to adjust to. Counselling with a psychologist enabled me to talk through the changes I was confronted with. However, I was astounded to discover that the average wait for a first appointment was approximately nine months, whilst for an appointment with a neuropsychologist, a waiting time of up to one year was considered the norm, such was the scarcity of such professionals UK wide.

I was subsequently transferred to <u>palliative care</u> services, the only route now feasibly available to my long-standing neurological team, which was a world then unknown to me but geographically much closer to home. Within weeks, I once again found myself surrounded by a new collection of faces, names and job roles, whilst the prospect of the initial meeting with the palliative care consultant filled me with dread.

▶ **Key Learning: Palliative Care** Palliative care is the care provided for life-limiting illnesses that cannot be cured. Its aim is to improve the quality of life of individuals by preventing and relieving suffering. This can involve psychological, social and spiritual support for both the individual and their family or carers. Palliative care can be provided for a long or short period of time. A particular form of palliative care is end of life care, which is care and support for people who are nearing the end of their life.

However, arriving at the location, nothing could have been further removed from the often noisy, chaotic and overbooked NHS clinics which I had attended over many years and become so accustomed to. Instead, I was greeted by a comfortable room with warmly coloured painted walls, a table with up-to-date magazines, fresh cut flowers and the offer of a drink on arrival, all combining to make me question if I was in the right building. As the sole patient for the afternoon clinic (a routine I was told for patients attending for the first time), the consultant, with a specialist nurse alongside her, spoke of what they were able to offer, but overwhelmingly the time was for you to ask any of the endless questions I recalled were swirling in my head. The offer of future appointments being held within my home was also hugely appreciated at a time when there was a sense of entering a different type of world.

What became particularly noticeable as I adjusted to now being under the umbrella of palliative care services was the number of doors that appeared to open to services which within the NHS had become increasingly difficult to access as eligibility criteria became ever tighter. For example, within a short time frame, access to a psychologist was available as and when/if needed, and a range of complementary therapies offered for the purpose of assisting mental well-being or relaxation. The allocation of a named specialist nurse who visited as and when I wished or needed has been a huge source of support alongside other members of the hospice community. Recent years within social care departments have increasingly seen a shift away from a 'named' or allocated social worker, occupational therapist and wheelchair service worker. I know this to have been a significant source of frustration and stress for many disabled people who depend on the involvement of such professionals to access the services they need to live their daily lives. All too often stories are told of health and social care professionals undertaking visits or assessments only for them to be followed up by a different individual. This impacts on the consistency of service which limits any working relationship to be formed and prevents effective communication between different professionals who may be working with the disabled person.

For a period of time, I was unable to access in-patient services of the local hospice due to having a non-cancer diagnosis. However, increasingly over the past decade, UK-wide hospices have expanded their services to patients living with life-limiting and progressive conditions, occurring from the recognition of need for a large number of people to whom little if any support was available outside of the NHS directly.

▷   **Key Learning: Hospice Care**   Hospice care is a form of palliative care. People tend to associate hospice care with dying, but this is not wholly the case as hospice care aims to provide care for people from the point at which their illness is diagnosed as terminal to the end of their life, however long that may be. Hospice care looks after the medical, emotional, social, practical, psychological and spiritual needs of the person who is ill and the needs of the person's family and carers. It is also the case that most hospice care is provided in the home and not in hospices. Hospice care is free, paid for through a combination of NHS funding and public donations.

I recall being fearful of my initial visit to the local hospice despite having endeavoured to dispel some of the myths which are arguably slowly beginning to shift about hospices and the care they provide. These may include, for example, that hospices are hidden away from the outside world and are locations that provide care solely to very sick people within their in-patient units. Conversely, it was with relief that I encountered an environment where all efforts were made (and continue to be made) to present a homely environment with individual 'bedrooms' with en suites, and during all admissions to the in-patient unit, the care has been nothing but first class. There is the inevitable reality that hospices are a setting where some people will spend their final days hopefully surrounded by loved ones. However, far from feeling like that, the hospice for me, over a period of time, came to (and continues to) signify a haven where any changes in my unpredictable condition will be monitored with every attempt to alleviate any symptoms as best as possible. It represents an environment where, as an in-patient, days can be spent as I wish depending on health status and where staff are available round the clock to tend to any needs, physical, emotional or psychological in nature.

Improving the Journey

Having now reached my fifth decade, as a young teenager pre-onset of impairment, I probably would not have given consideration as to how life would be aged 50. Realistically however, I would not have guessed that this milestone would have included the experiences, events, highs and lows that it has. For close to four decades, I have spent long periods of time within NHS settings across the UK in addition to extensive dealings nearer to home with a spectrum of health and social care professionals. Such experiences have undoubtedly ranged from the very positive to ones which to put it mildly left room for great improvement and a lot in between. Therefore, in attempting to bring together the diverse elements covered within this chapter, from a personal perspective, it will conclude with what I believe have been the significant changes that have taken place over close to four decades, both positive and otherwise. Additionally, I will consider what the impact of the shifts or changes that have occurred during this time have had on my life personally and likely those of many other adults living with a physical impairment in the UK in the early twenty-first century.

Disabled People and the NHS

Having had extensive contact with a wide range of professionals working within the NHS since the early 1980s, it is undoubtedly the case that for people living with a physical impairment, things have changed beyond recognition in many ways. During my years spent on hospital wards in the early 1980s, there were very few 'disabled' patients as disabled teenagers or children of school age were generally living within residential special schools out of view from society. Attending special school for three years, the norm was for a hospital consultant to hold clinics within the school with only the consultant and a physiotherapist typically present, the focus solely on the individual's 'condition'. My first experience of a ward of disabled adults was to come during a period of extensive specialist rehabilitation following spinal surgery where all decisions were made by the consultant, nursing staff, physiotherapist and a ward-based social worker. In contrast I recall there being little consideration for the patient's wishes, thoughts or feelings, and viewpoints of family members or carers likewise were rarely, if ever, considered.

Thankfully, today we have a very different NHS where disabled people are a visible part of any hospital population and where multi-disciplinary clinics exist alongside NHS support groups for those possibly requiring some extra support. In addition, there now exists a wide spectrum of professionals working within the NHS across both hospital and community settings who cater for the needs of people with physical impairments of all ages who wish to live within the community either independently, with support, or within family units. Whilst not denying the numerous difficulties and obstacles that most definitely continue to exist and which can cause a deep sense of frustration and upset, I believe greater efforts are being made to involve the person in decision-making with their wishes listened to and their voices heard. Whilst to a degree, efforts have been made over the past decade or so to focus on the psychological and emotional impact of living with an impairment (especially where an impairment has been acquired) in addition to the physical effects of a condition, much progress needs to be made, and sparse resources remain ever stretched. Long waits to see a psychologist or counsellor remain all too common, due in part to the continuing shortage of people working within this area and a lack of growth in funding in line with demand for services. However, if asked the question 'As a disabled person are your overall experiences of NHS care and support better today than they were in the early 1980s?', wholeheartedly my response would be 'yes'. There are, however, some areas such as community nursing and wheelchair services where getting support can be difficult, with waiting times for assessment and provision of equipment unacceptably long.

Social Services

In addition to extensive dealings within the NHS, like many other disabled adults, I have had long-term involvement with departments historically known as 'Social Services Departments'. Now, however, they often carry obscure names such as

'Social Care and Inclusion' or 'Social Care and Well-being Department', which in my mind serve only to confuse people and give no indication as to their role or purpose! Whether it be for aids to independent living or care support to live in the community or elsewhere, a large majority of disabled adults will encounter either an occupational therapist or social worker or both in their quest to access care and support. During my period of adjustment to becoming 'a disabled person', my experiences of a named social worker were overall positive. Information and help were given to complete applications for disability benefits, played significant roles in both restarting my education and identifying somewhere appropriate to live, thus highlighting the importance of continued social work involvement where long-term needs are evident. The eradication over the past decade or so of long-term 'named' social workers, which promoted consistency and enabled a working relationship between the worker and disabled person to be built, has led to long waits for a new worker to be allocated each time support may be required. This has impacted on joint working and communication with other care or health professionals who may be working alongside the individual.

In the early years, assessments of need were undertaken predominantly by social care professionals and care provided determined by a professional viewpoint with little input from myself as the service user. From the 1990s onwards, service users began to be placed more at the heart of the care planning process with the ability to play a role in managing their own care following assessment of agreed needs. Whilst legislation such as the *Direct Payments Act 1996* was widely welcomed for enabling individuals under 65 to have greater control of their care packages and day-to-day living, more recent years have worryingly seen direct payment budgets increasingly scrutinised. Additionally, the imposing of changing criteria has resulted for many in only the most basic needs being met such as funding for personal care needs and the essentials of daily living.

Community Care

Whilst the concept of community care has enabled some disabled adults to live independently (or semi-independently), the closure of day centres and other community resources due to local authority budget cuts are currently resulting in increased levels of social isolation, the very opposite of what community care was intended to bring. Furthermore, whilst the cost of many smaller aids now has to be met by the disabled person themselves, I believe that there are excessively long waits for aids and adaptations that will enable safe independent living as experienced personally by myself. This has additionally led to a current situation in which large numbers of disabled people living at home in accommodation that is not suitable for their needs, often supported by family carers, are facing a daily uphill struggle, anxiety and concern for what the future holds. Sadly, despite repeated statements from governments of late highlighting their commitment to good-quality social care, with promises to mend what is widely viewed as 'a broken system', there appears little to indicate any significant changes in funding in the near future which would noticeably improve this situation. Within my home area further budget cuts in 2019 have resulted in community alarm services which enabled disabled adults to live at home and summon help in the event of an emergency being removed due to the local authority ceasing funding. Among the 7000 disabled adults within the local authority for whom this vital piece of equipment enabled them to live at home in the knowledge help could be sought when needed, this has caused considerable upset. Whilst private providers have been quick to step in and offer the same service for between £200 and £250 a year, an answer as to how the necessary equipment should be paid for by the individual is one that is constantly ignored and has left many feeling vulnerable and at risk within their own homes.

Disability Benefits

For many disabled adults, difficult circumstances have been further compounded in recent years by changes to the main disability benefit Disability Living Allowance (for under 65s), with every recipient having to be comprehensively reassessed for the newly rolled out Personal Independence Payment (PIP). Whilst I personally agreed that some changes were required, undoubtedly the introduction of PIP has caused considerable stress for some disabled people, in particular those subsequently awarded either lower payments or none at all, only for their payments to be reinstated on appeal with wide criticism of the assessments undertaken. The current government would argue the introduction of PIP has enabled those with the greatest needs to have their needs more comprehensively met than was the case with Disability Living Allowance. However, PIP has proved to be controversial alongside the DWP's Employment and Support Allowance, which has arguably had a greater impact for individuals whose conditions or illnesses may fluctuate and are less visible or mental health related. With a UK population in which 1 in 10 adults now have a form of physical disability, trying to find a solution that fits all will continue to be an uphill struggle, and realistically there are no easy answers.

However, before portraying a scenario in which disabled adults in the UK with long-term needs face an uncertain and pessimistic future, I sincerely believe that in recent decades huge advances have been made in two associated areas: firstly, that of attitudes towards disability *per se* and secondly a vastly improved accessible society and disability awareness. As a wheelchair user through my teenage years, to venture outside was a huge challenge; accessible public transport was non-existent; likewise wheelchair-accessible vehicles and aids such as walking frames or wheelchairs were clinical and ugly-looking. Shops in high streets and public buildings had no need to consider disabled access as disabled people existed predominantly in residential homes in secluded locations away from public view. If my family took the challenge to take me out in public, I would be 'parked' outside shops while purchases were made, and I often attracted looks of sympathy or stares from passers-by. Whilst the first International Year of Disabled People in 1981 arguably had little noticeable impact, the implementation of the *Disability Discrimination Act 1995* led to gradual widespread changes in areas such as access, transport, a shift towards mainstream education and employment opportunities through the <u>Access to Work scheme</u>. These changes undoubtedly took time to occur, but in today's world, disabled access to shops, although not universal, is incomparable to later decades of the twentieth century. Public venues such as libraries, museums, theatres and concert venues now routinely have access policies for people with a range of disabilities while exhibitions such as NAIDEX (an annual three-day exhibition for disabled people and health and social care professionals working within the area of disability where new products are marketed alongside speaker events and more) and The Big Event (a two-day annual event where adapted vehicles and vehicle adaptations available on the Motability Scheme are able to be seen and tested) are two examples of how the disability market has expanded and has become 'big business'. As disabled people have become more visible in society, so a shift in improved disability awareness has ensued which I consider to be now unrecognisable to the level of awareness that existed through the latter decades of the twentieth century. It is in the context of these changes that I completed my PhD at Birmingham University in 2010. Hopefully, the 'Does she take sugar?' syndrome has been firmly consigned to history, never to re-emerge.

Some disability organisations argue that disability legislation has become weakened within the reformed *Equality Act 2010*, wherein disability, race and gender inequality were brought under the same umbrella. There are specific concerns in recent years around a reported increase in disability hate crime made in part possible by the rapid expansion of social media platforms where people can vent nastiness hidden behind a screen and in the knowledge that they will be unlikely to be identified. Recent years have also seen much reporting of increased numbers of disabled people living with financial difficulties as a result of both benefit changes and cuts to services previously funded by their local authorities, indicating arguably that progress made over recent decades has either stalled or gone into decline.

Undoubtedly for any person living with a physical impairment in the UK today, who by the nature of their impairment necessitates long-term involvement with health and social care agencies among others, daily life can undoubtedly bring challenges and highs and lows. However, as a veteran of long-term care, undoubtedly so much has changed for the better within the areas discussed within this chapter, and I have to remain positive that, despite hurdles along the way, things can improve further in the years ahead.

Commentary

This chapter presents a detailed account of issues and changes, both good and bad, that Julia has experienced over the time she has been living with her disability and receiving long-term care. Her account is of additional interest from the fact that embedded within it is a before and after perspective of living with her disability, which enhances the analytical lens from which she writes her perspective. The issue of long-term care should be seen as of particularly interest in relation to the demographic changes that are occurring within the population, and the expectation that more people living longer with life-limiting conditions, for example, dementia, will mean more people requiring long-term care (Sealey 2015). There are a number of key points that Julia makes which should be of interest to those interested in the lives of people living with a long-term disability and receiving long-term care.

One of the key points that emerges from Julia's account is the ongoing importance of social policy provision to her life over the last 40 years. Social policy has been important to meeting not only her long-term social care needs but also her health, education and housing needs. Significantly, social policy provision has been important not only to enabling her to meet critical and acute subsistence needs but also to meet longer-term participatory needs (Sealey 2015). This highlights why it is important to ensure that the social policy provision provided is geared towards meeting the needs of those requiring long-term care.

A key theme that is evident from Julia's account is the way that things have changed positively over the 50 years since her disability first emerged. Her account particularly highlights positive changes occurring in perceptions, legislation, support and provision. However, it should be noted that the changes that occurred in these areas should not be seen as singular, but as interlinked with each other.

For example, in terms of positive changes in perceptions, Julia recounts how when she was younger, being stared at was a common occurrence when she went out. This is not something that now occurs, and she identifies the introduction of disability legislation such as the *NHS and Community Care Act 1990* and the *Disability Discrimination Act 1995* as important to this change, as these helped in terms of raising disability awareness and visibility. The shift away from institutional care towards community care in particular was identified as important to this increased visibility.

Research from the British Social Attitudes Survey in 2009 suggested that attitudes towards disabled people in general were improving towards a more positive outlook (Staniland 2010). It has also been argued that the Paralympics of 2012 helped to change attitudes towards disabled people in a positive way (Deviren 2014). Concomitantly, it is arguable that the increased visibility of disabled people that resulted from legislation contributed to the change in perceptions. Similarly, legislation also increased support available to disabled people, such as in relation to the changes made that Julia highlighted occurred when she was at university and the introduction of Direct Payments. These changes have enabled disabled people to be more visible in the community, and also be more active in terms of raising the visibility of disabled people in the community and enabling them to raise issues relevant to them.

Julia highlighted how her social work manager commented on the fact that her employment as a social worker had had an important effect in improving the awareness and understanding of disability-related issues. Furthermore, this supports the changed emphasis in policy and practice away from the medical model of disability towards the social model of disability (Fillingham 2013). By this, it is apparent that by focusing on the social and environmental factors limiting what Julia could do, rather than on the physical impairments limiting what she couldn't do, it enabled her to attain a level of inclusion that impacted positively not only on her well-being but also the well-being of wider society. Julia did highlight that her earlier periods of time in education held a prevailing sense of acceptance of underachievement for disabled people, particularly within the special school she attended, and this is also something identified by both Charles Mark English-Peach in Chap. 4 and Mark Lynes in Chap. 8. In this context, it may be the case that such an acceptance of underachievement is restricting people living with disabilities from attaining wider inclusion in society.

Julia also identified a number of areas for improvement for those receiving long-term care. These include issues related in particular to structure and finance. As a consequence of her condition, Julia required both healthcare and social care, which are both structured and financed differently in the England. A key structural difference is that while most healthcare is universal and free at the point of use, social care is means-tested, and there are charges for most services. Partly as a consequence of these differences, a recent report from the National Audit Office (2018) described social care as a 'Cinderella service', meaning that it is the poor relation in comparison to the NHS. This is particularly evident if we compare the differences in funding that between healthcare and social care since 2010. In effect, while funding for healthcare has been at least maintained at 2010 levels, funding for social care has been consistently cut, principally due to the fact that local authorities funding has been cut in real terms by 28.6% between 2010/2011 and 2017/2018, and it is through local authorities that most social care is funded (NAO 2018). This continues a trend identified by Ranci and Pavolini (2015) of rationalisation and residualisation in long-term care in the UK, meaning that social care entitlement has been limited and restricted. This is reflected in Julia's observation that services have 'increasingly become difficult to access as eligibility criteria became ever tighter' and as has become evident in the change from Disability Living Allowance to Personal Independence Payment.

As identified by Julia, a necessary part of long-term care involves moving between healthcare and social care services. At points in her account there was an evident lack of cooperation between healthcare and social care services, and this was something that at times caused her issues in relation to accessing services. These included a lack of seamless care, fragmentation of care and a non-holistic approach to care, all of which have been identified as important rationales for the integration of health and social care (Heenan and Birrell 2018). Indeed, the integration of health and social care has been identified as particularly beneficial to individuals receiving long-term care (ibid.). The imperative towards the integration of health and social care has been something which has been evident in government documents since the late 1990s (Heenan and Birrell 2006). It is evident that implementation of integration has been slow, particularly in England in comparison to other parts of the UK (Heenan and Birrell 2018). However, more recently, this imperative has been codified in legislation such as the *Health and Social Care Act 2012* and the *Care Act 2014*, with a date of 2020 set as the date for integration of health and social care in every area in England (Johnson et al. 2017).

A related issue in this respect identified by Julia is the lack of continuity of care, due to both the lack of integration of care, but also due to a high turnover in the adult social care workforce. For instance, the NAO (2018) recently identified a turnover rate of 27.8% in the social care workforce, which it stated as disrupting the continuity and quality of care and also incurring higher costs in terms of recruitment and induction. For someone who received long-term care, this is an issue that recurs over time and so has recurring effects on the quality of care.

This also has relevance to the quality of care that is provided. Evidence has shown that continuity of care is important to better health outcomes in a number of ways (Cheng et al. 2010; Pelzang 2010). However, as Threapleton et al. (2017, p. 329) observe:

> There are often large divides between primary and secondary services or between health and social services and improving coordination…Transitions from inpatient to community care are hindered by ineffective communication, confusion over provider roles and respon- sibility and a diluted sense of individual responsibility when care spans many providers.

This is especially relevant to Julia's care which has spanned many providers. Julia does highlight that continuity of care is important to her and also where conti- nuity of care was lacking. This was particularly in relation to social care and a high turnover of social workers, and Julia observed how this had a negative impact not just on her relationships but also on the care she received. As stated above, this lack of continuity of care can be related to policy changes that have occurred contempo- rarily, particularly the lack of funding for social care in comparison to healthcare, something which has been compounded by austerity. However, the recent emphasis in policy is on personalisation/person-centred care, as set out explicitly in the *Care Act 2014*, and continuity of care has been identified as an important component of person-centred care (Santana et al. 2018). This suggests that if care is to truly become person-centred for those requiring long-term care, then the funding dispar- ity between health and social care clearly needs urgent attention.

Reflective Questions

1. What is the role for social policy in changing society's attitudes towards dis- abled people?
2. What are the benefits of integrating disabled people into mainstream society?
3. What social policies might you suggest that would give greater choice and con- trol over who provides care to you?
4. How adequately is social care funded in comparison to healthcare?
5. What specific needs does someone receiving long-term care have over someone receiving short-term care?

References

S. Cheng, C. Chen, Y.A. Hou, Longitudinal examination of continuity of care and avoidable hos- pitalization. Arch. Intern. Med. **70**(18), 1671–1677 (2010)

E. Deviren, *Paralympic Data from the ONS Opinions and Lifestyle Survey* (Department for Work and Pensions, London, 2014)

J. Fillingham, *Changing Needs and Challenging Perceptions of Disabled People with Acquired Impairments*, Phd Thesis (University of Birmingham, 2013)

D. Heenan, D. Birrell, The integration of health and social care: the lessons from Northern Ireland. Soc. Policy Adm. **40**(1), 47–66 (2006)

D. Heenan, D. Birrell, *The Integration of Health and Social Care in the UK: Policy and Practice (Interagency Working in Health and Social Care)* (Red Globe Press, Basingstoke, 2018)

L. Johnson, D. Rozansky, S. Dorrans, et al., *Integration 2020: Scoping Research* (Social Care Institute for Excellence, London, 2017)

National Audit Office, *The Adult Social Care Workforce in England*, HC 714 Session 2017–2019 8 February 2018 (Department of Health and Social Care, London, 2018)

B. Norwich, What future for special schools and inclusion? Conceptual and professional perspectives. Br. J. Spec. Educ. **35**(3), 136–143 (2008)

R. Pelzang, Time to learn: understanding patient-centred care. Br. J. Nurs. **19**(14), 912–917 (2010)

C. Ranci, E. Pavolini, Not all that glitters is gold: long-term care reforms in the last two decades in Europe. J. Eur. Soc. Policy **25**(3), 270–285 (2015)

M. Santana, K. Manalili, R. Jolley, et al., How to practice person-centred care: a conceptual framework. Health Expect. **21**, 429–440 (2018)

C. Sealey, *Social Policy Simplified* (Palgrave Macmillan, Basingstoke, 2015)

L. Staniland, *Public Perceptions of Disabled People: Evidence from the British Social Attitudes Survey 2009* (Office for Disability Issues, London, 2010)

D. Threapleton, R. Chung, S. Wong, et al., Integrated care for older populations and its implementation facilitators and barriers: a rapid scoping review. Int. J. Qual. Health Care **29**(3), 327–334 (2017)

Direct Payments: Rationalising, Processes and Improving

8

Mark Lynes and Clive Sealey

This chapter presents Mark Lynes' personal rationale and understanding of receiving <u>Direct Payments</u> (DP). Its key aim is to outline how the key concepts related to DP of choice, control and flexibility have had direct relevance to Mark's life. It will then outline the practicalities experienced related to the process of receiving and the outcomes experienced from receiving DP. It concludes by outlining some possible that could be made to DP to improve the lived experiences of recipients of DP.

The key aims of this chapter are:

1. To provide an understanding of the how key Direct Payments concepts of choice, control and flexibility relate to real life.
2. To outline the administrative and real-life challenges that recipients of Direct Payments face.
3. To outline improvements to Direct Payments for service users and carers.

Who Am I?

I am aged 48 years and live in Birmingham where I was born. I am the youngest of four siblings and uncle/great uncle to 11 nephews and nieces, aged from 1 year to 31 years. My personal interests are listening to audiobooks, watching TV, playing pool and watching most sports, including being an Aston Villa season ticket holder in recent years.

M. Lynes (✉)
Worcester, UK

C. Sealey
School of Allied Health and Community, University of Worcester, Worcester, UK
e-mail: c.sealey@worc.ac.uk

© The Author(s), under exclusive license to Springer Nature Switzerland AG 2021
C. Sealey et al. (eds.), *Social Policy, Service Users and Carers*,
https://doi.org/10.1007/978-3-030-69876-8_8

I was born in 1971 with cerebral palsy, which is a lifelong condition that occurs if a baby's brain doesn't develop normally while in the womb or is damaged during or soon after birth. Often, the exact cause is not clear. This impairment means that I am unable to walk or stand at all, and I am also unable to do most everyday personal care tasks such as washing, dressing, preparing meals, cleaning and driving. My impairment affects my left side more than my right side in terms of muscle strength and balance. However, I personally feel that my impairment affects me in almost everything I do, as I do things very slowly, including writing this chapter. In addition to cerebral palsy, I have also suffered from a lifetime of nervous stomach problems in relation to constipation which can result in me on some days, for example, throwing up before leaving the house. Although this has obviously had some impact on me, I have never let it stop me doing things, and it has become a lot less of a problem in recent years. My condition has not noticeably changed or had a noticeable impact on what I am able to do.

In terms of employment roles, I have been a disability outreach worker around local area agreements, which aimed to get people involved in their local district. I have also been an employment adviser. For 2 years I was a network officer for *West Midlands Regional Disability Network* where my main role was to facilitate a sub-regional network to improve their capacity building to improve services in their area.

I have done lots of other committee work, including chair of *Centre of Independent Living*. I was also the West Midlands representative on the *British Council of Disabled People* for 3 years, and for the last year I have been involved in the national service users' organisation *Shaping Our Lives* and am currently serving as a board member.

Choice, Control and Flexibility: A Biographical Rationale

The three key concepts that underpin the move to DP are choice, control and flexibility. I will now talk about how I came to be in receipt of DP, which has been a long journey. I will use my life experiences to highlight how issues of lack of choice, control and flexibility have impacted negatively on my life, as a way to rationalise why I see DP as important in enabling me to overcome these issues.

Rationalising Choice

From the age of 4 until I was aged 16, I attended what was then called Wilson Stuart Special School in Birmingham (it is now called Wilson Stuart School). I feel my greatest achievement there was to be able to take exams. This is because I didn't get the opportunity to study other than the basic level in all subjects, so my education basically consisted of maths and English. This was in part because the three schools on our campus did not have facilities for disabled students or pupils as we were called back then and was not really geared towards mainstream education. For example, there was no examination possible for disabled people.

I loved the school, as I made loads of friends and I did lots of sport competitions. However, reflecting back on this now, this has saddened me because you don't realise until you leave school what the effect of such a basic level of education and being denied an academic education will have on you in the future. I feel that this has had a serious impact on my life, as I had spent too much time catching up on the basics of what I needed to at least give me life choices, and I will give you two examples of this. One was at the age 25; I took a GCSE maths course for the first time. In one of these lessons, a reference was made to a GCSE history item. I had to raise my hand and say I had never been taught history. This was difficult because it was clear to me that this was routine knowledge, and this was really the first time I realised how different my education had been. There was also confusion from the course tutor on how to support me and continue with the lesson, as the course was one day a week. Another example of the possible impact was just a couple of years ago when I decided to apply for a social work access course, but I didn't pass some of the maths and English tests, although I did gain qualifications. I feel that the fact that I only studied these subjects for 9 months compared to 2 years minimum for most people contributed to the limitations of my education opportunities despite a decent level of what I call everyday education. However, at least I hope that my generation showed something to the powers that be to ensure that others could benefit. People often ask me what impact I think it's had on me, and the truth is I don't really know beyond the examples that I became aware of outlined above. However, if you imagine that educationally you are operating at a different level to your peers in society, but then are expected to operate at the same level pretty much as them in the real world, then it is bound to affect you. This is particularly the case when you become responsible for your choices in life and you are trying to improve your skills in a field. To put it another way, imagine all your achievements not to seem to be worthy enough just because of your background.

Between the ages of 17 and 19, I attended Derwen College for the Disabled in Oswestry, Shropshire. The main course I took was GCSE in office practice. I enjoyed my time there for three main reasons; the first was this college was my actual choice and not someone else's. What I mean by this is that without telling me, my school set up an interview for me at National Star Centre near Cheltenham, which is similar to Derwen. They did this by arranging a visit to the National Star Centre as a potential college placement, and while I was there, they informed me that an interview had been arranged. I had also visited Derwen and this was my preference, but they had not arranged an interview for me there. So, after several weeks of going back and forth, I agreed to go ahead with the Star Centre interview on the condition that I also had an interview at Derwen.

The second reason was that the course I took was the only one in the college where getting a qualification was a possible outcome. I saw this as a real chance to learn how to prepare organised written work academically. The course also allowed me to train in a fully operational office. This meant that I was able to get trained in tasks such as reception, switchboard, post room and banking.

The third reason was being away from home enabled me to learn how to make decisions about life with a different group of people in a safe place. There were quite a few periods of homesickness, but overall, I felt this was important particularly given my nerves issue due to my impairment. When I left Derwen, for all the above reasons, I felt much more grounded and able to begin to find my own identity as a person.

After 9 months back in Birmingham, I attended Bournville College aged 20–25. I studied a variety of subjects such as business administration, IT, business and finance, maths and English at BTEC, NVQ, GNVQ and GCSE levels. My thinking at the time about the subjects I chose was that I made the decision to study across a field rather than to take all levels in one subject, although I'm not sure I would make the same decision given my time again, but who knows.

Finally, in this section I wish to talk about aspects of my decision-making with regard to my education. The first is that with the exception of business administration, all my other courses at Bournville were mainstream classes, not special education classes. This meant I was aged 22 before achieving any sort of equality of education. Because of what I've seen and heard recently, I am 100% sure that I would not have achieved the things that will appear in the next section of this chapter without the additional support I received in mainstream education, rather than receiving separate special education.

Not so long ago, I watched two documentaries on Derwen College and National Star Centre. I was struck by how similar it was during my time there almost 30 years on, although Derwen College is now mainly a college catering for students with learning disabilities/difficulties, something that was starting to happen towards the end of my time there. The National Star Centre has remained more mixed. Watching the documentary, I felt students had the same life skills problems that the majority of students had when I was there, such as relationship issues, lack of disability awareness and lack of options after leaving. A friend I was speaking to who now works at Wilson Stuart School told me that students can now stay on for a further 3 years, which means they could leave aged 22. The reason given to me for this was the lack of resources and options elsewhere. My post-schooling experiences lead me to question this for a number of reasons, such as whether it enables people to move on if they are in the same environment for so long. Also, by enabling people to stay there until the age of 22, there is a tacit admission that there is a lack of resources and options for them to move on, but it is unclear how this lack of resources and options is suddenly dealt with when the person turns 22 and has to leave. I think it would be better to develop a range of progression options similar to the rest of society that provide life opportunities for disabled people and ensure all disability-related needs are met, rather than providing services that seems more about serving the needs of staff, family and carers.

Rationalising Control

While meeting my social worker to try to sort out life after Derwen, I was told about *Birmingham Disability Rights Group (BDRG)*. I then joined but didn't become active until I finished education at the age of 25 years. BDRG was all about promoting the <u>social model of disability</u> which in short says that my condition of cerebral palsy was an impairment and that my disability was the barriers put in place by society that prevents disabled people from having true equality. This barrier relates not just to usual things like ramps and general building access but barriers to wider issues like support to access employment opportunities and changes to care systems. The aim of focusing on these wider barriers is to ensure that people have more say in when and how they receive their care and ensure good standards and clear and accessible information both in digital and non-digital formats. BDRG tried to do this by largely providing administrative support to the *Direct Action Network* both locally and nationally, which as the name suggests was a direct action group primarily for disabled people to organise local direct action events. We also supported the creation of a *Disability Resource Centre* to implement rights into choice and control and service user-led services. BDRG also produced *Building Bridges*, which was a magazine that provided rights campaigning information and advice to members and others in their own homes.

▷ **Key Learning: The Social Model of Disability versus the Medical model of Disability**   When talking about the disability that a person is living with, there are two main ways in which we tend to define and describe the disability.

The medical model of disability is a way of talking about disability that emphasises the effect of the disabilities that the person has on what they can do. This means that there is a focus on the way that the disabilities of the person limits what they can do. For example, if we consider why a person in a wheelchair cannot access a building with steps, from a medical model perspective, we would say that the reason why this person cannot access the building is because they have an impairment that means they cannot use the steps. Therefore, the only way that the person would be able to access the building is if they did not have the disability in the first place. This is why it is called the medical model of disability, because it focuses on a medical solution to disability, meaning treating the disability that the person has.

The social model of disability is a way of talking about disability that emphasises the effect that society has on disabled people. This means that the focus is on the way that society limits what a disabled person can do. For example, if we consider the same example of why a person in a wheelchair cannot access a building with steps from a social model perspective, we would say that the reason why the person cannot access the building is because the steps limit their access. Therefore, it would be possible for the person to access the building if changes were made to the design and construction of the building, for example putting a ramp or a lift in place. This is why it is called the social model of disability, because it focuses on the way that society can both limit or enhance the lives of disabled people, in this case eliminating specific barriers that restrict what disabled people can do.

So that's how I started in the disability rights movement, and I was soon the group membership secretary and Treasurer of BDRG, and I also joined the board of the *Disability Resource Centre* for couple of years. However, in 1996 I joined an organisation that probably changed my life more than any other. This was called *The Search Team*, which was an organisation for all service users of <u>community care</u> services in Birmingham. The aim of this group was to receive information about services and consider how relevant they were to service user needs, and from this the Steering Group suggested changes to system and monitoring outcomes. I was vice-chair twice and chair between 1996 and 2012. I continued to do bits of focus group work with Birmingham City Council until earlier this year. It has helped me to keep busy, gave me a chance of employment and mostly importantly kept me out of the day centre. As I say, being in this organisation gave me an insight into wider social work policy such as how it worked and how it didn't work for service users, with partly implemented policies or initiatives due mainly to endless restructuring of staff teams at all levels or new management with different views on the usefulness of service users' involvement.

So, the above has allowed me to work with all sorts of people from different backgrounds with various levels of need; this also applies to local authority officers again at all levels. Over 20 years, this has given me a good knowledge of what service users think and a good knowledge of department messages both public and private about the way forward in their view. This work has also given me an awareness of how personal experience fits in to wider community and vice versa. This is why I feel this work has given me other opportunities I have talked about up to this point and as you continue reading.

As an adult, my first encounter with social workers was at the age of 19. I was leaving Derwen College, and I was allocated a social worker to look at options for moving back to Birmingham and to help me look at my long-term future. At this time, this was mainly done with my social worker accompanying me on visits to several colleges. I decided to return back to Derwen College, but this could not happen for some time, so it was also agreed between us to enrol at Bournville College; however that wasn't the end of my social worker's involvement. As I really enjoyed my time at Bournville, I decided to take what has turned out to be one of the most important decisions of my life and not return to Derwen. This didn't go down well at home as there were quite a few disagreements and arguments. However, my social worker held lots of meetings with me, performing the role of an advisor/ advocate in a process that lasted for 3 months or so with myself sorting out the college end of things and her leading on the home side. This pretty much brought to an end her two-year involvement with me.

My next social work encounter was one afternoon when my dad was taken ill and was hospitalised for a period. The next morning the <u>Emergency Carer Service</u> Services arrived to take over my care needs for 24 hours, despite the fact that I had arranged this previously with a care agency. This had its own problems, such as carers arriving early and late, and some knowing what they were doing and some not. However, my family became increasing distressed by the situation with the care team arriving before mom got home from hospital and mom became increasing upset at me having to go to bed at 8:30 pm. So, after 2 weeks, I decided to stay in a nursing home to enable me to support mom and dad to get the space they needed and allow mom to focus on looking after dad as he returned home from hospital.

From my experiences, many people believe that when you start receiving social care services, you keep receiving services for a very long time—this is actually not the case. It was 7 years on before my mom felt they needed to ask for respite care. And it was another 3 years after the first respite care before there was another need for respite care. The second period of respite care was set up using DP.

▷ **Key Learning: Emergency Carer Services** A concern for many carers and people they are caring for is what will happen if they fall ill or there is an emergency and they are suddenly no longer able to provide care for a temporary period. Emergency carer services provide replacement care in such circumstances. This requires the setting up of an emergency plan which would set out what would happen. This can range from simply contacting a family member or provided respite care itself. These arrangements are typically provided at an extra cost to the carer.

Another issue during this period was that my particular respite system was closed down, but to this day my dad has never been informed of this. Therefore, he did not know what to with leftover monies or what to do with the bank account; it was only because of my involvement with Birmingham City Council that we had any idea of what was going on. In terms of the social work role, I would say never assume the system knows what the service user knows and vice versa. Between June 2007 and 2011, I once again did not use services.

Rationalising Flexibility

I moved to Amberley Court, a BUPA run care home, which I found was like an out of body experience. The care home consisted of two floors of fairly small rooms, each with a TV room at the end. The only other rooms were two dining rooms, one activity room and a smoking room. As part of this out of body experience, the two things that really struck me was that you kind of left your previous life behind and you were expected to work around the system. Two examples of this were, although I was soon to be made redundant, I was still working whilst in the home, and the managers called a staff meeting to ensure that I was ready for work. The other thing that stuck me was the lack of personal care and the assumption that because most people wore incontinence pads, or most residents stayed in the home, everyone else would do likewise. To be fair, this wasn't because people were specifically prevented from exercising choice because staff didn't think we should but rather because of the following three things. First, for the majority of day, but not always I accept, only three members of staff were looking after us, if you include the nurse. This explains why staff could only do the basics for us. When you add to this the fact that staff worked 12-hour shifts most days, then it becomes understandable that, apart from ensuring <u>safeguarding</u> issues are dealt with, the culture of the home becomes focused unconsciously on meeting the needs of staff, which did happen most of time at least at some level.

The second reason was the attitude of the care home to residents' rights to a ful-filling life. As an example, there was no transport provided, which meant that only a few residents could leave the home on a regular basis. Additionally, there was also a lack of care staff available to support and no care staff to take us out on anything other than an occasional basis. This was also the case with regard to resources avail-able to activity staff. The third reason was lazy management and lazy listening, which meant that sometimes procedures would be signed off as being carried out without having been carried out. One example of this involving me was one night, a carer was putting me to bed, and I sustained a string burn. Because I was marked, I reported it immediately to the nurse on duty, but the next morning I found out I was not men-tioned in that morning's handover meeting, so I then reported to one of the managers but heard nothing. So, still marked, I waited until the weekend and reported it to a manager I trusted at the weekend, and he at least noted it. This brought home to me that whether or not all carers are good, bad or indifferent and the home had plenty of both, you have to have a system of values if you want quality.

I first met my allocated social worker 4 days after moving to Amberley Court. I found her hard-working but found her communication method and style very frus-trating. It felt as if she was managing my case in relation to other work, and I felt the fact that I was in a home and that she also had a few of her other clients there made it more convenient for her. In the first few meetings, the focus was on registering for housing and homeless stuff, but after that over the next 18 months in the home, our meetings usually focused on reviewing the service I received and my needs once I moved into a flat. The meetings went well and were quite constructive; however having said that, I found it quite hard to get my head around the level of support I would receive once I moved in the flat. There were two reasons for this: firstly because we were planning for something I had no experience of and, secondly because a lot of support I had been receiving in the care home would be denied to me once I left there, for example 24-hour care. I couldn't visualise life without the level of support that I was currently getting. My allocated social worker's approach was to put questions to me that she felt she would be asked by her managers and signposting me to other services with the aim of limiting the care package. Although I don't think it was intended on either side, there were nonetheless somewhat con-flicting agendas to this, as I felt I was the one co-ordinating the meetings for assess-ment and otherwise with up to eight support services or agencies.

One of the effects of this was that after 6 months of meetings with the housing association, they wrote to me withdrawing their offer of a flat due to their belief that all was not in place, particularly in regard to the care I would receive. I was also told by the housing association on the day I received the letter that the flat had already been allocated to someone else. However, after much toing and froing on that day, I was given three more days to sort things out. I think the *Supporting People Programme* should be re-established because, as I write, they are only able to operate a much-reduced service. They only get funded to provide support to two categories of vulnerable people, but if they were to re-establish the *Supporting People Programme*, co-ordinating administrative tasks with service users would mean that social workers would only have responsibility for certain meetings and doing specific tasks. Also, the service users would possibly feel more supported in having someone to talk through their issues with, which may lead to less questions for the social worker from all other parties on a case, freeing them up to do so-called more important work on the case.

▷ **Key Learning: Supporting People Programme** Supporting People (now
   called Housing Related Support) is a government programme set up in
   2003, which provides funding for a variety of housing-related support
   aimed at helping vulnerable people to live independently in their own
   homes and/or the community. Amongst others, it can support homeless
   people, people who misuse alcohol and drugs, survivors of domestic
   abuse and people with physical and sensory disabilities. It can provide
   a range of services including finding somewhere to live, dealing with
   rent arrears debt and budgeting, learning domestic and social skills to
   maintain independence, applying for benefits, finding training and
   getting an emergency help alarm for the house. It does not cover
   personal care services, such as help with dressing, shopping or meals.
   Some services are free; some require payment. Prior to 2009, the money
   provided for Supporting People was ringfenced, meaning that it could
   only be spent on Supporting People services, but this is no longer the
   case and has led to an inevitable reduction in Supporting People
   programmes. This is despite that fact that evaluations of Supporting
   People programmes have consistently found that they provide a
   significant net beneficial return, meaning that the outcomes they
   produce are significantly more than its costs (Jarrett 2012).

At the end of 18 months at Amberley Court, I had taken part in meetings and assessments involving all the following separate services to greater and lesser degrees:

- The care home
- Social work
- Homeless service
- Disabled person homeless service
- Occupational therapy
- Home adaptions
- Supporting People
- District nurse services

- Housing association
- DP

These disjointed experiences along my social care journey have led me to view social care as essentially process-driven, focused on outcomes rather than being genuinely person-centred. Outcomes seem to be arrived at through a mixture of poker, workforce management and duplication of effort. What I mean by this is that the assessment process is a game of poker because, as a service user, you are trying to get the most care to meet your fluctuating 24-hour needs, whereas your social worker is asking questions to you in order to meet your essential needs in the cheapest way possible. I feel this is dangerous because service users are living life on a tightrope more and more these days, particular when you consider wider cuts to other support services, which mean you might need more expensive care in the future because inadequate care provision is more likely to go wrong.

This is compounded by my experiences of workforce management, meaning that new people come in, existing people are moved around, and nothing happens for at least 6 months policy wise. And in relation to duplication, this is where you find that someone in the same department is working on the same thing as someone else without each other's knowledge.

My Experiences of DP

Following on from discussion with my social worker while at Amberley Court, I first became involved with DP in 1998 when I appointed a Personal Assistant Organiser, responsible for giving support to service users who needed help recruiting Personal Assistants (PAs). On a personal note, this job was the first time I employed a PAs funded by the Access to Work Scheme.

▷   **Key Learning: Personal Assistants (PAs)** Where a person in receipt of DP directly employs their own support worker, that person is known as a Personal Assistant (PAs). A PAs can be employed to provide a wide range of care and support needs as identified in the assessment of needs of the individual. This can include amongst others driving, washing, toileting, help with paperwork, shopping, ironing, meal preparation, educational activities and help with medication. The key benefit of employing a PAs is the flexibility that it enables individuals having in meeting their needs. However, this means that the care is provided on an employer-employee basis and that the employer, that is the person in receipt of DP, has responsibility for all the employer-related legal, financial and practical issues that this entails.

It became clear to me from discussions from my PA that, despite the challenges there might be, a DP was the best option for many people like myself, but by no means all, to plan their lives with a degree of flexibility. This was further highlighted by my experiences in the care home which indicated that DP would be the best way, if not the only way, for me to have as much choice and control as possible. What I mean by this is that when I was in care, there was nothing person-centred about the organisation where incontinence pads took priority and presumptions that nobody would want to get a job were the order of the day, despite the best efforts of some individual staff. This led me to make the decision that when the time came, I would use DP.

Experiences of the DP Process

In September 2012, I moved to my flat, living on my own for the first time. I sorted out the care required by the housing association by hiring their care service for 6 months. I was cared for by a regular team of six. I hired the service using my DP which was assessed at over £1600 per month, as part of the assessment processes mentioned previously. The care team were very good indeed. However, there were problems with my experience of the agency system, as I was only getting 21 hours per week care instead of the 32 hours per week I had paid for, and there were a few times where no one turned up at night. So, 6 months after learning to live independently, I decided not to use the care agency anymore.

When I first employed a PAs, I just employed two people, one for weekdays and one for weekends, but I then took someone on for nights as well. I currently employ one PAs with responsibility for care and one with responsibility for driving. But I have employed up to four PAs at a time, one weekday morning PAs, one evening PAs, and one weekend and bank or cover PAs. Now that I do causal work in five different venues, my DP team makes my work commitments possible, with the right amount of negotiations and flexibility, despite just as many challenges for them as individuals.

Because of my professional experience, I have so far recruited PAs from previous experience of them for trial periods or recommendations from people I knew. This is fine, but two things that are important are that you are true to yourself; what I mean by this is that if you're a formal person, then shortlisting and interviewing might be for you, but if this is case then I would suggest you need to put aside the costs of at least two recruitment processes. If you are more like me, then you must gain knowledge of recruitment and how you might conduct the process and what your role might be on the day and who else you might need help from and what their role might be. Another tip I have is about the job description, which is to have at least in your head a traffic light system approach, with 'green' being what you would like the person to do, but if the candidate has no experience it's not that important; 'amber' being things that are quite important, but the candidate might still be offered the job even though they can't do all the tasks; and finally 'red' being that a candidate must have these skills and abilities to be offered the job. This is also good from your point of view as it might allow you to easily identify the right candidate. There are other assessment systems such as scoring out of 5. Another reason the traffic light approach is good is that it allows you to identify what is important to you when you have someone working in your home, and more widely, it allows you to decide if any areas are off limits or if there are any tasks needed to be done before a certain time. This might be useful if you have a family or other people who use your home on a regular basis.

Finally, in my experience it is a good idea to have some idea at least in your head of tasks that you want doing daily, weekly and monthly. Prepare a contract for signing, and setup procedures for engagement with friends and family, particularly if they are working at family occasions. I think my approach has been a bottom line one. There are two main reasons, the first being that as I have no family living with me, as long as things get done within reason it doesn't matter when. The other reason is I hire them to do the job, so let them do it their way and intervene only when necessary.

Financially, apart from knowing how to manage budgets or at least knowing how to get support with this responsibility, there is no additional financial commitment if you have a DP. However, you may still have to make a contribution, depending on your financial situation, under the Fairer Charging System, but this is the case whatever type of care you receive. In my experience, many DP recipients have an increasingly small budget these days, which means PAs are very often required to do spilt shifts and therefore from your PAs point of view travel costs are a big issue. But I feel clear and fair arrangements are essential, particularly when public transport is part of the picture.

▶   **Key Explanation: Fairer Charging System** This refers to the way that a local authority is allowed to calculate a charge for directly providing a service. This could include services such as meals delivered to the home, domiciliary or home care, and adaptions to the home. In effect, it means that if an individual is assessed as needing a service and chooses to have that service provided by the local authority, the amount they charge should not exceed the cost of providing the service. Local authorities do have some discretion in terms of whether to charge for services, and this means that charges for services can vary from local authority to local authority, but where they do charge, they have to adhere to the principle of fairer charging.

Beneficial Outcomes

DP aren't always easy, but in my view, it is the best way of me getting the same level of support provided by my dad for over 40 years until he became ill 7 years ago. Sadly, my father passed during the writing of this, but the combination of DP and my father allowed me to be me. For example, by allowing me to choose my PAs, I could get a car as I was able to employ a driver. Although I was able to work outside of Birmingham before DP, it has made these opportunities much easier and quicker than it was beforehand, as travel by both car and train with a PAs is easier and, at times, more affordable. I have also found that DP have allowed me to do more evening activities fairly easily. Also in the last 2 months while recruiting for a new person, I was able to put in the job description a range of start times in line with my work commitments, whereas in the care home, this took some considerable arranging or a while to filter down to frontline staff however well-meaning they were. I have also been able to agree to take on a self-employed person which meets more of their needs, therefore making it easier to retain their services for longer. However, I would advise people to double-check their responsibilities towards self-employed people particularly if they only work for you.

I would recommend DP to anyone, whatever you decide to do with it whether that is employing staff, buying services or buying equipment. Your local council will give you more information on what you are allowed to spend your DP on. However, you would need to know your answers to 'what if' questions, that is what happens if your PAs can't come in to work.

Improvements to DP

Finally, I would like to speak about my views on the wider DP system in relation to other parts of the care system. At the moment, I get £21,000 per year in DP. Previously, I have employed up to four people at the same time. But over the last 5 years I have seen an increasing pressure on resources, with PAs needing the maximum number of hours possible, given the increasing costs of living. This then causes issues with retaining staff because of spilt shifts, pay rises and time off issues. There are several reasons in my view. There has not been an increase in the hourly rate of £10.96 per hour since 1998 to my knowledge. I have done lots of work with Birmingham City Council on DP, and the council team have worked on it for a long time, and apparently, they can't remember an increase either.

A few years ago at a providers' meeting, they were given figures that showed that depending on which service user group they are working with, the provider would receive between £11.28 and £11.48 per hour, and until recently a provider would be also be allocated an Account Manager by Birmingham City Council, plus other forms of support. In contrast to the above, a DP recipient just gets one amount to employ PAs, to pay employment costs and to arrange holiday and sickness cover. We are also now responsible for providing a workplace pension fund for any employee who takes it up either now or in the future, from the same budget. I would resolve some of the above by paying recipients 14 payments per year instead of the current 13 payments. This extra payment would go into a separate bank account from care hours account to pay for employment costs and payroll and recruitment support costs and most recently workplace pensions. I would also re-establish a national Independent Living Fund. The fund should have three functions, the first being to meet care costs that local councils cannot meet in exceptional circumstances in regard to DP recipients, with, for example each local council allowed to apply successfully five times in 4 years.

▶ **Key Learning: Independent Living Fund** The Independent Living Fund (ILF) was a discretionary scheme designed to support people to live independently within their communities rather than living in residential care homes. It was mainly used as a top-up fund to give extra money to disabled people to help people pay for carers and personal assistants. Many of the people who received the ILF would otherwise have had to move to residential care homes. The crucial point about the ILF is that it was administered independently from other benefits that individuals received. However, the government closed the ILF in England in 2014 and transferred ILF funding to local authorities to absorb into their general funds for disabled people.

Another function I believe an ILF type body should have is funding to enable PAs to go on training courses, including covering backfill costs of replacement staff. A disabled person, as employer, could be able to make an application to this fund up to, say, three times over 2 years for courses that will lead to improved services and skill development. The third function would be to hold a national bank register of cover staff.

I would introduce a DP option to use for all different types of provision such as day care or hobbies groups or at least the costs for someone to attend these and other activities. From my own experience of being made homeless over a 24-hour period, I know that it is best not to introduce DP during a crisis situation, and a proper review of a person's situation, once the crisis has passed, is recommended practice. I feel that someone from a DP support provider and a social worker should attend the review process, and then before choosing a provider, interviews should be arranged where required so that people make an informed choice about their support provider as well as their care support. An alternative option might be to employ social workers in the DP administrative support team to provide impartial advice at this stage.

Finally, I would look at the system and introduce better awareness about how local authorities' support models for care providers compared to others, so that there is a care system rather than numerous care systems. I would also have a basic care rate and a personalisation care rate review to ensure that care homes and others deliver what they are being paid for, rather than a 'one-size-fits-all' service for all service users, as by doing this you will ensure that there is better knowledge of actual costs of care.

In recent years, there has been the welcome development of free courses put on by *Skills for Care*, but there are still issues such as who pays for cover staff costs and travel for employees who are attending the training. I have also found a reluctance from PAs to take up training because of the spilt shifts issue meaning that training may eat into free time. Another reason is because of second jobs and family pressures.

I am not saying that the above goes far enough or indeed that all the details are right by any means, but I think similar ideas would provide more support to employers, to give employees more security and to see the job as a career opportunity. Most of all though, I would put some balanced investment back into the personalisation agenda instead of cuts of recent years, with the aim of making DP a workable model for more people and save the care sector money in the long run.

Commentary

This chapter above by Mark Lynes provides some relevant and interesting insight into the process, rationales and outcomes from his lived experience of receiving of DP. Before commenting on this specifically, it is relevant to note that the chapter highlights an issue for disabled people that is also highlighted in the chapters by both Charles English-Peach and Julia Smith in this book. This is the low expectation of disabled people in the education system. Mark outlined this as something which impacted on his achievement in later life, and research has shown to be a factor in the low achievement of disabled people (Chatzitheochari and Platt 2018). It suggests that this is an issue which is impacting significantly on the future well-being of disabled people and one which needs to be addressed.

To contextualise DP briefly, the essence of DP is where a local authority gives the service user the money to buy their own social care services that they are assessed as needing, rather than the local authority providing the service themselves. The service user then takes responsibility for providing for their assessed care needs. This requires the service user to become both the consumer and the purchaser of the services they need. This is mainly done through the employment of PAs, as indicated in the account above.

DP have been a part of the successive governments' personalisation agenda since 1997, following legislation introduced in 1996. Successive legislation over the last 20 years has changed local authorities' responsibility to provide DP from a *power* to a *duty*, and the type of service users who can receive DP has also been increased over the same time (Jarrett 2016). The recent *Care Act 2014* further enshrined the use and implementation of DP in a contemporary and future context, and this has led some to claim that in the future, DP will be the default rather than the exception for adult social care (Glasby and Littlechild 2016). Moreover, there is the proposal to extend DP to health care (Department of Health and Social Care 2018), as seen in Julia Smith's chapter.

The key rationale for the personalisation agenda has been to give people genuine choice and control over their own lives (Gaylard 2016). As seen in the Mark's account above, DP have been important in enabling and enhancing these aspects of his life, which reflects previous research that the use of DP leads to an improvement in feelings of choice and control from service users (Glasby and Littlechild 2016). A specific example of this is in relation to who Mark could employ and the power to change employees when he felt that they were not providing an adequate service. Another important aspect of the personalisation agenda is enabling flexibility within an individual's life, as enshrined recently in the *Care Act 2014* (Jarrett 2016). This is reinforced by the ability to employ different PAs for different times of the day, which have enabled Mark to work and do other things in his life. This can be seen as additionally enhancing his self-determination, independence, quality of life, personal dignity and integration into the wider community, wherein:

> Direct Payments are viewed as facilitating people to live in the ways that they choose rather than being given services to match preconceived assumptions about what is needed and how individuals should live. DP provide greater flexibility and reliability over when, how and who provides the support that people need. (Spandler 2004, p. 192)

In this context, an obvious contrast can be drawn between Mark's account of his sense of independence and personal dignity while in the care home and while in receipt of DP. It is evident that in relation to both of these, there has been a significant improvement while in receipt of DP, and this has had a knock-on effect in terms of improving his integration into the wider community, vis-à-vis his ability to work flexibly. As Glasby and Littlechild (2016) observe, this is significant in terms of the emphasis in policy given to supporting disabled people to engage in paid work; it also suggests that DP can have a 'ripple effect' in terms of having an impact that spreads further than the initial impact (ibid.).

A specific issue with DP identified in Mark's account is in relation to the support provided to service users to enable them to administer and manage the DP process, such as the employment of PAs. This was also an issue identified in a report from the House of Commons Public Account Committee (2016, p. 10), which stated that DP users:

> need support to be an employer, to manage aspects such as salaries, pensions, sick pay and even the possibility of having to take disciplinary action against their employees. We heard that without support to do this, some users are reluctant to take on the responsibilities of a DP. In 2012, Skills for Care, the body funded by the Department of Health to provide practical tools and support to help develop the adult social care workforce, published good practice guidance for people employing personal assistants. Skills for Care conducted research in 2014 that found that not all local authorities are providing adequate support to users who employ personal assistants.

Mark also identified that training needed to be provided to those in receipt of DP to enable them to understand the process better, and this was something that was also highlighted by Simon Heng (2015) in his account of being in receipt of DP. A key aspect of DP is that it creates an 'employer-employee relationship' which, as Barnes (2006) observes, introduces a level of complicity into the nature of caring, which is not something that neither PAs or service users are usually trained for.

Linked to this were financial issues related to the receipt of DP that Mark highlighted. Specifically, he suggested that there needed to be an extra payment to pay for additional employment and administration costs. Another issue of agreement between Mark and Simon Heng relates to the negative impact that the demise of the Independent Living Fund (ILF) has had on service users. Both identify the importance that the ILF had in enabling service users to access funding at exceptional times and to meet the additional responsibilities linked to DP, which for service users can be very significant and suggests that there is a need for such provision in policy.

There have been developments in DP in through the use of payment cards to process DP. This is where the service users' allocated funding is loaded onto a payment card. According to the Independent Living Strategy Group (2018), 69 local authorities reported that they used payment cards for DP. While this offers the potential for more financial freedom for services users in terms of how they spend their allocated fund, the reality is that these cards are being used more as a way for local authorities to tightly control how service users spend their allocation, through, for example restrictions on cash withdrawals. In other words, because spending on the cards can be restricted to certain items, it is being used as a control and micromanage how DP are used (ibid.). Such a development threatens to roll back the freedom, flexibility and independence that the introduction of DP was supposed to initiate, and has initiated, for disabled people (Brindle 2018).

Mark's account highlights a concern that a continued lack of increase in the amount of DP received is causing issues related to the recruitment of staff. This is something that has been exacerbated by the fact that, as someone who directly employs PAs, he is responsible for all financial aspects of their employment, including pensions, holidays and sickness cover. This reflects a concern highlighted by Scourfield (2005) that the low levels of DP can impact on the recruitment and retainment of staff. Mark observes correctly that there has not been an increase in the rate of DP since 1998. In the ongoing context of central government austerity, and especially in relation to the unique impact that austerity is having on local authorities' budgets, it may be the case that this an issue that will have a continuing impact on DP.

Mark's account highlights that DP have resulted in some significant positive intended consequences for disabled people. In particular, it is clear that DP have improved the choice and flexibility of care available to disabled people, as intended. It is also clear that DP have unintendedly widened the perceptions of disabled people through the increased horizons this system brings into sight. For instance, rather than being contained within residential care, DP have enabled disabled people to improve their opportunities for activities and interaction within the community, for example, work and leisure, which is an important way to overcome the prejudice and stigma that exists about disabled people. It may also be relevant to overcoming the lower expectations that people have about disabled people, such as that Mark experienced in his schooling and which research has shown to be a factor in the low achievement of disabled people. However, it is also evident that there are two main issues which are impacting of the overall effectiveness of DP. The first is its complexity, in terms of the requirements needed to be able to apply and administer. This is very likely impacting on the extent to which DP are being taken up. The second issue is its underfunding, which is impacting on its overall effectiveness in terms of the type of care providing and the level of care provided. This has very likely been exacerbated in the context of austerity and is very likely something which will continue to have a limiting impact in the foreseeable future.

Reflective Questions

1. How could education and social policy be used to overcome the culture of lower expectations regarding children attending special schools?
2. Should Direct Payments be offered to all people who request it, or should it be restricted, based on strict criteria?
3. How could policy changes overcome some of the funding issues identified in relation to Direct Payments?
4. Do the benefits of Direct Payments outweigh its limitations?
5. How could social policy improve the choice, control and flexibility for people using Direct Payments?

References

M. Barnes, *Caring and Social Justice* (Palgrave Macmillan, Basingstoke, 2006)

D. Brindle, Council tightens reins on personalised care. The Guardian 12th June (2018). Available via https://www.theguardian.com/society/2018/jun/12/councils-tighten-reins-on-personalised-care. Accessed 8 Feb 2019

S. Chatzitheochari, L. Platt, Disability differentials in educational attainment in England: primary and secondary effects. Br. J. Sociol. (2018). https://doi.org/10.1111/1468-4446.12372

Department of Health and Social Care, *A Consultation on Extending Legal Rights to Have for Personal Health Budgets and Integrated Personal Budgets* (Department of Health and Social Care, London, 2018)

D. Gaylard, Book review. Br. J. Soc. Work **48**(1), 274–275 (2016)

J. Glasby, R. Littlechild, *DPs and Personal Budgets: Putting Personalisation into Practice 3e* (Policy Press, Bristol, 2016)

S. Heng, Is relying on social policy benefits over a long time an easy life? in *Social Policy Simplified: Connecting Theory with People's Lives*, ed. by C. Sealey, (Palgrave Macmillan, Basingstoke, 2015), pp. 218–232

House of Commons Committee of Public Accounts, *Personal Budgets in Social Care* (House of Commons, London, 2016)

Independent Living Strategy Group, *Payment Cards in Adult Social Care. A National Overview 2017* (Shaw Trust, Bristol, 2018)

T. Jarrett, *The Supporting People Programme*, Research Paper 12/40 (House of Commons Library, London, 2012)

T. Jarrett, *Social Care: DPs from a Local Authority (England)*, Briefing Paper Number 03735 (House of Commons Library, London, 2016)

P. Scourfield, Implementing the community care (DPs) act: will the supply of personal assistants meet the demand and at what price? J. Soc. Policy Soc. **34**(3), 469–488 (2005)

H. Spandler, Friend or for? Towards a critical assessment of DPs. Crit. Soc. Policy **24**(2), 187–209 (2004)

The Lived Experiences of Limiting and Limited Policy, Practice and Services

Dionne*, Dorothy*, and Clive Sealey

The chapter is unique in that it is written from the parallel perspectives of Dionne* and Dorothy* (pseudonyms), twins of Jamaican heritage who, as the text shows, had similar reasons for being defined as children in need, but different lived experiences of being looked after by the local authority. The chapter presents their accounts together but separately to highlight the individualised nature of their experiences. It should be noted that for most of the chapter, they are describing the same incidents. While there are similarities in their accounts, there are also differences, which provides several reference points for discussion at the end of the chapter in terms of possible improvements to practice for social workers working within this field.

The chapter considers how practice could be improved when working with children identified as a 'child in need' and a 'looked-after child' by a local authority. Both of these are defined legal terms within the *Children Act 1989*, as shown in Table 9.1.

The focus of this chapter is highly relevant in the context of the fact that over the last decade or so, the number of looked-after children in England has continued to steadily increase (Department for Education 2017), in the light of several cases which highlighted failings in the child protection system, in particular Baby P. It should also be noted that the primary reason for children requiring to be looked after was due to abuse and neglect, at 61% (ibid.), something which is also relevant to this chapter.

Dionne* (✉) • Dorothy*
Birmingham, UK

C. Sealey
School of Allied Health and Community, University of Worcester, Worcester, UK
e-mail: c.sealey@worc.ac.uk

C. Sealey et al. (eds.), *Social Policy, Service Users and Carers*,
https://doi.org/10.1007/978-3-030-69876-8_9

145

Table 9.1 Legal definitions of 'child in need' and 'looked-after child' from the *Children Act 1989*

Legal term	Definition
Child in need	They are unlikely to achieve or maintain or to have the opportunity to achieve or maintain a reasonable standard of health or development without provision of services from the local authority
	Their health or development is likely to be significantly impaired, or further impaired, without the provision of services from the local authority
	They have a disability
Looked-after child	Is provided with accommodation for a continuous period for more than 24 hours
	Is subject to a care order
	Is subject to a placement order

These definitions only apply to England and Wales

The main aims of the chapter are:

1. To detail lived experiences of being defined as a child in need and a looked-after child.
2. To consider limitations of the current system for taking children into care.
3. To highlight improvements that could be made to the care system.

Who Are We?

Dionne

My name is Dionne, and I am 35 years old. I work as a social worker for adults for a local authority, having previously worked as a traffic warden for 11 years. I qualified to work as a social worker in 2015 and have worked as one continuously since then. I have started my Post-Qualifying training and am considering working as an Approved Mental Health Practitioner. I do enjoy working as social worker. For a number of years, I have done a lot of work for the University of Birmingham on their social work course, providing a service user input. This has mainly involved speaking to students about my experiences, as a way for the students to get a service user perspective.

I have had a range of experiences with social workers which I feel have led me to becoming a social worker. These experiences have been both good and bad. These include being a looked-after child and being both a foster carer and a kinship carer for my youngest sister at the age of 25. I will talk about these in more detail below, but I will start by outlining the circumstance which led me to become a looked-after child.

Dorothy

My name is Dorothy and I am the twin sister of Dionne. At present I am living on my own and work in several fields, including cleaning, security and bar work. Like Dionne, I have done work at for the University of Birmingham on their social work course to provide a direct service user perspective to social work students, and have done this on and off for many years, but it is very intermittent. I am also a user of mental health services.

For the first part of my life, I lived with my twin sister and younger sister and my Mum. I had a stepdad, as my real dad was not around and has never been. I first went into the care of the local authority when I was very young but don't remember much about this. I have been in care several times since, and I do remember these. All of my siblings have been in care, except my younger brother who has never been taken into care.

What Were the Circumstances That Led to Us Being Taken into Care?

Dionne

Initially, my Mum ran her own business as a music promoter and as a model and was very successful during this time. However, my Mum separated from my stepdad and met a new partner. They had my baby sister when I was about eight, and it was at this time that she started to take drugs. My Mum separated from my sister's father, but the negative impact of the drug taking was already having an impact, both professionally and personally. For example, she lost her business, and her ability to care for us was limited. This led to our first contact with social services, as we were being left alone for long periods of time, both days and night. At this point, my Mum was not really functional and spent most of her time in her room with other people, I can only presume taking drugs although I never actually saw her do this. Most of the other times, she was out of house, and the three of us were left on our own. During these times, we had to look after ourselves, which we were somehow able to do. In effect, due to my Mum not really being functional, I was running the household at the age of eight, looking after my sisters, cooking, cleaning and making sure my twin sister and I went to school.

However, we had a fear of spiders, and when these appeared in the house when we were alone, we would leave the house crying, which would draw attention to the fact that we were alone in the house. This led to the police being called and ultimately social services. This happened a number of times and led to us being put in emergency foster care several times. We were allocated a social worker who I found nice and who did not really want to remove us permanently from our home and so always found a way to return us back home. However, eventually it was taken out of her hands, and all three of us were removed by the police into emergency foster care. As a consequence of this, the social worker went off sick and had a breakdown. Reflecting back, however, I would say that it was the right decision to have us removed, for the reasons outlined above.

Dorothy

I am a firstborn twin. I am also a user of mental health services. I was born in another part of the UK and moved to the area I live in now at the age of two and a half. By this time, my Mum had divorced, and we were now living with my first stepdad.

I was probably about six years old when I became aware of the problem my Mum had with drug taking. Previous to that I had found drug-taking paraphernalia but had not known what they were. And when my Mum used to lock herself in her room, we used to think that she was just smoking; we didn't know that she was taking drugs. Mum didn't really look after us but kept leaving us with other people; we were innocent, and we didn't know what was what. I thought Mum was partying, and it took a fair while for us to realise what she was really doing. We just learnt to look after ourselves when she was taking drugs. My focus was my younger sister who I was always looking after and felt I'd been her carer from birth really. It was my role, just automatically.

I think we slowly realised the seriousness about what Mum was doing, while there had been pipes and equipment before, but as we got older, we began to understand what these were. By the time we had returned from being in care, we were getting sent to the phone box to call drug dealers for Mum. We thought we had been taken into care for neglect; no one had told us about the drugs issue the whole time. Mum never took drugs in front of us, but everyone else in the house did.

What Are Our Experiences of Being in Emergency and Long-Term Foster Care?

Dionne

As it was an emergency removal, me, my twin sister and younger sister were all taken with only the clothes on our back. We lived in emergency foster care for two months, and only had two pairs of clothes during this time, the ones we were removed in and a pair that was bought for use, and we alternated between these clothes during this time. We were also required to be checked for sexual abuse, despite there being no record of this in our notes. For this, we were examined by a male doctor, and I was very traumatised by the intimate examination that he undertook, which I had not been warned about.

This period in emergency foster care was not a happy time. We missed two months of school while in there. The foster parents also had kids older than us, and I felt that they resented us. They would not allow us to play with their toys. Also, we were placed not too far from where we had grown up, and so everyone knew what had happened to us in terms of being in foster care, and so we were teased about this. This was a significant reason why throughout our time in care, we were reluctant to let people know of our circumstances, which probably impacted on the provision we received.

Eventually we were found long-term foster carers, but not for all three of us together. The plan was to keep me and my twin sister together and send my younger sister to a separate foster carer. They also wanted to send us to white foster carers. I was 10 or 11 at the time, but I strongly refused both of these plans. Because of this, they changed the plans and sent my twin and younger sister to live together and me on my own. We were only given 30 minutes to say goodbye to each other.

We were both sent to live with Black foster carers, mine being a woman aged 50–60 years. During this time, we were allowed to have contact with each other, and it became apparent that our foster carers had very different approaches to our care. My sister's foster carer did not allow her to do anything; it was all done for her; instead emphasis was placed on books and allowing her to concentrate on schooling. For example, she was not allowed to play outside or to cook or clean. As a consequence, she was never allowed to learn to be independent. My experience was the opposite of this. I feel that these two experiences were too extreme and that there should be some balance in term of the emphasis in foster care.

I was in this foster care placement for about a year and a half. At the age of 13, I was returned to my Mum's care, and my two other sisters returned about 6 months later. My Mum had been asking for us to be returned and had had to undergo an extensive assessment to ensure this happened. However, she did everything that was asked her, such as coming off drugs. We were also asked if we wanted to go and live back with our Mum, and we said 'yes' to this. In this respect, I think it is good that our voices were heard.

Dorothy

The first time I can remember going into care was when I was around 10, when my twin sister and I were separated and I was placed with my younger sister in foster care. The reason for going into care was not really explained at all; we were just taken from our house. We lived in care for about four years.

I got on really well with my foster carer, and I still see her occasionally and call her auntie, and my memories of a foster home and the woman who cared for me was lovely. I know my relationship with my foster carer was different from that of my sisters. I was taught to do all kinds of things such as sewing and cooking, and even now I can make my own clothes. I do think that it was good that my foster parent had the same cultural background as me, as this enabled me to interact with her more than if otherwise. One thing I do remember is that we went to church almost every day as my foster carer was very religious. Although all the material things I wanted were provided when I was in care, I did miss out on the emotional aspect of being in a family such as praise and confidence. My foster mum loved me and still does, but she had a very different way of living and showing love as a very strict Christian. There were many hugs though and these were important.

Even when I was in care, I was looking after my younger sister. This affected me in many ways, such as in schooling as, for example, I had no time to do homework. My behaviour was also problematic, but I had no help with this. I was also suspended from school quite a few times, until eventually I just didn't go back. I felt suicidal at times at school, but if anyone asked, I said everything was OK, and this was accepted. Both my sister and I learnt to keep how we feel to ourselves, partly due to a fear of authority and the implications of saying what was really happening and how I really felt. Another issue we had was a lack of consistency of teachers. At our school we mainly had supply teachers, and so it was hard to build trusting relationships to enable us to confide in teachers. I also had to change schools a few times when moving in and out of care.

What Happened When We Were Returned Back to Our Home?

Dionne

Once back living with Mum, there was no monitoring of her or of us, we were effectively left on our own again. Initially, things were fine, my Mum started a new relationship, and she also had another baby girl. Once this relationship ended, though, my Mum returned back to drugs, and our house effectively became a drug den. This meant that I had to return to caring for my siblings, meaning that I missed a lot of school. I do agree with the decision to return us; however, I think that bearing in mind our previous history, I think our return should have been monitored more effectively. Later on, I reviewed my case notes, and it showed that during this period, there were 187 complaints in relation to our family from neighbours and others, and yet we were allowed to remain there. We had allocated social workers during this period, but the case notes also showed that the social workers made up bogus case notes of visits made, probably due to fear from where we lived regarding the drugs dens. So despite being on a full <u>care order</u> and the Child Protection Register, I do not feel that we were protected as we should have been.

Consequently, I experienced and witnessed a lot of things that I should not have experienced. This included drug raids, violence towards my Mum, a murder and threats from weapons. Ultimately, I felt that I had to leave that house, and so I managed to rent a flat at 15 and live with my twin sister, while my younger sister remained living with my Mum. I did this by selling drugs to finance my living. The alternative to this would have been to enter the sex trade, and so I saw this as the lesser of the two evils. I felt that I was left with no alternative. I had asked my then social worker for financial help, but all that she arranged for me was to receive £17.50 a fortnight, which was no way enough. So, I was left to find a way to ensure that we had enough money.

I sued social services for their incompetence in relation to mine and my twin sister's particular circumstances, and they settled out of court.

Dorothy

When we came out of care and went back home, things became much harder, and I think that's when my mental health stuff began. I think there is a relationship between these two things. I was returned to my Mum at around the age of 13, to what was essentially a drug house. I lied to get back to live with my Mum as I wanted to be with her so much. This also happened when I was returned back to the house, I would lie and say everything was alright so that I could stay living with her. The social workers did not do anything about this. One of the reasons for this I believe was that the social workers were scared and intimidated by my Mum, who could be quite vociferous in the way she made a point. So I think the social workers found it easier to just leave us alone and not challenge what she said. I don't think it made any difference whether or not we went into care—Mum was going to go down the road she had chosen no matter what.

We attended <u>family centres</u> for assessment to ensure that it was okay for us to go back and live with our Mum; however, there was no real help when we moved back in with our Mum from care. My Mum did try to get back to normal and had to prove this to get us back, but once we were home, all of this stopped, and we were left to our own devices. So, things went back to how they were. It was evident that the house was not good when we lived there, and the social workers should have known this, but they did not, or they did but did not do anything. This was incompetence from either being too scared or too inexperienced to know. I feel this contributed to the failure that occurred once we returned home. This had significance conse-quences for me. For example, I was selling drugs at the age of 13/14 in order to get money to live and run the household with my sister.

▷   **Key Learning: Family Centres** Family centres were first set up during the 1970s, but it was the *Children Act 1989* which specifically placed a requirement on local authorities to provide family centres (Ranson and Rutledge 2005). There is no set model of family centres, and they can provide a variety of preventative and/or reactive functions. This included providing parenting programmes in the form of therapy and support where children have been taken into the care of the local authority, in order to enable them to return to the family.

How Have Our Experiences of Care Impacted on Us in the Long Term?

Dionne

I feel that my circumstances have meant that I have always had to be an appropriate adult to my family throughout my life. This has meant that at times I have felt that my life had to be put on hold, and I have made sacrifices, either financially, time-wise, education-wise or personally. I am seen and have been described as a miser-able person, and I'm not much of a hugger. I have been independent throughout, but I also learned to keep myself to myself.

In addition, my circumstances also made me want to try to ensure that my young-est sister did not have the experiences I had. Unfortunately, she did end up in the system and moved around a lot, including in kinship care with relatives in Manchester, before eventually being brought back to the local authority in which we all live.

In my opinion, the number of placements and disruptions she encountered, including different parenting styles, boundaries and expectations, resulted in some challenging behaviour. During this time, I was trying to foster my younger sister, but she had been allocated a social work assistant (SWA), who did not seem to understand the processes. This led to delays; subsequently my sister was in care for five years before being considered for an assessment for fostering by me. Due to my concerns with the limitations of the foster care application, I chose to apply for kin-ship care. I was working at the university and had also began working as a traffic warden. Thought-out the entire process, I was supported by my twin sister, but only one of us was permitted to be named on the application. As I was already a parent, we decided to put the application in my name. I completed the relevant Form F application but got the impression that from the SWA assigned to my case that she was ticking a box in this process and did not really believe that I could or should foster my sister.

Eventually, the SWA made recommendations to the fostering panel, and a meeting was set up to make a decision. However, no one turned up at this meeting or at three other subsequent meetings, and the recommendations that the SWA had made were ignored. The SWA apologised for this and wrote an addendum to her original report with a recommendation that I should be allowed to foster and kinship care for my sister. When the meeting was held at the fifth time of asking, she was told that her recommendations had been rejected. The reason given for this was that my sister had become settled in her foster placement and school. As there were delays in getting the panel together, my sister moved from primary to secondary school. It was stated that as she was settled in her new school, it would disrupt her if she was required to move placements and live with me. This was despite the fact that my sister's school was a distance of approximately 10 miles from where she lived, so she had to do this journey by bus every day. Despite all our efforts, my youngest sister remained in long-term foster care, outside of the family until the age of 18.

Dorothy

I've needed help with my mental health for a long time; there are times when I am feeling suicidal, for example and really need help. I've been like this since I was 13; I remember feeling very confused and alone; I just woke up in hospital; I was living at home with my mum at the time, having been in the care system before. Subsequently, I have suffered from anxiety and deep depression. I may have been independent when I was younger, but I was left alone to work it all out for myself, and in particular no one ever spoke to me about my mental health. I only really understood that I had ongoing mental health issues in 2010, the first time when I was 26 years old. I have had counsellors in the past but not at the moment. I have had a Community Psychiatric Nurse (CPN) for the past nine years, linked in part to the relationships I have had but also to my childhood experiences. I feel that the CPN is focused too much on medication and the emphasis is on me taking medication, not on any therapy. There is also a lack of continuity in terms of the CPN nurses that I see. The CPNs now are so various I don't know who they are, and so many of the people who come to the door don't even seem to know what my situation is. There is no continuity of care, because they are too busy.

When I reached 18, I was provided with some care leavers' aftercare such as advice, which was OK, but pretty limited—just a bit of training and skills. My aftercare worker was pretty good and made sure that I did stuff I was supposed to do. I also have to say that I think that because she was Black this did help. However, overall, when I left the system, I did not feel that there had been adequate aftercare support. No one has ever spoken to me about what it was like to grow up with a Mum with drug problems or how to deal with my own mental health, never mind everyone else's. You're given a piece of paper and told to ring these organisations, but I can't do that—I get too anxious.

▷   **Key Learning: Care Leavers' Aftercare** Up to the year 2000, there was no
     requirement on local authorities to provide care for looked-after children
     after the age of 16. However, there has since been a range of legislation
     that have provided a legal responsibility for care leavers' aftercare. The
     Leaving Care Act 2000 raised the age of local authorities' responsibility
     for care leavers to 18 for all care leavers and to 21 if they were in
     education. The *Children and Young Person Act 2008* extended this
     responsibility to 21 for all care leavers or 25 if they are in education
     (HM Government 2016).

There is really no help out there for people over 25, and once I hit that age, there
was no support. I needed someone to work with me, to help me to try and get my
confidence back. They just wanted to get me on a scheme or straight back into work
and I couldn't do that then or now. When I was in care, aftercare finished at 18; it is
now 25, and this is a really good change, but I think it should be longer, to support
into further adulthood. I feel that if I had had aftercare up to 25, my life could have
been very different. Someone to help, talk to or listen when I need them would have
been really good. But they only have emergency teams, so they only see me when
things get really bad; they can't help the rest of the time.

It is not easy if you have mental health problems, and I feel the process for this
has made it worse. I also have a lot of debt, much of which is due to me not feeling
I care about life. I pay council tax and am in arrears; I didn't understand about
applying, though they just took off my money—no one told me—I've always tried
to pay it when I can, and the Citizens Advice are saying they will work with me to
help. One thing that has contributed negatively to my mental health is having to
apply for Personal Independence Payment (PIP). I have also found a local organisation that I'm hoping to help me, but it's scary to go, and I don't know if they will be
able to help. I need someone to help me phone, because I don't know what to say.
Instead, they tell me when to come, and I come, but when I get nervous or scared, I
just can't just go out there and deal with it all. If I feel under pressure and afraid to
go out, the thought of going on a bus is too much for me, but it's too far to walk. I've
had doctors' appointments, and I've had to say 'oh sorry, I mean I am up and ready,
but just can't get out of the house'. I am on three types of anti-anxiety medication;
they all have little side effects and work better taken in a certain order, but no one
told me that, and I had to work it out by making mistakes. They've changed my
medication so much and not told me why—you just get what you're given. If something isn't working, they just swap one type of medication with another.

I don't want to be like this for the rest of my life. I want to work, be more confident and have a better life. But I need the right support for that to happen. I am
looking forward to the next chapter of my life to include a better job and a family
and with a baby. Despite everything I've gone through, I still feel I can offer much
to a baby.

How Could Provision Be Improved for Children in the Care System?

Dionne

I think some key issue that my circumstance brings to the fore in relation to social services is when to intervene, as whilst I agree that it was right for the local authority to intervene and that care was the best thing for me and my sisters, this is often inconsistent. If the evidence exists for intervention, as in mine, my twin sister and middle sister's case, then they should intervene, for example where basic care needs are not being met, such as clothing, food financial support, access to social activities and emotional support. If, however, the case does not really insist for intervention, then they should not intervene, as in the case of my youngest sister. Additionally, I also feel that looked-after children face specific penalties that impact on their development and well-being in later life that are not considered by social services as the corporate parent of the child.

The Assessment Framework Triangle has lots of grey areas, one of which is that it focuses too much on parenting and not enough on support for the parent or caregiver. As an example, while foster carers get respite care, this is not the case for parent or caregiver, and in some instances, it may be that such a focus on the needs of the parent/caregiver can prevent the need for further disruptive intervention.

▶ **Key Learning: Assessment Framework Triangle** The Assessment Framework Triangle refers to a specific way to determine whether a child is in need and what these needs require. It is usually presented as a triangle, with safeguarding and promoting the child's welfare in the middle of the triangle. Outside of the triangle are the three interrelated factors of 'child's developmental needs', 'parenting capacity' and 'family and environmental factors'. The key rationale for representing it as a triangle is that it foregrounds that all assessment, planning and provision of services should focus on these three key factors with the focus on the child's welfare at the centre. (See: https://www.scie.org.uk/publications/introductionto/childrenssocialcare/waysofworking.asp for a diagram of the framework.)

I think that one of the key social work practice points is the importance of communicating with relevant other service users and professionals. In particular, there should be a real emphasis on maintaining contact with siblings and extended families. It is also important that in child protection, the voice of the child is heard to ensure that their needs are being met. This should include not just things such as food, warmth, shelter and clothing but also things such as emotional support, boundaries, routine and love. The last of these points is very significant but often not promoted in the care system, as often people are scared of blurring boundaries. So, it may be the case that what a child requires is for their current caregiver to say that to them that they love them, but this is not something that is seen as appropriate. Social workers also need to spend more quality time with service users, not time that is merely tokenistic. There needs to be accurate record keeping and ensuring that they make decisions made with full information, based on relevant research and reading of the case, and not going in blind and making judgements based on assumptions, as this will mean that they are more likely to work with the service user, not against them. There should also be backup plans for children that have been removed that include things that affect the quality of care that the child can receive, for example backup plans for their social worker going off sick.

My experiences in foster care also lead me to believe that there should be a standard level of care provided in this type of environment. In particular, there needs to be more awareness in showing support and love to the child as a consequence due to circumstances. To do this, foster carers need better knowledge of circumstances from which the child has come, as this will better prepare them for the potential issues in the placement. They should be able to see all the child's notes, not just a snapshot with just the good bits, but the not-so-nice bits that comprise what the child is. They should also be trained.

There should also be a set amount time that children spend in foster care, and this should be adhered to. This could be done through a tier-level approach, based on circumstances of the child and which people work towards, as shown in Table 9.2.

The key benefit from the proposal below is that it would provide a clear pathway for children to leave foster care based on their circumstances, and this in turn would enable foster carers to plan accordingly. At present, often foster carers do not know how long the child will be in their care and so are unwilling or unable to plan the care accordingly.

My views on ethnic matching in have changed over time. If I had been asked when I was younger, I would have said that it was very important to make sure there is a cultural match in placement. However, I now feel that as long as the child's cultural and emotional needs are understood, then this is not really necessary. This is because we are living in a multicultural society and have access to a broader range of information, and people are much more aware of how important this is.

When children are returned to their parents, there should be a level of return monitoring based on the circumstances of the case. For example, in our

Table 9.2 Proposed foster care tiering system

Top tier (complex cases)
Initial two-week period foster care
Can be extended under specific circumstances
May apply in circumstances where further information is required
Middle tier (less complex cases)
Max two weeks of foster care
Focus on providing long-term care
Focus on getting the child to go home
Lower tier (simple cases)
Max three days of foster care
Short-term arrangement
Child may be going back home, that is respite care

circumstances, it was clear that drugs were still impacting on the ability of my mom to care for us after we had returned, and so there could have been more support in place for her. I feel she should have been allocated a social worker to have helped her to deal with the issues that she had. However, birth parents do not often get this help, and this would be something that perhaps would help them to cope with the stresses of caring for their children again.

When young people leave care, it is obvious that some people are falling through the net and struggling to adjust. One of the main reasons for this is the lack of financial support that is provided for them. There should be some level of financial support, and guidance and support throughout the start of their adulthood, as it is evident that people leaving care do need more support than they are currently given.

The process of applying for sibling care should be made simpler, as there are too many hoops to jump through. There needs to be acknowledgement that you are putting yourself forward to support a family member, which will ultimately mean that children are not being put in care. Additionally, there needs to be some changes to the process. For example, those applying for sibling care have less training, support and information which should have a social worker to help them through the process. Also, the kinship assessment as it currently is based on the ability to care for the child, not to care for children. The consequence of this difference is that it slows down the process considerably and does not offer equality for those seeking to foster or the children involved who should be at the heart of it all.

Dorothy

My experiences of social workers are not very good. Firstly, I had too many social workers, and this meant that there was no consistency of care. Whenever there was a change of social worker, we would get asked the same questions as we had been previously asked, the answers to most of which was in our care notes, such as how long we had been in care. This made it clear to us that the social workers were not reading our notes and so made us feel that we were not involved.

Secondly, they never showed any knowledge of our case as required. I don't feel that we necessarily needed to be put in care all the times that we were; I feel that the social workers could have worked with us to keep us together as a family. They also didn't check really that it was safe to go back or to stay there.

We did actually make a complaint to Birmingham Social Services and were going sue them for neglect, but they settled out of court. We found out all about this from reading our files later on, where it was clear that the social workers were aware of what was going on yet they did nothing.

I think to improve social work training, social workers should make themselves more aware of what is happening in the life of the child. Most of them came to the house and left, without trying to understand our circumstances, and this meant the underlying issues that we had were never dealt with. Social workers should also try to work with the family, not prioritise taking children into care. They should also try to build relationships with people, not make themselves seem scary. One thing I do remember is the stigma associated with being seen with a social worker, and so trying to remove this stigma would be good. I do think that social workers are responsible for too much, and bearing in mind their responsibilities, they do not get paid much. They should be paid more than doctors, as they have more responsibilities. They should also have more training.

The services I would have liked in relation to social services when I was in care would have been effective monitoring when we were back with Mum. A social worker keeping us informed about what was happening and, for instance, telling us how they thought Mum was doing. This would include enough social workers to be able to work effectively with the family, as no one ever worked with us and Mum, just us in isolation and Mum alone. This didn't really help is learn how to live together.

I thought the services I received between 16 and 18 with aftercare workers were actually some of the best support and advice I was offered in this time—but once that ended, there was nothing. One of the main limitations of the service is having cut-off ages when you are no longer entitled to services, both on leaving care and in relation to mental health.

Aftercare services should also include a service I can use when I need it, rather than when they decide I can be fitted in. In particular, someone who understands about benefits and can help me get my finances straight and understand the system more. Also, a named person to work with, as currently it's a different person every time, and some of them speak down to me like I am a silly child, so I can't build any relationship with them. Sometimes now I get so anxious I just lock my door and close out everyone. I need someone to help me build skills and confidence that I can turn to before I hit an emergency crisis point. This could include continuous support from a CPN or similar person—I've never had a support worker.

Beyond that, I don't know what support I really need, because no one has told me any options or anything.

Chapter Commentary

As outlined in the introduction to the chapter, while Dionne and Dorothy had similar experiences from being in need, they also had individualised experiences of being looked after. There are some evident differences in their recollections, which is perhaps not surprising considering the passage of time. Notwithstanding these differences, their accounts do provide relevant reference points for analysis of interventions for children in need and children looked after by the local authority.

In relation to the similarities, these are most evident in terms of their status of being a child in need. The most obvious are their experiences of social workers before, during and after being looked after. In terms of before, it is evident that they believe that social workers could have intervened earlier in their situation in terms of removing them from their home. So, for example, they both talk about the fact that social workers and the police were called numerous times to their house as a consequence of a number of incidents, and numerous complaints made to social services about the family. However, despite this, there was an emphasis on not talking action, rather than taking them into care, despite the obvious signs that their parent was failing to provide them with basic care. There are numerous possible valid reasons why this decision was taken, the most obvious of which is the possible negative outcomes that looked-after children can have in comparison to non-looked-after children (Department for Education 2018). However, a closer analysis of this data shows that while on some measures, the outcome for looked-after children is worse than for non-looked-after children, this is not as straightforward as it seems. In particular, when comparing looked-after children with children in need (i.e. identified by the local authority as in need but not being looked after by them, but very likely looked after by their family), then looked-after children do considerably better than some other children on a range of measures. This is significant as it suggests that a child remaining in need for a long time has significantly more negative outcomes that a looked-after child.

Additionally, numerous serious case reviews over the years have shown that a delay in decision-making can contribute to the negative outcomes that children experience. As a consequence, when such children do eventually enter care, they do so with greater degrees of difficulty than perhaps necessary (Davies and Ward 2012). Moreover, while research has shown that there are limitations within the care system, the majority of children say that the care system does provide a safe environment for children and that it was the right choice for them (Biehal et al. 2014).

A possible reason for this outcome is also provided in the accounts above, in terms of the relationships that Dionne and Dorothy had with their social workers. Notwithstanding, the positive relationship reported by Dionne with one particular social worker, in general there was a lack of meaningful relationships built up with social workers. Numerous possible reasons were provided for this, such as the lack of continuity of social workers and the fear from social workers themselves in terms of the environment in which they found themselves. What is clear is that the lack of positive relationships between Dionne and Dorothy and their social workers impacted significantly on the outcomes, which reflects the findings made by Professor Eileen Munro in her review of child protection systems in England (Munro 2011). This review provided evidence which showed that the only factor that could be evidenced as improving the outcomes for children in need is the relationship between the child/family and their social worker. Linked to this is the response observed by Dionne when she tried to challenge care, wherein she was seen as being difficult and awkward, an observation also made by other services users when trying to do the same (Parkhill and Wall 2019).

In terms of similarities during their time in care, the most obvious is the emotional impact that being in care had on Dionne and Dorothy. In particular, both individuals articulated that their experiences have led them to internalise their feelings and not feel that they were able to express them, so, for example they had a fear of authority which impacted on their ability to express their true feelings when it may have been beneficial for them to do so. In both instances, this has had negative short-term and long-term impacts on them. Dionne made the point that there needs to be more emphasis on not just the practical needs that looked-after children have but also their emotional needs, which in the context of the traumatic experiences that they would both have gone through would see highly appropriate. A key priority identified by the NSPCC (2018) for children in care is supporting the emotional well-being of looked-after children and young people throughout the system, and the experiences above provide support for this.

Whilst in care, they were both cared for by Black foster carers, which reflected their ethnic heritage. Historically, ethnic matching has been seen as very important to effective fostering outcomes for Black, Asian and Minority Ethnic (BAME) children. However, this has shifted politically recently to the promotion of placements of children of minority ethnic heritage with white families, principally in order to avoid delay in adoption where no families of a similar ethnic heritage are available (Wainwright and Ridley 2012). There is evidence that the promotion of matching BAME children with BAME foster families can be effective. However, the evidence presented by Dionne suggests that this may not always be as essential as previously thought, primarily due to greater understanding. Additionally, there may be a requirement for greater pragmatism in relation to this as a consequence of the relatively high number of unaccompanied minors seeking asylum which has led to significant increases in terms of looked-after children.

In terms of similarities after being looked after, there are two key points to be made. The first is the lack of aftercare support provided to the family as a whole, as opposed to just the children, after leaving care. For example, Dionne commented how her mother had worked hard with social workers to enable them to leave care and go back to live with her. However, once back with the family, this work and support virtually ceased, meaning that they were unable to continue to live there and found alternative temporary accommodation for her and her sisters. This suggests that work with children in need and looked-after children needs to take a whole family approach, meaning an approach that does not just focus on the child's needs but also the family's needs. This is an approach that both Dionne and Dorothy feel would have been beneficial to them.

Also relevant is the lack of support and help both felt available once they had left care, similar to the experiences of Charles English-Peach in Chap. 4. This included not only financial support but also emotional and practical support. At present, support for care leavers ends either at the age of 21 or 25, depending on their educational status. Research shows that the outcomes for care leavers is much worse than the general population on a number of measures, including housing, health, education, unemployment and involvement with the criminal justice system (HM Government 2016). There have been several recent pieces of legislation and policies designed to ameliorate these outcomes. The most recent of these has been the requirement for local authorities to publish the support that they provide care leavers (the 'local offer') (Roberts et al. 2019). One important point highlighted by Dorothy was trying to navigate the social security system as a care leaver and the lack of assistance to enable them to do this. However, the general point made by both Dionne and Dorothy was the need for greater support for longer, beyond the current age restrictions, and their experiences provide support for this.

As stated above, there were also differences in terms of the experiences by Dionne and Dorothy. The main difference was in relation to the type of foster carer, which itself seemed to lead to different relationships with the foster carer. In particular, the level of <u>attachment</u> shown in each placement differed markedly. An obvious point to make here is that parenting is not a 'one-size-fits-all', and different people have different parenting styles. However, these parenting styles can have an important influence on the level of attachment that a child has with their new family, which in turn can have an important impact on the longer-term outcomes that they have (Howe 2011). Therefore, while different parenting styles are relevant, the point made by Dionne that there needs to be a certain basic standard of fostering is also relevant in this context. Dionne provides a model for providing clarity for foster carers in terms of how long a child will be with them, in order to enable them to plan and care accordingly. This or something similar could be a way to ameliorate the differential experiences that can be present in foster placement.

Also evident are the different mental health outcomes of Dionne and Dorothy. In particular, there is great emphasis in Dorothy's account on the negative mental health impact. This is perhaps not surprising when considering the high proportion of looked-after children who have mental health problems that require professional support, which can be up to five times greater for looked-after children than for non-looked-after children (Bazalgette et al. 2015). An important contributory factor to this has been the lack of support provided post leaving care, as detailed above. An example of this lack of support is in relation to <u>Child and Adolescent Mental Health Services (CAMHS)</u> support, which effectively stops when a child reaches 18, after which there is the need to access adult mental health services which have significantly longer waiting times. In the context of the very high level of mental health need prevalent among looked-after children, this area requires specific policy focus.

Reflective Questions

1. How typical do you think the experiences of Dionne and Dorothy are in terms of other looked children? What can be learnt from their insights?
2. Should the current policy whereby children in need/looked after have separate social workers from their parents/caregivers continue, or should there be a whole family approach to working with families?
3. What social policies (housing/financial guarantees/counselling support/job schemes) could be introduced to improve the experiences of looked-after children leaving care?
4. Could CAHMS policy change to prioritise the health and well-being of looked-after children? What would be the advantages/disadvantages of such a model?
5. Is the social policy of ethnic matching still important when considering the placement of looked-after children in foster care?
6. How might social policy initiatives attract more foster carers from ethnic minority backgrounds?

References

L. Bazalgette, T. Rahilly, G. Trevelyan, *Achieving Emotional Wellbeing for Looked After Children* (NSPCC, London, 2015)

N. Biehal, L. Cusworth, J. Wade, et al., *Keeping Children Safe: Allegations Concerning the Abuse or Neglect of Children in Care* (NSPCC, London, 2014)

C. Davies, H. Ward, *Safeguarding Children Across Services: Messages from Research* (Jessica Kingsley, London, 2012)

Department for Education, *Children Looked After in England (Including Adoption), Year Ending 31 March 2017, SFR50/2017* (Department for Education, London, 2017)

Department for Education, *Outcomes for Children Looked After by Local Authorities in England, 31 March 2017, SFR 20/2018* (Department for Education, London, 2018)

HM Government, *Keep on Caring. Supporting Young People from Care to Independence. DFE-00165-2016* (HM Government, London, 2016)

D. Howe, *Attachment Across the Lifecourse: A Brief Introduction* (Red Globe Press, Basingstoke, 2011)

E. Munro, The Munro review of child protection: final report, CM8062 (2011)

NSPCC, Looked after children (2018). https://learning.nspcc.org.uk/children-and-families-at-risk/looked-after-children/. Accessed 7 June 2019

I. Parkhill, K. Wall, The journey to care – reflections of a service user. Disabil. Soc. (2019). https://doi.org/10.1080/09687599.2019.1649815

S. Ranson, and H. Rutledge. *Including families in the learning community. Family centres and the expansion of learning* (York: Joseph Rowntree Foundation, 2005)

N. Roberts, T. Jarrett, T. Powell, et al., *Support for Care Leavers*, Briefing Paper Number 08429 (House of Commons Library, London, 2019)

J. Wainwright, J. Ridley, Matching, ethnicity and identity. Reflections on the practice and realities of ethnic matching in adoption. Adopt. Foster. **36**(3), 50–61 (2012). https://doi.org/10.1177/030857591203600306

Chantele Harvey Head and Joy Fillingham

The chapter will present the lived experiences of Chantele Harvey-Head to detail the impact that living with an undiagnosed mental health disorder over a long period of time can have on an individual and consider the effectiveness of services tasked with providing treatment and support to people living with a mental health disorder.

Overall, it is estimated that one in four people in the UK experiences a mental health problem each year; this includes common mental disorders such as anxiety and depression to less common mental health disorders such as a psychotic disorder and autism spectrum disorders (McManus et al. 2016). Perhaps more significantly, the trend over the last 20 years is for an increase in the number of people suffering mental health disorders, particularly women (ibid.) Moreover, having a mental health disorder is one of the largest single causes of disability, with sickness absence related to mental health accounting for 70 million sick days per year in the UK (ibid.). There are also substantial increases in the numbers of young people acknowledging mental health issues (Pitchforth et al. 2019).

Chantele's account below presents her lived experience of living with bipolar disorder, previously known as manic depression, from a very young age to the present. Bipolar disorder is estimated to affect around 2% of the population, with similar rates for men and women (Marwaha et al. 2016).

▶ **Key Learning: Bipolar Disorder** Bipolar disorder is a lifelong mental health condition which affects 1 in every 100 people at some point in their life. It is a condition of extremes, as is mainly characterised by repeated and alternating episodes of either depression (feelings of low

C. Harvey Head (✉)
Birmingham, UK

J. Fillingham
Department of Social Work and Social Care, University of Birmingham, Birmingham, UK
e-mail: j.fillingham@bham.ac.uk

C. Sealey et al. (eds.), *Social Policy, Service Users and Carers*,
https://doi.org/10.1007/978-3-030-69876-8_10

mood and lethargy) or mania (feelings of very high mood and jubilation). These episodes can last between 3 and 12 months. Between episodes of depression and mania, there may be periods of 'normal mood'. The exact cause of bipolar disorder is unknown, but it is thought to be a complex mix of physical, environmental and social factors. Treatment for bipolar disorder can include medical, psychological and lifestyle interventions.

Chantele's account details her experiences of living with her mental health condition from childhood through to adulthood and the long-term impacts of not recognising her condition early enough, as many individuals have such conditions without realising what they are encountering. Her account also details her experiences of what happened when a diagnosis was finally made and she sought and was provided with help, and whether the help provided was as appropriate as it could have been.

The main aims of the chapter are to:

1. Outline the impact of living with an undiagnosed mental health condition in childhood.
2. Detail the lived experience of the importance of timely and accurate diagnosis of mental health conditions.
3. Explore current treatment, support and provision for individuals experiencing mental health disorders.

Who Am I?

I am Chantele, I was born in 1978 at New Cross Hospital, in Wolverhampton, a little place in the Midlands. My parents were 20 and 19 years old respectively when they met. I have a brother and two sisters. My brother and I have the same dad and my sisters both have a different dad. We had a nice upbringing; money was tight but there was warmth and love for all of us.

I don't really know how they met just bits and bobs that I've picked up over the years. I didn't grow up with my Dad; he was around at times; I know that because of the photos my Mom has, but I don't really remember him being around in my early days. He was born in Britain and sent back to Jamaica when 9, where he stayed until 18. When my Dad started getting into trouble, they sent him back to Britain. I didn't have much contact with him at all until my daughter was two years old; my husband went behind my back and got in touch with him, I wasn't happy but that's another story for another day. The lack of regular contact with my father when I was growing up had an impact upon me, and I felt I missed out on having a father figure and that this added to the challenges to my mental health.

My Mom on the other hand I grew up with, and she has told me things in her life that Hollywood movies are made of. I didn't really learn to deal with adversity as Mom insisted everything was fine—even when it clearly wasn't. She had a hard upbringing with plenty of downs and not many ups that then took a toll on our relationship. My Mom and I didn't get on for many years, and growing up I have early memories of feeling alone, different and helpless.

What Were My Childhood Experiences of Developing Mental Health Issues?

I started school in 1999 in Erdington in Birmingham. I liked school but had a temper so was always getting suspended. I was diagnosed with dyslexia when I was 23 and was sent for testing from my college at the time. So, when I was at school, I didn't understand why I felt so stupid. Having dyslexia (difficulty with words and numbers) always made me feel behind other people so I tried to hide it and used to push people away; this used to make me feel small and worthless at times, and I would retreat into myself and have darker thoughts; I was very good at sports as I found it a release. I missed a lot of school due to illness: stomach problems, and I used to cry a lot which I now realise is an early symptom of mental health. The impacts of missing so much school made me feel estranged from my peers, and I didn't feel as if I fitted in. I stayed at the same school despite the repeated suspensions; I didn't think any other school would have me. I recognise now that the stomach problems were Crohn's disease but did not know this at the time. I have now suffered with this for 20 years.

> **Key Learning: Dyslexia** Dyslexia is a learning difficulty, which unlike a learning disability means that it does not affect a person's intelligence. Instead, it causes problems with reading, writing and spelling. Therefore, indicators of dyslexia usually become most evident when a child starts school, and their attention is on learning how to read and write. It is estimated up to one in every ten people in the UK has some degree of dyslexia. The exact cause of dyslexia is not known, but it can be genetically inherited. Dyslexia can also be linked to other problems not directly connected to reading or writing, such as poor short-term memory, poor organisation and time management, problems with concentrating and a short attention span. Dyslexia support in schools is usually through special educational needs support, but where there is a need for additional support then a formal Education, Health and Care plan (EHC) can be requested.

The teachers didn't want to help and would prefer to put me in detention or isolation. It felt like I was different from everyone else and was being punished for it; girls thought I was trying to be hard because of my moods and how the teachers treated me, so would try to start fights to prove they were not scared of the crazy girl. This made me angry and sad, and I would do my best not to retaliate, but it was always me that got in trouble, making me feel more depressed and anxious (this is where everything and anything would make you scared or afraid, constantly panicking). I was not provided with any help whatsoever at school, not even from CAMHS.

▶ **Key Learning: Child and Adolescent Mental Health Services (CAMHS)** CAMHS are specialist NHS mental health services for children and young people only, up to the age of 18. CAMHS provides help and support for problems like depression, anxiety, self-harm, stress, bullying, eating disorders or self-esteem. For children under 16, a referral needs to be made to CAMHS by parents, teacher, social worker or GP; over 16s can self-refer. CAMHS are multidisciplinary teams consisting of services that can include psychologists, psychotherapists, psychiatrists, nurses, occupational therapists and clinical social workers. CAMHS are provided by a range of organisations including NHS mental health and community trusts, local authorities and the private and voluntary sectors. Once a referral is made, CAMHS offer assessment, diagnosis, treatment and support. Services often include a waiting list.

The first time I had any interaction with a mental health representative was when I was 13 and had tried to commit suicide, as a result of the breakup of a relationship and the fractured bond with my parents. I remember waking up in the hospital and the doctor telling me I needed to grow up. It made me feel much worse about myself and made it harder to seek help after that time. This led to feelings of shame and unworthiness.

At times I would consider suicide and self-harming, both of these things have been a factor throughout my life and still arise to this day. I still at times when I'm in a dark place return to self-harming as the pain makes me feel something which reminds me that I am alive. The trigger which began these emotions was breaking up with a boyfriend when I was 13; it was at this time I didn't see my dad and realised he too had abandoned me. I tried to talk to my Mom about it, but because she insisted that everything was great when it really wasn't, other relationships became more important to me as a result. I don't think Mom understood what I was going through; there was a breakdown in our relationship for many years as a result of this.

My second suicide attempt was when I was 16 and had a breakdown; I was looked after by the GP at home. I still am unable to identify the trigger for this event. The GP came around once a day for a week to check on me, and then the contact stopped, and no further treatment suggested. I still feel no help was offered. It wasn't until I was 31 and was taken to the doctors by my husband after we had watched a Stephen Fry documentary on TV about bipolar, and we both thought I could have it. So, after doing the recommended online test in which I scored highly, he took me, and the doctors were made to listen to what I had to say. My husband recognised that I appeared to have lots of warning signs outlined in the programme, such as tearfulness and insomnia.

How Significant Was Getting a Mental Health Diagnosis?

I'm not really sure how I got through all these years, without really understanding what was happening to me. There were so many dramatic events from my point of view and lots of crying. When I had my first daughter in 2002, I was forced to go to a mother and baby unit to assess my ability to care for her. I was given help and felt that the place was quite nice—and when I left, I felt sure I would be able to look after my daughter on my own. The breakup of my relationship with my daughter's dad again led me to spiral again into a breakdown. It was confusing because I couldn't understand that I wasn't normal, and I just didn't know if it would ever stop.

In between the ages of 16 and 31 I used to drink and take recreational drugs to help cope with the thoughts in my head; I used to go clubbing a lot, and being drunk or high was a great escape from everything else.

After school I took a year out to do a YTS scheme and then went to college to do performing arts which it I got a BTEC in. I did a year at university after that; I didn't complete the course due to my undiagnosed mental health problems. The university offered zero help towards any mention of mental health; I would say it was mainly disregarded and ignored by the people I reached out to. The effects were substantial, for example I couldn't sleep, eat or engage with others, which meant it was impossible for me to fully commit to the course.

My work life has always been hard, trying to explain why I need certain days off or why my temperament would change hour by hour. By this time, I had received no help with my mental health. I have worked in clothes shops and supporting the welfare of children and young people, but the people I worked with did not understand all of my reactions and indeed at the time neither did I. Now I have started working with the University of Birmingham to help students understand about conditions such as mine, and I feel I am beginning to have a voice and build confidence.

The diagnosis helped me understand myself further. It was only made at the instigation of my husband taking me to the GP after seeing a documentary. It was at that time I saw how my mood can fluctuate between 'high', meaning I'm feeling extremely happy and wanting to do something constantly, for instance, painting or decorating. This isn't as good as it sounds as it can make me disappear for days at a time with no concern for how my friends and family are feeling. Being on a 'down' is the complete opposite, where I can stay in my room not talking to anyone for weeks on end and have suicidal feelings. The explanation given to me regarding bipolar was awful—they didn't even have a leaflet on the topic and instead gave me one regarding depression.

Prior to being diagnosed with bipolar, I struggled to get help from anyone at my GP practice, and I was regularly told that I just needed to cheer up. No friend was particularly supportive at this time—they didn't understand what I was experiencing and couldn't relate.

Getting diagnosed was one of the best days of my life as it finally made sense why my head was so jumbled. All the things I had said or done to myself and other people wasn't just because I was different but because there was actually something wrong with me. I know it sounds silly to say I was happy that I was 'sick', but it was a relief to know that maybe I could be on the road to being normal. Now to be honest I hate the word 'normal' because I've always been a bit different, but at least for some days I could experience being normal.

What Treatments Have I Received for My Conditions?

I was put on medication for my bipolar which didn't have the right effect; it basically put me into coma (made me like a zombie from walking dead). My husband and I didn't know any better, so assumed this was a normal reaction; there was no follow-up by any doctor. After two years we went back and were sent to see a specialist at a local unit (this is a treatment centre which is a place where people with all sorts of mental health issues are seen by doctors who focus just on mental health), who changed my medication. My medication has probably changed six times over the past eight years without much explanation. I was never offered any form of treatment beyond medication.

I was diagnosed with Crohn's disease around four years ago; it is not a condition which will go away, but something I have learnt to manage. I don't talk about it much. More recently I have managed to be seen at the hospital regarding my Crohn's disease. I only managed to get back in after I hadn't heard anything from them for a long while, so I managed to work up to calling them. This is a big thing for me due to my anxiety (something else I deal with, which causes me to get very nervous and panic over things other people find normal), so once I had contacted someone at the hospital, they said they had discharged me due to me not getting in touch with them sooner. They said they had sent a letter six months earlier, but as I hadn't replied I was off the list. So now I had to get an appointment at my GP's which in itself is a miracle; they had to refer me back to the hospital, who then sent me out an appointment, a process which took six weeks from my first phone call. I mentioned my mental health to them many times, but it was never spoken about by any health practitioner. Had they acknowledged my mental health issues and tried to see the whole picture, I feel I could have received help that recognised the whole of me rather than the specific element they were focusing upon.

How Do I Reflect on the Treatment and Support I Have Received?

Now that I have been diagnosed for some time, that happiness I felt has turned to anger and frustration. How could I have been left like this without support or diagnosis for so long? I had self-harmed and almost killed myself over feeling the way I did, and I would have left my daughter without her Mom, let alone all my friends and family. Luckily, we see a lot more in the news and on TV; there's mental health week, and numerous charities are out there to help people like me. My life could have been different if I had been treated earlier; maybe I would have finished university or carried on dancing; I'll never know, but at least I'm here now telling my story.

I feel not being diagnosed for so long has had a lasting impact on my life that I believe will never go away. I have a feeling of being let down by the NHS, my GP and even friends and family which has given me trust issues that I still have with new people I meet and lifelong friends. The NHS were not sending me much needed appointments, and the care was fractured and inconsistent. GPs appeared to be sending me away without solutions when I was struggling; it felt like a permanently revolving door to the surgery at times. I have occasionally told a friend some of the issues I was experiencing, and they would appear sympathetic and then go and tell other people about my business.

The most positive thing to come out of all of this is my psychologist (this is someone who talks to you and helps you understand what you're going through and tries to help you feel better) who has been so important in getting me and my family the help I need. I met her when I went to an awayday to understand the bipolar; my psychologist was there and recognised that I needed additional support, and so she took me on as a patient. It was purely by chance and the individual actions of the psychologist I met which resulted in me having such support. She has suggested <u>art therapy</u> in addition to medication, since then I have started art therapy which is very draining mentally but has also been a big help as I always come away feeling more positive. I enjoy art therapy—it seems a little outside my comfort zone, but I am sticking with it.

> **Key Learning: Art Therapy** Art therapy is a non-medical form of therapy that involves the use of a range of creative techniques such as drawing, painting, collage, colouring or sculpting to help people to address underlying psychological and emotional health issues such as emotional, behavioural or mental health problems, learning or physical disabilities, life-limiting conditions, neurological conditions and physical illnesses. There is no need to have any previous experience or expertise in art. Art therapy functions on the basis that the nonverbal messages, symbols and metaphors found in an individual's art lead to a better self-awareness and understanding of their underpinning feelings and behaviour, and this better understanding enables the individual to address unresolved emotional conflicts, improve social skills and raise self-esteem.

She has helped get my medication changed to a point where on good days I feel normal; she has also made sure my Community Psychiatric Nurse (CPN) sees me more often. My CPN is meant to visit to help me get back into the community, though realistically this doesn't happen. My CPN helps look after my mental health only, not my Crohn's even. She only comes about every four to six weeks; I have been on waiting list for certain groups for over a year.

> **Key Learning: Community Psychiatric Nurse (CPN)** A CPN is a registered mental health nurse who works in the community, as opposed to working in a hospital or other institution. This means that they visit service users in their own homes, in out-patient departments or in GP

surgeries. However, most still work as part of a Community Mental Health Team and work alongside psychiatrists, occupational therapists, social workers, psychologists and support workers to support people over a period of one to two years. CPNs can administer medicines, provide psychological support and work closely with family members and carers to keep an eye on service users. They can also help individuals to talk through their problems and give practical advice and support.

What Could Be Improved for People Living with Mental Health Problems?

The most immediate change I would like to see is that people with mental health issues such as bipolar could be treated as a human with respect and interest. I feel we are patronised, scrutinised and treated as cases rather than people.

I do feel I haven't been given enough help or support from my doctors or the mental health team. I feel they could have seen me more often, and when I tell them I'm ok when it's obvious I'm not, they could be more forceful with helping. Some of the challenges I have found when dealing with these conditions continue to have long-term effects on me and my future. I feel the financial side of not being able to work consistently and the complexity of the benefits system have never properly been explained to me. I have found out, for example, that I have previously been entitled to benefits which could have helped me, but no one had even told me that these existed, despite me asking for help and information regularly.

I am on a variety of medications, some of which appear to interact with each other negatively. If the medications are changed, which happens quite often, I would expect a doctor to monitor the side effects of such treatments, but none of them even appear to know what medications I am taking. However, unless I pursue them, no follow-ups happen. I have had Crohn's disease which is clearly linked to stress and mental health issues. For example, when I have anxiety, my stomach gets all into knots, and I can become very weak and unwell. No one has considered the medications I am taking or whether they are compatible. Each is concerned with treating the symptoms of an immediate condition, not trying to identify what is happening and why.

My GP surgery has no continuity and I never get to see the same doctor two visits running. Having different doctors see you every time and having to explain again my situation is draining and makes me feel like they don't really care, and at times I am made to feel that if I don't say I'm ready to end things, I won't be seen; unfortunately this seems to happen regularly. The most important aspect would be that they should speak to me and engage with me as an individual, rather than categorise me and leave me isolated.

Summary

Living with mental health has a daily impact on my life. I can some days be the most fun-loving and carefree person in the room and have my kids laughing and playing with me. Other days where every little thing can set me off and put me on edge, it makes me sad knowing my kids know there is something wrong with Mommy, especially my eight-year-old son. I feel like he deserves a normal Mom, and there are days I don't see him much as don't want him to see what I see in myself. This makes it hard to be motivated some days, and it is struggle, but it's a fight I'm going to keep on fighting, as losing someone to mental health is one of the hardest things I've had to experience, and I don't want anyone else to go through that. So, no matter how dark it gets, I know I have a support network to help me in the shape of my husband and children.

Commentary

Chantele's account provides a vivid and considered long-term account of her experiences of living with an undiagnosed mental health disorder. What is evident from her account is that it is through a combination of her determination, the support volunteered by her psychologist and her personal support networks that Chantele has faced these experiences and has sought, and continues to seek, appropriate help. There are likely to be many people encountering the same conditions, without sufficient personal or support capacity who are trapped by assumptions, expectations and, as Chantele calls it, fractured and insufficient care. It is also evident from her account that there are key lessons to be learnt for practitioners and policy-makers in order to improve provision for people living with a mental disorder. Before discussing this, there are some similarities in Chantele's account with other contributors to this book that are important to note.

The key similarity is the lack of continuity of care from professionals, in terms of Chantele not seeing the same professional. Instead, Chantele detailed that she would see different professionals at successive appointments for diagnosis and treatment. This chimes with the accounts of numerous other contributors in this book's other chapters. The Care Quality Commission (2017) has detailed that a lack of continuity of care for mental health service users is detrimental to the quality of care received. More specifically, Biringer et al. (2015, p. 763) highlight this as particularly significant point of analysis, wherein they argue that 'improving personal continuity in mental health and welfare services should be a number one priority'. This is because of the importance of 'trusting relationships' to recovery, while the absence of such a relationship is observed as leading to stress and anxiety and impact on recovery, as experienced by Chantele. So, this similarity in Chantele's account highlights an important limitation in the way that treatment has been provided to her.

Another similarly in Chantele's account is the emphasis on inappropriate medical treatment for her condition, as also experienced by Charles English-Peach in

Chap. 4. The specific similarity between Chantele's and Charles' account is the negative social impact that such inappropriate medical treatment has had, in terms of suppressing their ability to function within society, and that it was only after alternative non-medical interventions were used that their conditions improved. NICE guidelines do state that people with bipolar disorder should be offered non-medical interventions (NICE 2014 [2020]) and have been demonstrated to improve healthcare at a reduced cost (Morriss 2015). This did happen, but only much later in her care, suggesting that this guidance is either not known or not being adhered to by practitioners. Additionally, the implementation of such processes is not mandatory, and there are no mechanisms by which health professionals are monitored to identify and decide upon whether this is followed or not.

It should be noted that debates around inappropriate prescribing are not new but have been prevailing for decades, and yet the situation remains (Bauer et al. 2018). What is apparent in Chantele's account is the positive effect that therapy as a form of treatment had on her condition. This suggests that for some service users, therapy could be a better alternative to medication. Chantele's account also highlighted the importance of community mental health to the positive progression of her condition. In this context, the emphasis in the NHS Long Term Plan (NHS 2019) on both the community mental healthcare provision and access to psychological therapies should be seen as a positive step in the treatment of mental health disorders for some, not all, service users. The issue of course is whether the funding will be made available to allow this transformation to happen.

It is also notable that the negative experiences that Chantele detailed in her childhood continued well into her transition to adulthood, due to the sustained un/misdiagnoses of her condition into her adult life, as also evident in Charles' account. The attitudinal responses of professionals are also again evident here, whereby Chantele's behaviour was presumed to be as a result of her personality, rather than her condition. This particularly negatively impacted on her work and university life, the latter of which was specifically acknowledged as an issue that needs attention in the 'Future in Mind' publication (Department of Health 2015). In particular, the Office for Students (2019) suggests that mental health disorders are underreported and so underdiagnosed at universities, with stigma being a significant reason for this. It also suggests that universities need to do more to identify and support those students who experience mental ill health during their time at university, something which is borne out in Chantele's account.

A prevailing theme that runs through Chantele's account is the lack of diagnosis of her condition, from when she was young through to adulthood. She detailed displaying behaviours indicative of suffering a mental health disorder from an early age, but her behaviour was viewed as a disciplinary issue and resulted in repeated exclusions from school. Even her suicide attempts were largely seen as attention-seeking, without attempting to explore other possible reasons for her actions. This is significant because research shows that over half of mental health problems in adult life start by the age of 14 and 75% by the age of 18 (Department of Health 2015). The evidence is also clear that early diagnosis is important and will help the individual deal with their condition in later life (Duffy et al. 2017). However,

Chantele's experiences reflect the evidence that there is a specific issue of underdiagnosis of mental health conditions in children and young people (Alderwick et al. 2015). The development of CAMHS in England and Wales in 1995 was meant to overcome some of these issues by providing a specific mental health service for children and young people. A lack of robust, good quality evaluation studies of CAMHS means that a definitive judgement on its effectiveness is not possible, but there is tentative evidence to suggest that it has had a positive effect on some mental health outcomes (Rocks et al. 2018). In particular it is evident that CAMHS is a positive move away from previous mental health guidance that focused mainly on naughty children (Kerfoot and Williams 2005), as experienced by Chantele. However, the CAMHS model has been criticised for creating barriers that mean that children are falling in gaps and so not receiving the care that they require (Department of Health 2015). There has also been funding pressures which has seen cuts in CAMHS and has led to long waiting lists and variations in service between regions (Office of the Children's Commissioner 2018). In addition, there is an observed large treatment gap in the provision of CAMHS, in terms of access to treatment and the geographical variability of treatment (Crenna-Jennings and Hutchinson 2020), which risk repeating the errors in diagnosis that Chantele experienced and which undoubtedly contributed to her negative mental health experiences in later life.

In December 2017, the then government published a consultation on children and young people's mental health and published a response to this consultation in 2018 (Department of Health and Social Care and Department of Education 2018). This proposed specific measures to improve metal health support in schools and colleges, most notably having a Designated Senior Lead for mental health in all schools and colleges, and a maximum four -week wait for access to specialist NHS children and young people's mental health services. These are both positives measures which, from Chantele's account, are much needed and could make a significant positive impact. However, there also needs to be attention to two key issues evident in Chantele's transition which remain unresolved in recent government publications. These are that different regions can stipulate different ages when responsibility for care passes from CAMHS to adult mental health services and the appropriateness of adult services to deal with the issues faced by young people (Department of Health 2015).

Chantele related the importance of getting a diagnosis for her mental health disorder, and this is quite important as it provides a legal entitlement to treatment through the *Mental Health Act 1983[1987]*. However, as her experiences showed, getting a diagnosis did not guarantee that the treatment provided would be appropriate to her condition. One of the reasons for this related by Chantele was the sole focus on her mental health condition to the exclusion of other comorbidity factors impacting on her well-being, such as her Crohn's disease. This reflects a wider inability to see her mental health condition as part of a wider 'whole', and requiring a 'whole system approach', meaning a system that aims to meet all the needs of a person with a mental health disorder. To relate this back to Chantele, this could mean recognising that changes in her bipolar medication will impact upon her

Crohn's disease or that bipolar episodes or the instances of substance misuse that she detailed can have an impact on her ability to work.

> **Key Learning: Comorbidity** In its simplest terms, comorbidity refers to when one medical condition is negatively having an effect on another condition. In more specific terms, it refers to how one main condition is being directly made worse by one or more additional conditions. To take type 2 diabetes as an example, this is a main condition on its own; however type 2 diabetes can also be made worse by other comorbidity conditions such as high blood pressure, which can also occur independently of type 2 diabetes. In relation to mental health, comorbidity between a mental health and medical condition refers to when a medical condition negatively affects a person's mental health conditions.

The link between unemployment and mental health is especially prevalent, with the key point that they can feed off each other to limit the well-being of individuals (Kousoulis et al. 2013). The growing awareness of the significance of Adverse Childhood Experiences (ACEs) also makes this a highly relevant point. Moreover, this highlights that what is required is a determination to understand and treat in a more comprehensive manner the causes of mental health, whether they be medical or social. This reinforces the importance of better early intervention and prevention to positive mental outcomes; however, the current context of austerity raises significant concerns as to whether this approach is feasible in either the short or long term.

Reflective Questions

1. How does diagnosis impact upon an individual?
2. How have limited perceptions of Chantele impacted upon the support she has received, and what social policies might be put into place to ensure greater consistency of support?
3. At what stages within her experiences could intervention have been helpful?
4. How could different social policies have prevented the piecemeal approach to healthcare provision that shaped Chantele's experiences?
5. How did Chantele identify her conditions and find help, and what might this tell us about the need for different policies and practices in the diagnosis of bipolar conditions?

References

H. Alderwick, C. Ham, D. Buck, *Population Health Systems. Going Beyond Integrated Care* (King's Fund, London, 2015). https://www.kingsfund.org.uk/sites/default/files/field/field_publication_file/population-health-systems-kingsfund-feb15.pdf

M. Bauer, O.A. Andreassen, J.R. Geddes, et al., Areas of uncertainties and unmet needs in bipolar disorders: clinical and research perspectives. Lancet Psychiat. **5**(11), 930–939 (2018). https://doi.org/10.1016/S2215-0366(18)30253-0

E. Biringer, B. Sundfør, L. Davidson, et al., Life on a waiting list: how do people experience and cope with delayed access to a community mental health center? Scand. Psychol. **2**, e6 (2015). https://doi.org/10.15714/scandpsychol.2.e6

W. Crenna-Jennings, J. Hutchinson, *Access to Child and Adolescent Mental Health Services in 2019* (Education Policy Institute, London, 2020). https://epi.org.uk/publications-and-research/access-to-child-and-adolescent-mental-health-services-in-2019/

Children's Commissioner for England, *Children's Mental Health Briefing*. https://www.childrenscommissioner.gov.uk/wp-content/uploads/2019/02/childrens-mental-health-briefing-nov-2018.pdf. Accessed 05 December. 2019.

Department of Health, Future in mind (2015). https://assets.publishing.service.gov.uk/government/uploads/system/uploads/attachment_data/file/414024/Childrens_Mental_Health.pdf

Department of Health and Social Care and Department of Education, *Government Response to the Consultation on Transforming Children and Young People's Mental Health Provision: a Green Paper and Next Steps*, (Cm 9626, 2018).

A. Duffy, S. Goodday, I.C. Passos, et al., Changing the bipolar illness trajectory. Lancet Psychiat. **4**(1), 11–13 (2017). https://doi.org/10.1016/S2215-0366(16)30352-2

M. Kerfoot, R. Williams, Setting the scene: perspectives on the history of and policy for child and adolescent mental health services in the UK, in *Child and Adolescent Mental Health Services: Strategy, Planning, Delivery and Evaluation*, ed. by R. Williams, M. Kerfoot, (Oxford University Press, Oxford, 2005), pp. 3–39

A. Kousoulis, K. Angelopoulou, C. Lionis, Exploring health care reform in a changing Europe: lessons from Greece. Eur. J. Gen. Pract. **19**(3), 194–199 (2013). https://doi.org/10.3109/13814788.2013.779663

S. Marwaha, N. Sal, P. Bebbington, Bipolar disorder, in *Mental Health and Wellbeing in England: Adult Psychiatric Morbidity Survey 2014*, ed. by S. McManus, P. Bebbington, R. Jenkins, et al., (NHS Digital, Leeds, 2016), pp. 220–237

S. McManus, P. Bebbington, R. Jenkins, and T. Brugha, *Mental health and wellbeing in England*. (Health and Social Care Information Centre, 2016).

L. Morriss, Nut clusters and crisps: atrocity stories and co-narration in interviews with approved mental health professionals. Sociol. Health Illn. **37**(7), 1072–1085 (2015). https://doi.org/10.1111/1467-9566.12285

National Health Service (NHS), The NHS long term plan (2019). https://www.longtermplan.nhs.uk/publication/nhs-long-term-plan/

National Institute for Clinical Excellence (NICE), Bi-polar disorder: assessment and management (2020). https://www.nice.org.uk/guidance/CG185

Office for Students, Mental health: are all students being properly supported? (2019). https://www.officeforstudents.org.uk/publications/mental-health-are-all-students-being-properly-supported/

J. Pitchforth, K. Fahy, T. Ford, et al., Mental health and well-being trends among children and young people in the UK, 1995–2014: analysis of repeated cross-sectional national health surveys. Psychol. Med. **49**(8), 1275–1285 (2019). https://doi.org/10.1017/S0033291718001757

Quality Care Commission, The state of care in mental health services 2014–2017 (2017). https://www.cqc.org.uk/publications/major-report/state-care-mental-health-services-2014-2017

S. Rocks, M. Stepney, M. Glogowska, et al., Understanding and evaluating new models of child and adolescent mental health services in south-east England: a study protocol for an observational mixed-methods study. BMJ Open **8**(12) (2018). https://doi.org/10.1136/bmjopen-2018-024230

Lived Experiences of Domestic Abuse, Domestic Violence and Intimate Partner Violence

Janine*, Eva*, David John Sambrook Gowar,
and Peter Unwin

This chapter is about social policies surrounding <u>domestic abuse (DA)</u> <u>and</u> <u>domestic violence (DV)</u> and <u>intimate partner violence (IPV)</u> in the UK and is informed by survivor experiences from both women and men, as domestic abuse and IPV towards men is a little-known phenomenon.

▷ **Key Learning: Domestic Abuse and Domestic Violence** Domestic abuse and domestic violence are terms which are often used interchangeably. At the time of writing, there is no statutory definition of domestic violence and abuse. The Government aims to include one in a Domestic Violence and Abuse Bill, when that is legislated for. However, there is a non-statutory definition that is used across the Government. This defines domestic violence and abuse as:

> Any incident or pattern of incidents of controlling, coercive or threatening behaviour, violence or abuse between those aged 16 or over who are or have been intimate partners or family members regardless of gender or sexuality. This can encompass but is not limited to the following types of abuse:

- Psychological
- Physical
- Sexual

Janine* (✉) • Eva* • D. J. S. Gowar
Worcester, UK

P. Unwin
School of Allied Health and Community, University of Worcester, Worcester, UK
e-mail: p.unwin@worc.ac.uk

© The Author(s), under exclusive license to Springer Nature Switzerland AG 2021
C. Sealey et al. (eds.), *Social Policy, Service Users and Carers*,
https://doi.org/10.1007/978-3-030-69876-8_11

- Financial
- Emotional

Controlling Behaviour

Controlling behaviour is a range of acts designed to make a person subordinate and/or dependent by isolating them from sources of support; exploiting their resources and capacities for personal gain; depriving them of the means needed for independence, resistance and escape; and regulating their everyday behaviour.

Coercive Behaviour

Coercive behaviour is an act or a pattern of acts of assault, threats, humiliation and intimidation or other abuse that is used to harm, punish or frighten their victim.

The new statutory definition proposed for the Domestic Violence and Abuse Bill is very similar to the definition above, except that sexuality is replaced with sexual orientation and the term financial is replaced with economic.

While the terms 'domestic abuse' and 'domestic violence' are often used interchangeably, domestic abuse is a broader concept which can include forms of abuse other than physical violence and is defined as 'an incident or pattern of incidents of controlling, coercive, threatening, degrading and violent behaviour, including sexual violence' (Women's Aid 2020). IPV or DV are the terms likely to be used where there is physical or sexual threats or actions, but not where the issues concerned were, for example, those of psychological/emotional abuse/financial abuse, harassment or online abuse.

▷ **Key Learning: Intimate Partner Violence (IPV)** Intimate partner violence refers to a type of domestic abuse which is carried out specifically when people are in an intimate relationship. The relationship can be in the form of dating, cohabiting or marriage, and can occur either inside or outside the home. The World Health Organization (WHO) defines intimate partner violence as 'any behaviour within an intimate relationship that causes physical, psychological or sexual harm to those in the relationship', and this shows that IPV encompasses a range of behaviours, including physical violence. It differs from domestic abuse in that domestic abuse can refer to abuse carried out by anyone in the household, such as when a parent hits a child, which is not classed as IPV.

The topic of DV gained public and professional prominence in the 1970s, prior to which such issues were seen primarily as private concerns only. Despite this new profile, and a raft of legislation and policy, domestic violence remains a core societal problem. The Office for National Statistics (ONS 2019) estimated that some 7.9% of women and 4.2% of men suffer domestic abuse in the UK.

In this chapter, Eva and Janine speak about their mixed experiences in accessing support from DV services, while David gives voice to a male perspective, particularly reflecting on his experience of professionals' attitudes. The chapter will cover those experiences, relating them to societal attitudes and UK government policy, and make recommendations for best future practice and policy.

The main aims of the chapter are:

1. To give voice to the lived experiences of survivors of domestic violence and domestic abuse.
2. To compare and contrast the psychological and practical complexities and consequences of involvement across a range of domestic abuse situations.
3. To detail and analyse initiatives put in place to try to combat domestic abuse and make recommendations for improving outcomes and practice.

Janine's Story: Who Am I?

I am Janine, aged 60 years, and working at the University of Worcester as a member of the IMPACT service user and carer group. I am a survivor of domestic violence.

I moved to the country town of Harlston* 6 years ago to try to escape F (the perpetrator of my abuse). Since then, I have been discharged from secondary mental health services, so am dependant on my overstretched GP but I need more help. The DV has exacerbated my mental health problems, and post-traumatic stress disorder (PTSD) makes me uncharacteristically anxious, paranoid, secretive, fearful and introverted.

> **Key Learning: Post-traumatic Stress Disorder (PTSD)** Post-traumatic stress disorder (PTSD) is a mental health disorder that can develop when someone experiences a traumatic, scary or dangerous event. While all people experience short-term stress at the time of a traumatic event as a natural physical reaction to protect from harm, most people will not experience further trauma after the event. However, some people continue feel stressed or frightened after the event even when they are not in danger, and when this continues for a significant period of time and interferes with relationships or work, this is symptomatic of PTSD. A specific diagnosis of PTSD requires evidence that the person relives the event from time to time, changes their routine as a consequence of the event and reacts to specific triggers linked to the event, and that cognition and mood is affected by the event. Sometimes PTSD can appear months or years after the event that caused it. PTSD is often accompanied by depression, substance abuse or one or more of the other anxiety disorders.

Unfortunately, I cannot envisage my circumstances improving until F dies or confesses to his crime and is imprisoned. If the latter happened, I would feel vindicated, but worried about the repercussions.

The Paucity of Support Services

I now receive very little support from health and social care services, and my GP surgery is massively oversubscribed. I recently had to phone 114 times in quick succession to get an appointment with a nurse, who decides if you are ill enough to see a doctor. Last year, following a suicide attempt, I was directed to Mindhealth*, a primary care service where I saw a psychologist for 12 × 1-hour sessions. It was good to have this time, which was helpful but frustrating and upsetting as there wasn't much he could do to relieve my anguish. Last year I attempted suicide again and was put on the waiting list for a six-day 'Managing Emotions' course, but the waiting list is almost 1 year long, which means it is of very little use to me. I have been taking antidepressants for about 22 years and am keen to benefit from other forms of intervention. Since my DV experiences, I have also been prescribed tramadol to help me cope when I become too anxious, plus some medication to improve the gynaecological problems caused by a violent assault.

Before the DV necessitated my move to Harlston, I visited the same psychiatrist at a local hospital for about 15 years. I received a good service there and attended cognitive behavioural therapy (CBT), both individually and in a group. There was a community psychiatric nurse available most mornings. Unfortunately, my need for more mental health support coincided with the services being reduced, due to budget cuts. The mental health unit in Harlston has recently told me that they can only help seriously ill patients, so I was discharged back to primary care.

▶ **Key Learning: Cognitive Behavioural Therapy (CBT)** Cognitive behavioural therapy (CBT) is a short-term psychotherapy treatment used to help treat a wide range of mental health issues, from sleeping difficulties or relationship problems, to drug and alcohol abuse or anxiety and depression. The key aim of CBT is to change the way that a person thinks about the difficulties that they are having, as a way to change their behaviours. The focus is on moving away from negative thought images, beliefs and attitudes that a person may have in relation to the issue towards more positive thinking as a way to change the way that the person behaves. This is what the notion of cognitive thinking relates to, as it refers to the way that a person thinks about something. In short, if you change the cognition, you change the behaviour, or put in another way, if you change the negative thinking, you enable more positive action. Two key aspects that distinguish CBT from other psychological therapies is that it is relatively a short therapy of about 5–10 months in duration, and CBT can be undertaken largely by the individual at their own pace, under guidance from a therapist.

I then turned to the voluntary sector for help but again found that waiting lists were months long—the counsellor I worked with in a voluntary rape and sexual harm support service was excellent, but this limited input was all I could benefit from as other services at this organisation were rationed.

I was made aware of private providers of therapy, but I could not afford these as I have not been able to return to my profession since the DV, and I am not eligible for incapacity benefits since I was discharged from secondary care. I have lost count of the financial costs of my DV experiences and live on the poverty line, made worse by the fact that I have had to move house several times due to continued harassment from F, despite him having been bailed to stay at least a mile from my home. I was homeless for 3 months, sofa surfing. My car was broken into and then vandalised. Indeed, my mental health is so fragile; I am virtually unemployable.

On a prosaic note, my prescriptions are now free as I just turned 60. I do try to practise yoga, as it makes me feel calmer, and I go to dance classes and the gym, which help my mood. These I have to pay for. The police confiscated several phones and a laptop, as F kept breaking his bail and contacting me. I only ever got one phone back and that was broken. If my case had successfully gone to court, I would have been eligible to apply for expenses, but the Crown Prosecution Service deemed that my mental health was not robust enough to withstand cross-examination, so F escaped justice.

Looking to the future, I would like to get treatment from a mental health specialist regularly. My GP is great, but he can't be an expert in every field and is so busy I would only go to see him if I was desperate. I believe that a psychiatrist should only prescribe mental health medication and believe it is unacceptable that I have not had a medication review for several years. I would also like a service especially for DV survivors, even an informal group would help, as my experience is extremely isolating. My counsellor at the rape and sexual harm organisation suggested I should set up one up myself! Maybe in a previous incarnation I could have done that, but my self-confidence is now far too low. I would also like the NHS to be more creative about the techniques they offer, for example exercise or art therapy.

Eva's Story: Who Am I?

I am Eva, in my early 40s, a female survivor of domestic violence.

I grew up with domestic violence, and my first relationship was domestically violent and started when I went away to university. I picked the biggest drug baron I could find and started using drugs and alcohol as a way of numbing everything that had gone on at home. He said to me that if I ever finished with him, he would tell everybody what I was really like, which immediately tapped into my own low self-esteem and just gave him carte blanche to do whatever he wanted to do, basically. He took all my money, and he raped me numerous times. He told everybody what I was 'really' like, which made me paranoid, and I was paranoid anyway because of the drugs, and I got into trouble with the university because I wasn't attending my lectures, and I just left the university even though I was in my final year, and I vowed never to go back. I went home, which was not good because my family weren't pleased with me. Then I got a place at another university, where a lecturer said to me 'if you don't curb your addictions, you're going to end up prostituting yourself to fund them', which struck a real chord with me and I started to sort myself out.

Reflections on Help Provided

There were several offers of help at university such as telephone services and free counselling, but a mixture of fear and shame meant I did not take these up. I eventually got my degree at yet another university, having been kicked out of my second one due to my terrible reputation of being a bit wild with the drink, and in my final year (again!), I got put into a mental health institution for a month. I was told to go to my lectures and to come back and write my essays while I was still resident in the mental health institution. I met a consultant psychiatrist there who was to work with me for the next 20 years, which was not helpful to me, despite this duration. All I wanted to do was talk as I was desperate to unburden myself of all what had happened to me, but she did not have the time, the resources or the inclination. The net result was that I didn't even talk about my domestic violence experiences and how they were at the root of many of my mental health issues.

The psychiatrist and her team spoke with me about psychosis and depression and post-traumatic stress disorder (PTSD) but never enabled me to talk about the real issue—domestic violence. I come from a family where my dad was domestically violent, but he 'won' me in a custody battle with my mum, so my trust of authority figures was virtually nil. I went on to take a series of domestically violent partners, but I've been single for 8 years now, and my mental health has never been so good. I remember attending a domestic violence course once where they said don't ever tell a new partner that you've been domestically abused for fear they would exploit that, so I have always bottled everything up. There's something about my vulnerability or inability to communicate that triggers violent responses in men, so I don't want to replay it.

I sometimes reflect on why I did not take up more help and remember an alcohol counsellor once saying that sometimes people need help to be helped, and I could understand this, but my paranoia about other people knowing meant I could not use local services, and I lacked the funds to travel to services elsewhere. Fear was always with me, and I learnt very early on, or I felt very early on, that you couldn't be honest with your psychiatrist; you couldn't be completely honest because they wouldn't be able to handle what you were saying to them. I was scared that if they knew the extent of my worries and the experiences, I had suffered that they would lock me up and throw away the key, as I was obviously such a bad person.

The advice I would give to professionals running services for domestic violence would be to underline and really reassure people what they say will be contained and safe. When you're in a domestically violent relationship, you just need reassurance because the whole world doesn't feel right—you've been gaslighted, you've been manipulated, you've been raped, and you've lost all sense of identity and purpose. I think face-to-face services are best, though I did occasionally use telephone services—the Samaritans I rang twice, but they just signposted me to Mindhealth* although I was so poor, I couldn't get on the train to actually physically get there. Now that I'm older, I can see a lot of what was going on, but even the best services would have struggled to help me as I was such a closed book. I held on to that sentence that the counsellor had said, about needing help to be helped—I knew I needed help, and I was, in some ways, crying out for help, but I didn't know how to connect and was in complete denial of the pain I was suffering.

▶   **Key Learning: Gaslighting** Gaslighting is a term that has come to prominence recently to describe a specific type of psychological manipulation. In personal relationships, it refers to efforts to destabilise the victim and delegitimize the victim's beliefs by manipulating their perception of reality. This is done by one partner stealthily using denial, misdirection, contradiction and misinformation to make the other partner question their own recollection, understanding and/or opinion of an event or events. For example, the person doing the gaslighting may deny that an incident has happened, or that it happened the way it did, with the intention of causing the other person to become upset or frustrated by their seeming inability to accurately recall the event. Over a long period of time, this can cause a person to become wholly confused and question their intellect and mental health, further causing anxiety, depression and other mental health disorders.

I don't think the bad memories ever leave you, and in my experience, I think my mind flooded with it all, and that's what tipped me over into psychosis and depression.

How to Improve the Current System

Overall, my experiences as both an inpatient and outpatient of mental health services were that they further victimised and disempowered me. They assumed control which didn't 'hold' me psychologically, but which mirrored the abuse I had suffered in the domestically and emotionally violent relationships that I had been in. They thwarted my freedoms, medicated me till I didn't know my own name and patronisingly assumed the position of 'We know best'. At best, this encouraged rebellion in me, at worst, muteness.

To have been in a place where I could trust my psychiatrist and the team and move forward in the process of healing and not be placed in the 'sick role' would not have taken much time and effort on their part. I feel now, as I did then, that more understanding of the pain I was in and a more humanising holistic approach would have been better than what was on offer, hence the muteness. I was not willing to trust or let go and so become even more vulnerable. Mental health services are not mothering. They do not (I believe for legal reasons) administer reassurance or hugs which are quite often what are needed during and after periods of distress. They never even once offered me the dignity of having an open or frank discussion.

The isolated victim, as in my case, becomes further isolated and dependent, which again compounds and mirrors the persecution felt in the abusive relationship. It is difficult to come to terms with abuse, let alone being at the mercy of a consultant psychiatrist and their team. Again, this fuelled my paranoia, psychosis and depression. The helplessness and depression I felt when a letter arrived for an appointment with the psychiatrist is an indication that something about the mental health system doesn't work. It's not a 'one-size-fits-all' situation.

A solution to all the enduring stress and distress I had suffered was when I approached a solicitor I knew in Alcoholics Anonymous who signposted me to a women's service that was offering a 12-week course for victims of domestic abuse. This was my salvation. It was in this network of women where I found connections, through sharing experiences, coffee mornings and lunches, which freed me from my isolation. I learnt that what I was feeling was OK and merely human responses to the trauma I had suffered. I was *not* and *am not* an 'interesting case' as one psychiatrist put it!

David's Story: Who Am I?

I am David, a man in his early 60s, and a male survivor of domestic violence. I am a white middle-class male who worked in Social Services and further education for most of my working life. I endured escalating levels of violence and abuse from my wife for 6 years which began almost imperceptibly with occasional fits of unwarranted jealousy and paranoia. As these became more frequent, they led to me not being allowed out on my own for fear of the consequences and eventually exploded into episodes of violence and sexual torture. Yet I did not perceive the physical and sexual violence to which my wife subjected me—or the severe emotional, psychological and financial abuse—as 'domestic abuse', which, to me, was what men did to women, because that is how Western society has traditionally defined it.

Attitudes Towards Male Victims of Domestic Violence

Men who suffered domestic violence from women have traditionally been viewed as weak and subjected to ridicule and public shaming. My wife was arrested twice for assaulting me: on the first occasion, I had had to lock myself in the garage as she had been chasing me with a knife. On the second, the police took photographs of my bruises and scratches and of the damage she had wreaked on furniture and ornaments. She was not charged on either occasion: on the second, after releasing her without charge, the police even returned her to my house (despite the fact that she was not living there as we had separated 3 months previously) at 4.30 am supposedly for her to collect our 17-month-old daughter. It took nearly an hour to convince them that this was not a good idea. I asked if a male perpetrator would have been returned in this way, but this elicited no response.

When I eventually made the decision, after 6 months of specialist counselling and having suffered for 18 months with terrifying visual and physical flashbacks, to report the sexual and physical abuse to the police, the first thing the (female) officer said to me was 'you said she used to handcuff you and squeeze your testicles: you must have enjoyed it or you would have reported it sooner'. Again, I asked if a female complainant would have been challenged/disbelieved like this, and again I got no answer.

Legal Struggles and Allegations

The battle through the courts which ensued after my wife was arrested for assaulting me was Kafkaesque in nature. Over a period of 6 months I was subjected to a catalogue of false and malicious allegations: there was a new one about every 2 weeks. The most serious of these—that I had sexually abused my older children and that I was having an inappropriate relationship with an unspecified child at the school at which I was then working—led to a full Child Protection Investigation by one Council and a full Position of Trust investigation by another. I was suspended from work for 3 months pending the outcomes. Both investigations completely exonerated me, and I was able to return to work with my Disclosure and Barring Service check still clear.

After I finally managed to extricate myself from my abusive relationship, I felt a huge sense of relief. My son, who was 11 at the time, felt it too—no longer would we fear my wife's return from work, wondering what was in store. The violence and abuse to which I was subjected have left me with physical and mental scars, but it is the continuing aftermath that has affected me even more than that. The emotional and psychological barriers to forming new relationships, and psychosexual problems, refuse to go away. I naively believed that the Family Court and the social workers would help my children and me, but the unfortunate reality is that, several years on, I am still fighting for justice and for the truth to be acknowledged. The false allegations have had a deep and lasting effect on me mentally and emotionally, with sleep problems and anxiety, and practically in terms of having to get official bodies to accept that the allegations were indeed false. It took more than 2 years for the Council concerned to fulfil my data protection request, which eventually revealed that they had accepted all the allegations as having been true without question, and a further 12 months for them to agree to append corrections to their files. My son, who is now 17, has also been affected; he has told me of many instances of emotional and psychological abuse, including threats to 'get him adopted' when he was only eight, and I feel guilty every day for not having picked up how he was being abused. My relationship with my daughter, who is now ten years old, remained close until shortly before her ninth birthday when her mother stopped her having contact with me, despite this action being in breach of a court order. I have now not seen my daughter for 18 months, despite her having a psychological assessment which concluded she was showing strong indications of alienation. I am continuing to fight for justice for her, and her right to have a meaningful relationship with both her parents, but the effects of the Covid-19 pandemic on the Family Court have meant that these efforts have been delayed.

How I Survived

I have only survived the last 6 years thanks to the support of my children and my sister and because I was lucky enough to find the Stonham Group (now closed due to austerity cuts) which provided support for male victims of domestic abuse, which made me realise I was not alone, and gave me some strategies for coping and understanding. I am dealing, as well as I can, with the effects of post-traumatic stress disorder (PTSD) and have been waiting to see a psychologist for 18 months. My financial circumstances effectively mean that I will become homeless when I reach the age of 75—if not before—because that is when my mortgage expires, and I will not be able to pay it off, and there is no equity there. Becoming a member of IMPACT, the service users and carers organisation at the University of Worcester has been hugely helpful to me in regaining some sense of self-worth. I have read widely on the subjects of narcissistic personality disorder and parental alienation in an attempt to understand the mechanics of the abusive relationship. After nearly 4 years of being quite sure I would never want to be in a relationship again, I met someone—also an abuse survivor—and we are helping each other to regain some trust. I have found the exposure therapy with my counsellor and sharing my lived experience with social work students very therapeutic and have also contributed creatively to the Survivors UK website.

▶   **Key Learning: Exposure Therapy** Exposure therapy is a type of behaviour
     therapy that is used to treat a range of mental health disorders such as
     generalised anxiety disorder, social anxiety disorder, obsessive-
     compulsive disorder and PTSD. As the name suggests, the method of
     exposure therapy is to directly expose the individual suffering from the
     disorder to what is causing the disorder. This is done to an increasingly
     stronger degree in a controlled environment. So, for example, someone
     suffering from arachnoid phobia (fear of spiders) would be exposed to
     spiders, varying in size and number as the treatment progresses. The
     rationale for doing this is that exposure helps to overcome anxiety or
     distress by extinguishing the fear that an individual has. There is
     evidence that exposure therapy is particularly effective for treating
     PTSD (DiMauro 2014).

Nobody should have to go through what I have been through. The dual stereotypes of the violent man and passive woman undoubtedly obscure the existence of male victims of domestic violence, and because men are also unlikely to view their own victimisation as either domestic violence or a criminal assault, they are unlikely to seek help and will experience difficulty finding any even if they do, as services for men are still few and far between. However, the undeniable year-on-year increase in male victims is hopefully bringing about a growing recognition within society—if not from government—that intimate partner violence is not simply a gender issue, but an issue of power and control within intimate relationships.

Commentary

The above narratives portray serious shortcomings in both attitude and reach of services available under current social policy. It is apparent that the problems in negotiating attitudes and systems which Eva and Janine highlight as experienced by women and which led to them being misjudged and victimised by the system are also experienced by men. Feminism took up the cause of domestic abuse of women in the 1970s, with the world's first women's refuge being opened by Erin Pizzey in 1971 (Pizzey 2011). Pizzey described herself as a family systems theorist, believing in keeping families together where possible and urging absent fathers to see children. Research spanning over 40 years has consistently found that men and women self-report perpetrating domestic violence at similar rates, but women are twice as likely as men to be injured or killed during a domestic assault. The Crime Survey for England and Wales (CSEW 2019) estimates of domestic abuse are based on a relatively broad definition covering male and female victims of partner or family non-physical abuse, threats, force, sexual assault or stalking. The latest figures (Office for National Statistics (ONS) (2019)) regarding long-term trends show little change in the prevalence of domestic abuse over recent years. The Crime Survey for England and Wales for the year ending March 2019 estimated that 5.7% of adults (2.4 million) were victims of domestic abuse. This rising trend is thought to reflect factors related to reporting and recording and does not provide a reliable indication of current trends. According to the ONS (2019), women are statistically twice as likely to be affected by domestic violence (1.6 million women and 786,000 men experienced domestic abuse in the year ending March 2019). David's above narrative shows that the effects on men are also devastating. The latest figures from the Crime Survey for England and Wales show little change in the prevalence of domestic abuse in recent years.

Significantly, out of the 1,316,800 domestic abuse-related incidents and crimes reported in the year ending March 2019, 746,219 were recorded as domestic abuse-related crimes. This represents an increase of 24% from the previous year and suggests that the police are charging more adults with having committed criminal offences, a great contrast with earlier decades. Flatley et al. (2010) had found that young women up to the age of 24 years were the group most likely to experience domestic violence, and the ONS (2019) still indicated that women aged 20–24 years were significantly more likely to be victims of domestic abuse than women in any other age group.

Feminist writers understood domestic violence as the natural extension of men's patriarchal attitudes towards women, leading men to feel they had the right to control their partners, using violence if necessary (Lawson 2012). Feminists campaigned successfully to bring the issue into the public arena, thereby securing resources to establish services to help victims. This activism and advocacy led to governmental and public acceptance that 'domestic violence' was synonymous with violence against women; David's testimony above emphasises that men are also significantly affected.

Feminist activity, plus changing public opinion, led to changes in legislation including the *Domestic Violence and Matrimonial Proceedings Act 1976*, which provided the police with powers of arrest for the breach of injunction in cases of domestic violence and allowed women to obtain the right to stay at the matrimonial home. A further significant piece of legislation was the *Housing (Homeless Persons) Act 1977*, which refers to persons who are homeless or threatened with homelessness which helped domestic violence victims with re-housing. This was followed by the *Domestic Proceedings & Magistrates' Courts Act 1978*, which amended the use of injunctions to prevent further violence in the home. *The Domestic Violence, Crime and Victims Act 2004* was designed to bring the above legislation together under one *Act*, giving legal protection to victims of domestic violence. Since that time voluntary sector campaigns such as Zero Tolerance (https://www.zerotolerance.org.uk/about/) and government initiatives have tackled the structural causes of domestic violence. The *Domestic Abuse Act 2021* provides a statutory definition of abusive behaviour as:

Behaviour is "abusive" if it consists of any of the following—

- physical or sexual abuse;
- violent or threatening behaviour;
- controlling or coercive behaviour;
- economic abuse;
- psychological, emotional or other abuse

and it does not matter whether the behaviour consists of a single incident or a course of conduct.

For the definition of abusive behaviour to apply, both parties must be aged 16 or over and 'personally connected'. 'Personally connected' is defined in the *Act* as parties who:

- are married to each other
- are civil partners of each other
- have agreed to marry one another (whether or not the agreement has been terminated)
- have entered into a civil partnership agreement (whether or not the agreement has been terminated)
- are or have been in an intimate personal relationship with each other
- have, or there has been a time when they each have had, a parental relationship in relation to the same child
- are relatives

This above definition is likely to be expanded when the proposals in the proposed *Domestic Abuse Bill* become law.

Many steps have been taken to try to safeguard women and men at risk of domestic violence; much of such violence is doubtless still going unreported. Eva's testimony above gives a range of reasons why she did not report certain issues relating to her situation and illustrates also the complexities, including mental health considerations, which prevent disclosures and access to services. David's testimony highlighted ongoing prejudice in 'the system' towards men as victims of DV, and he is currently pro-active in talking about his experiences to professionals and students, hoping that his openness will play a part in bringing about some cultural change.

A two-year Europe-wide initiative aiming to combat domestic violence launched in 2011 was aptly entitled 'The Iceberg Project', reflecting that much of the violence is hidden below the surface. This project found that in cases of stalking and physical violence, the perpetrator was likely to be male, whereas when females were the perpetrator, then acts were more likely to be of a less physical nature. The report highlighted the ongoing effects on health (particularly mental health), learning, confidence and relationship development and suggested a range of initiatives to improve policy and services (Lees et al. 2013). These suggestions included survivors of domestic violence being encouraged to tell their stories, of challenges to be made whenever prejudicial comments are expressed by others and by teaching students on professional qualifying courses about the realities of domestic violence and the part they have to play in tacking this scourge on society from day one of their training.

Based on the 2012 definition, the government published its 2016–2020 strategy to end violence against women and girls (VAWG) (HM Government 2016). This included £80 million of dedicated funding to provide core support for refuges and other accommodation-based services, rape support centres and national helplines. A further £20 million was announced in the 2017 Spring Budget. Included within this £100 million total is a £15 million new Violence Against Women and Girls Service Transformation Fund to support local domestic abuse service provision.

The strategy's vision was that by 2020:

- There is a significant reduction in the number of VAWG victims, achieved by challenging the deep-rooted social norms, attitudes and behaviours that discriminate against and limit women and girls and by educating, informing and challenging young people about healthy relationships, abuse and consent.
- All services make early intervention and prevention a priority, identifying women and girls in need before a crisis occurs and intervening to make sure they get the help they need for themselves and for their children.
- Women and girls will be able to access the support they need, when they need it, helped by the information they need to make an informed choice.
- Specialist support, including accommodation-based support, will be available for the most vulnerable victims, and those with complex needs will be able to access the services they need.
- Services in local areas will work across boundaries in strong partnerships to assess and meet local need and ensure that services can spot the signs of abuse in all family members and intervene early.
- Women will be able to disclose experiences of violence and abuse across all public services, including the NHS. Trained staff in these safe spaces will help people access specialist support whether as victims or as perpetrators.

Services developed alongside such positive government initiatives with some 400 specialist domestic violence organisations now provide refuge accommodation for women in the UK with approximately 4000 spaces for over 7000 women and children. Males are less well provided for with only some 70 spaces being available, whereas specialised services for communities such as LGBTI people and Gypsy Roma Travellers are non-existent. Ten years of austerity measures in the UK, however, have led to services for domestic violence being cut, which together with legal aid cuts have greatly limited the potential of the above strategy. Janine's testimony demonstrated the lack of such facilities and suggests that the above government strategy has a very long way to go before it translates into everyday practice. Indeed, the recent experiences shared in this chapter by Janine, Eva and David demonstrate the continued paucity of resources, their inaccessibility and the fact that abusers are still able to find ways around the system.

One evident similarity between the three accounts is the prevalence of PTSD, as they all mentioned the occurrence of this in their accounts. The significance of this occurrence is supported by research which shows that PTSD is the most common type of anxiety associated with domestic violence (Duxbury 2006). This suggests that there is a specific need for trauma-informed psychological services for domestic abuse survivors, and specifically that there needs to be an awareness that domestic abuse survivors are suffering from psychological trauma, especially in generalist services such as GP surgeries who can often miss the symptoms of PTSD in the context of domestic violence (Ferrari et al. 2016). Indeed, Trevillion et al. (2013) observed that domestic violence training for clinicians improved the psychiatric outcomes of domestic abuse survivors.

One evident difference between the experiences of Janine and Eva compared to that of David is the response from the police that David experienced, detailed by David as stemming from stereotypes of male DV. In particular, David's account supports the observation by Dutton and White (2013, p. 12) that 'gender stereotypes profoundly affect our perceptions of the seriousness and preferred outcomes'. What this means is that that male victims of DV are often either not taken seriously or not listened to at all, which makes them less likely to seek out relevant professions. Such approaches risk worsening the impact of DV on men. Without a qualitative shift in thinking in this area, some of the benefits that have occurred from taking steps to take DV seriously from a woman's perspective, such as its public health benefits, risk being undermined or subverted when men are the survivors.

Prevalence statistics of all types of domestic violence remain high, and the challenges ahead remain great, especially with awareness of recent worrying trends regarding young people becoming involved in abusive relationships (Barter et al. 2009). The changing nature of sexualities will doubtless also produce future dilemmas and challenges, but the more individuals such as Eva, Janine and David speak out, the greater the chances are that fairer, equitable and more effective services will become available. Policy-makers and service providers need to listen to survivors and include them meaningfully in design initiatives from start to finish. The proposed *Domestic Abuse Bill* will hopefully lead to better services overall which will meet the aspirations of previous government and voluntary sector initiatives and mean that the narratives of Janine, Eva and David are never repeated.

Reflective Questions

1. How should the laws and policies on DV have better helped Janine and Eva?
2. What key social policy recommendations would you make to improve future services?
3. 'Eva' thought that staff members rarely took the time just to be with her and to listen—how might you ensure that your service always had time for individuals?
4. Why do you think David had such a discriminatory experience in a range of settings?
5. If you witnessed a male being treated discriminatorily in your service, what would you do, and what laws and policies would support your actions?
6. What social policy initiatives would encourage men to speak up more widely about their experiences of domestic violence and abuse?

References

C. Barter, et al., *Partner Exploitation and Violence in Teenage Intimate Relationships* (NSPCC, London, 2009). https://www.nspcc.org.uk/globalassets/documents/research-reports/partner. Accessed 12 June 2020

J. DiMauro, Exposure therapy for posttraumatic stress disorder: a meta-analysis. Mil. Psychol. **26**(2), 120–130 (2014). https://doi.org/10.1037/mil0000038

D. Dutton, K. White, Male victims of domestic violence. New Male Stud. **2**(1), 5–17 (2013). https://www.newmalestudies.com/OJS/index.php/nms/article/view/59/59

F. Duxbury, Recognising domestic violence in clinical practice using the diagnoses of posttraumatic stress disorder, depression and low self-esteem. Br. J. Gen. Pract. **56**(525), 294–300 (2006)

G. Ferrari et al., Domestic violence and mental health: a cross-sectional survey of women seeking help from domestic violence support services. Glob. Health Action **9**(1) (2016). https://doi.org/10.3402/gha.v9.29890

J Flatley, et al. (eds.), *Crime in England and Wales 2009/10: Findings from the British Crime Survey and Police Recorded Crime*, Home Office Statistical Bulletin 12/10 (Home Office, London, 2010). http://www.homeoffice.gov.uk/publications/science-research-statistics/research-statistics/crimeresearch/hosb1210/. Accessed 24 June 2020

HM Government, New definition of domestic violence (2012). https://www.gov.uk/government/news/new-definition-of-domestic-violence. Accessed 11 June 2020

HM Government, Ending violence against women and girls strategy: 2016 to 2020 (2016). https://assets.publishing.service.gov.uk/government/uploads/system/uploads/attachment_data/file/522166/VAWG_Strategy_FINAL_PUBLICATION_MASTER_vRB.PDF. Accessed 23 Apr 2020

J. Lawson, Sociological theories of intimate partner violence. J. Hum. Behav. Soc. Environ. **22**(5), 572–590 (2012). https://doi.org/10.1080/10911359.2011.598748

S. Lees et al., Domestic violence: the base of the iceberg. Br. J. Midwifery **21**(7), 493–498 (2013). https://doi.org/10.12968/bjom.2013.21.7.493

Office for National Statistics, CSEW Crime in England and Wales: year ending June 2019 (2019). https://www.ons.gov.uk/peoplepopulationandcommunity/crimeandjustice/bulletins/crimeinenglandandwales/yearendingjune2019. Accessed 02 June 2020

E. Pizzey, *This Way to the Revolution: A Memoir* (Peter Owen Publishers, London, 2011)

K. Trevillion, S. Byford, M. Cary, et al., Linking abuse and recovery through advocacy: an observational study. Epidemiol. Psychiatr. Sci. **23**(1), 99–113 (2013). https://doi.org/10.1017/s2045796013000206

Women's Aid, What is domestic abuse? (2020). https://www.womensaid.org.uk/information-support/what-is-domestic-abuse. Accessed 10 June 2020

Christine Ransome-Wallis, Bob Conner, Barbara Pugh,
and Peter Unwin

This chapter will explore the lived experiences of several informal carers and examine whether social policy supports them in their caring roles. As set out in the Introduction chapter, the definition of 'carers' used in this book relates to anyone who provides unpaid care by looking after an ill, older or disabled family member, friend or partner. This excludes those who provide care as formal payment for this caring, such as through employment. According to this definition, carers are typically friends or family. They may be eligible for a Carer's Allowance or a means-tested Carer's Premium, depending on the number of hours they spend caring. This means that this chapter is not concerned with paid care workers who are essentially employees of domiciliary care agencies or residential/nursing homes. Informal carers are key to all health and social care services, and many policies and initiatives have been introduced in order to improve service delivery and the quality of life for carers.

Since the 1990s governments have increasingly recognised the role that carers play in supporting an increasingly ageing population, and a range of estimates suggest that, without such carers, the costs to the NHS and statutory care services might be in the region of £132 billion per year in the UK (Carers UK 2019), which is the equivalent of the budget of the NHS itself. There are estimated to be approximately 8.8 million adult carers in the UK in 2019, compared to 6.3 million adult carers recorded in the 2011 (Carers UK 2019), these figures reflecting an ageing population, which suggests that carers will be more important in the future. This makes

C. Ransome-Wallis (✉)
Birmingham, UK

B. Conner • B. Pugh
Worcester, UK

P. Unwin
School of Allied Health and Community, University of Worcester, Worcester, UK
e-mail: p.unwin@worc.ac.uk

© The Author(s), under exclusive license to Springer Nature
Switzerland AG 2021
C. Sealey et al. (eds.), *Social Policy, Service Users and Carers*,
https://doi.org/10.1007/978-3-030-69876-8_12

understanding their specific needs and requirements an important priority for policy and practice.

The chapter presents the different lived experiences of three carers, Christine, Bob and Barbara. Christine's narrative is concerned with caring for her elderly mother, Bob addresses the issues involved in caring for a spouse who is living separately in a residential care home, while Barbara reflects on having cared for a son with learning difficulties throughout his childhood, through institutionalisation and onto living independently in the community. A key theme that emerges from these accounts is that while the role of informal carers is recognised and valued in contemporary society, the necessary support systems are not in place, and many informal carers make financial and personal sacrifices to the detriment of their own health and well-being. Based on this point, recommendations will be made regarding best future practice.

The main aims of the chapter are:

1. To outline the lived reality of being a carer.
2. To highlight the benefits and consequences of providing adequate support to carers.
3. To consider and recommend improvements to current and future carer policies.

Christine's Story: Who Am I?

I am Christine, and I cared for my elderly mother for almost 15 years. I was happy to do this, but as my story below tells, caring came at a great personal, career and financial loss. I was trying to work in a very demanding, well-paid job working very long hours and trying to care for mum in the evenings. However, suddenly one day I just keeled over so that was me finished. I was diagnosed with a complete breakdown. It took a year to get my health back, and I was really forced into early retirement and full-time caring. My story below begins shortly after my mum had been discharged from hospital, having had a leg amputated.

The Assessment Process

As part of her discharge, Mum needed an assessment by a social worker. I can laugh about it now, but it was our first encounter with a social worker. Mum was in her wheelchair, and after declining a cuppa, the social worker began on her questionnaire which was all she looked at. She merrily ticked boxes, but then Mum and I looked at each other in disbelief when she asked: 'Is this a temporary condition?' Mum went quiet, so she asked the question again and mum said: 'Well I did think I'd try and grow another leg'. The social worker didn't bat an eyelid but carried on working through the questionnaire. 'And can you use a hoover?' she asked. Mum pointed out it was a wooden floor, so we didn't need a hoover.

We did get some help which meant I could still work, leaving home at 7 am and returning circa 7 pm. I would set Mum up with a sandwich or something for lunch, and she would prepare the evening meal which I cooked when I got home. She could just about manage during the day herself. Obviously, I did the washing and cleaning, but then she got to the point where it became harder for her to cope so well, and there was no increased package from the NHS or the local authority, so I had to cope. There is always an assumption that the carer can pick up the slack.

When assorted social workers came to assess Mum's needs each year—never the same one twice and never having read the notes—they totally ignored me and were only interested in Mum, 'the service user'. I might be her daughter and live-in carer, but there was no interest in engaging with me. I got to the stage of sitting behind her, shaking my head and mouthing 'Nooooo!' to some of her answers because she was painting a totally unreal picture. She did know how to do the things she was claiming to do; she just didn't do them anymore! Consequently, social workers were going away wondering why they had wasted their time on someone who could do so much for herself, and I had to do much more because I had no choice. Looking back, she was in denial about how little she did do although she didn't realise the implications of what she was saying, and I didn't want to upset her by telling her.

The Effect on a Carer's Career

I soon understood what being a carer entailed: 'Yes, I'm here and I'm quite happy to look after her but don't I get any breaks?' When she went to the day centre— which she didn't always if she didn't feel like it—she was picked up at 10 am and back before 3 pm, but it gave me time to mop the kitchen floor which I couldn't if she was there because there would have been black tyre tracks. Her going off gave me time to clean the house, rather than do things I might choose. I didn't have a life of my own, but after the breakdown, I did recognise the signs of crisis looming again and did something about it.

Not working was a shock to my system. We had a nice house which had been adapted for Mum but no income to maintain it, and we still had all the outgoings. Finances nosedived so I used up all my savings and went from having an excellent salary to living on benefits. It was desperation and it certainly wounded my pride to go on benefits and we had to cut down accordingly. My self-esteem plummeted. I'd never claimed anything from anybody. Going to the job centre was totally humiliating. I lost it and sobbed so much I was taken into the manager's office and given a cup of tea. On the jobs front, had I looked at the available work? Yes, I had perused what was on offer, but it was all skilled work—skills I didn't have—like a roof tiler, a Balti chef and a plumber. Asked what my last job had been, I said 'Communications Manager' and was asked 'So you want a manager's job then?' She didn't understand the kind of work I had done all my life would not be advertised in a job centre, but 'manager' was the only word she focused on. Maybe I could have managed the local supermarket or Aston Villa?

Experiences of the Carer's Assessment

A <u>Carer's Assessment</u> was what I was entitled to and I met another social worker. She agreed I could have four hours of help a week which was better than nothing. They could do the washing for me. I said I could load and empty the machine whilst talking to mum. They could do the shopping for me. Well shopping is a break for me. In frustration she barked 'Well what *do* you want?' I didn't know there was a list I could choose from, but she totally missed that I needed a break from my mum. I wanted someone else to sit and talk to her so that I could escape. Living with someone that closely becomes a strain and you get on each other's nerves. Sometimes it did blow up. She would drive me absolutely crackers by pushing and pushing me, even goading me, and in the end, I would flare up and say something I regretted, but it was my fight back. She would sulk and snivel, decide she didn't want her evening meal, go to her bedroom and come down the next morning right as rain, and life would go on. It can get very tense at times when you are so close and there is no break for either of you. It wasn't easy for me and it probably wasn't easy for her. I'm all she'd got and her world was diminishing.

> **Key Learning: Carer's Assessment** The *Care Act 2014* gives carers over the age of 18 the right to have a separate and free assessment of their needs from local authorities. This means that a carer can request to have an assessment to see if they are entitled to things that might make their life easier as a carer. This can include financial, emotional, physical help and also advice, training and support. However, it should be noted that while there is a right to an assessment, there is no automatic rights to any services, as this will be determined from the assessment. While the Carers' Assessment is different from the needs assessment for the person being cared for, they can be carried out at the same time if requested.

If I could have had some me-time, I might have gone for a swim, just doing what I wanted. I'm a carer; get me out of here! Coffee with friends was less likely; friends start dropping off because you can't get out, and they had long stopped coming to me because mum would always hog their attention, being someone different for her to talk to. Carers should be entitled to some life of their own, but it doesn't work out like that, and they just become more isolated.

My real bonus came when a helpful social worker assessed the situation at home and suggested mum went for a week's <u>respite care</u> every so often in a ward just used for that purpose at a nearby hospital. I was told she wasn't ill, so I should not visit every day but could pop in if I wished. For me, that week soon passed. I spent three days de-stressing, one day enjoying my freedom and then three days gearing up to her coming home. But mum absolutely loved it. She had worked in the NHS when she was younger, she only ever read doctor and nurse romances and she met lots of new people. She also made a couple of new friends. With one, they planned to both come in together so they could meet up again. It was like going on holiday for mum, her week away every two months, and she looked forward to it.

▷ **Key Learning: Respite Care** Respite care refers to where the carer takes a temporary break from caring while the person they care for is looked after by someone else. The key aim of respite care is to enable the carer to take time out to look after themselves, or have respite, so that they do not become exhausted and run down, and so unable to continue to care. Respite care could be for a few hours or for a longer time. Types of respite care can include going to a day care centre, going to stay at a residential care facility or another carer looks after the person being cared for in their home. Respite care could be agreed as part of a <u>Carer's Assessment</u> and be funded by the local authority as part of this assessment or be self-funded.

Care in the Care Home

Mum was admitted to hospital after a serious fall, and while she was in hospital, she contracted the *C. difficile* bug (although we were told she'd been put in a single room because she'd had 'a bit of diarrhoea'), and we only learned the truth sometime later. Mum had weakened so much; she'd lost the use of her leg. Staff shortages combined with mum saying she didn't feel well enough for the physio or to get dressed led to her further loss of independence. However, because mum had all her mental faculties to the day she died, staff were led by her requests. From my point of view, this was detrimental, but no one listened to me, and, if I tried to ask anything, I was seen as a nuisance with comments like 'Why do you want to speak to the doctor?'

Three months on came the news I'd been expecting. They couldn't do any more for mum and needed the bed. We had always assumed that she would come back home so the discharge assessment was arranged. The social worker and occupational therapist (OT) came round to check the house over. There was a major problem. Mum was a large lady, and because of her stump, they had given her a wider wheelchair which alas was an inch wider than my door frames. They could squeeze her into a normal sized one to get her through the front door but then what? The OT offered that they could widen my door frames. However, having the lounge door widened 3" to the right would have taken out one side of the fitted kitchen units and to the left would have blocked the way to the dining room. There were more doors to consider. I listened in disbelief at this major work to make my home wheelchair friendly. I asked cautiously whether I would have to pay but was assured 'they' would. So I asked how much it might be. 'We could do it for about £90k' said the OT. For a woman of 89, I thought, incredulous. Is this value for money for taxpayers?

I told mum the gist of what had passed. She said it was ridiculous and announced she wanted to go into a home. She decided that she just wanted to be looked after all the time and to stop being a burden on me. She wouldn't have it that she wasn't, but the lady wasn't for turning. We discussed whether she wanted a small cosy place or a larger one with lots going on, which of her elderly friends might want to visit, but this was totally new to both of us.

The hospital social worker gave me a six-inch-thick file with details of every home in Birmingham and the surrounding area. The next day I was on tour, learning as I went along. I felt a sense of responsibility because I was having to choose mum's last home knowing she would leave there in her box. I wanted her to be happy for however long she had left but I felt very alone sorting it. I also had the social worker on the phone daily with her recurrent 'Have you found somewhere yet? We need the bed', which piled pressure on as Mum became a 'bed-blocker', and it was my fault. I saw four or five homes a day and then at the end of the week I found the perfect one. It wasn't far from my home, it ticked all my boxes, the staff I saw were friendly and engaged, and there was lots of space for getting round in a wheelchair. The only downside was that they were refurbishing four rooms and couldn't take Mum for three weeks. I left a message for the social worker with my good news.

The next day, the social worker rang me. 'We can't wait that long. I've found her a bed. It's in a shared room, but she can have a single room when one comes available. It won't be long'. As it transpired, this was the home that was number two on my list so I agreed mum could go and have a look. By the time she arrived the next day, a single room was available. She cast a cursory look round and said 'Yes, this'll do', so we began making plans to move her.

I brought personal things from home, her own clothes, toiletries, photographs, the TV from her bedroom and she settled in. A month passed and a social worker visited to assess that she was happy and wanted to stay. Had she not been, she could have moved. She had a space in the nearest lounge right by the TV, and I noted she had taken over the remote so that she could watch her programmes. Mum also enjoyed the quizzes, which she won, although she refused to have one resident on her team because she shouted out the answers. She seemed happy, but it was me having problems struggling with being a free agent after being a wife, a mum, a daughter and a carer—I'd lost track of who I was. I struggled emotionally. It was my house but our home. Mum was still everywhere but she was never coming back, and she wasn't dead. I had to come to terms with this as my life and I could do what I wanted. Mum's not sick, I don't have to visit every day, and she's looked after. When I went to visit mum after I took a much-needed long holiday, her eyesight had deteriorated to the extent that she could no longer read her puzzle magazine and then lost interest in the TV because it was hard to see. One day they had a residents' meeting, and I was one of only two carers who attended. Mum was one of only three or four residents who knew what day it was. The manager was suggesting possible activities such as the man who came in and showed films on a blank wall or maybe they might like a trip out to see the Christmas lights. I reminded her that mum's sight was going, and she said she couldn't know everything. I became increasingly concerned about attitudes and standards in the home, more so as mum's faculties deteriorated.

Finding My Voice

The final crunch for me came when mum fell out of bed one night smashing the bedside table, knocking the buzzer out of reach, and she was on the floor for a couple of hours before being found by the night staff. I didn't know this until later. I was just told she'd fallen out of bed and refused to go to hospital. Fortunately for me, a couple of weeks later, a social worker came to do her annual assessment. After going through what she liked about the home, he asked was there anything she didn't like. 'Well I didn't like falling out of bed', she said. You could almost see the alarm bells going off in his face.

A case conference was organised for three days later. Mum and I were both invited to attend but she chose not to go. Admissions to the home were stopped immediately. Everyone was round the table at the case conference, and I learned from the police inspector that mum was one of three safeguarding incidents they were investigating there.

▷   **Key Learning: Case Conference** A case conference is a meeting held by the local authority to discuss safeguarding concerns that an adult may be at risk of harm. There is a legal requirement to hold a case conference if there is such a concern. The aims of the case conference are to establish if there is an actual risk of harm and, if so, to determine what the harm may be and agree what needs to be done to protect from harm. The case conference is attended by the individual concerned, together with family/friends, professionals involved in providing the care such as a care organisation representative, social worker and doctor, plus investigating authorities such as the police.

The social worker outlined why we were all there and then I was asked if I wanted to say anything. Did I!!!! Suddenly I had a voice. The care home manager appeared bored, her boss was sinking lower into his seat, and I was just saying things I'd raised before which had been ignored. I finally felt vindicated. Admissions were stopped for about five months and I can never thank that social worker enough.

▷   **Key Learning: Safeguarding** Safeguarding is the legal requirement to take action that promotes the welfare of children and adults, and to protect them from harm. Often the primary focus in safeguarding is on protecting from harm. However, these two elements of safeguarding should be seen as inextricably linked, in that promoting the welfare of children and adults, such as through ensuring that their needs are met, is an important way to protect them from harm, through making them less at risk of harm. As an example, if an older adult is provided with services that enable them to maintain mobility, they may be less likely depend on other people for their needs and so less likely to suffer from abuse or harm. All organisations that work with or come into contact with children or adults at risk of harm are legally required to have policies and procedures to ensure safeguarding in practice.

I wish I could say everything was hunky dory after that but it wasn't. When mum's end was imminent, I was told she wouldn't last the weekend, but she lasted three weeks. When her happy release finally came, I went to collect the death certificate from the doctor round the corner, but the home hadn't informed her. I went back to the home who said it had been done, but when they checked the record book, it hadn't.

I have learned so much and hope that, in our own ways, mum and I provided voices for all those residents who didn't have one or anyone to speak up for them.

Bob's Story: Who Am I?

I am Bob Conner, a retired actor, and I cared for my wife, Pat, at home for several years until her dementia needs required residential care. Fortunately, Pat's care home is nearby, and I am still able to visit every day.

Pat was in her early 60s when I first began to notice small changes in her behaviour. She worked in a law office, only five minutes' walk from our home, and she started to work increasingly late, blaming it on staff cuts and workload. However, one day when she still had not come home by 8:00 pm, I walked to her office and found her working at her desk with no one else in the building except the security officers. I took this as one example of several signs that she was finding it increasingly difficult to cope.

On another occasion, when she was about to go shopping, she came back into the house and asked me if I could show her where the ignition switch was in her car. Eventually, after many small and strange incidents, she came home one day with a dent in her car that she claimed to know nothing about. After making enquiries I found that she had been involved in a minor collision for which she had no recollection, subsequently agreeing to give up driving.

Over the next eight years Pat's mental and physical capacities continued to deteriorate, and, now in my 70s, I cared for her at home. Throughout the last two years of being cared for at home, Pat required constant care and attention right down to eating, dressing and toileting, and she would have been at significant risk had I not been around.

Becoming a Carer

I had to give up my career, which I loved, to become a full-time carer and received an <u>Attendance Allowance</u> and home care, but the latter turned out to be a 20-minute visit around 9:00 am to dress and wash Pat. Often the carer didn't arrive until well past that time, and by the time she arrived I'd already done the job. The cumulative physical and emotional effect on me of full-time caring was tremendous. Not only was it a 24/7 job, but I had to watch someone who I dearly love get progressively more bewildered every day. Pat would look at me, sometimes with fear and sometimes with pleading in her eyes, and the memory of those looks can reduce me to tears even now.

▷   **Key Learning: Attendance Allowance** Attendance Allowance is an income benefit providing extra money for those over the State Pension age who need regular help with <u>personal care</u> for six months or more. It is non-means-tested, which means that it can be claimed regardless of person's financial circumstances. For those who are terminally ill, Attendance Allowance can be claimed straightaway. There are two different rates paid depending on the level of care required, with the higher rate paid for those requiring more care.

A turning point came when Pat suffered a pulmonary embolism and was hospitalised. She was, of course, cured, but the doctor suggested that perhaps home was no longer the right environment for her and she was discharged from hospital into a care home. Sadly, she did not meet the criteria for <u>nursing care,</u> and although Social Services pay a large proportion of her care costs, I still have to find quite a large <u>top-up fee</u>. When it came to discussing costs, I find officialdom to be immediately on the defensive, mainly interested in spending as little as possible—Pat's well-being was considered second to the cost and my well-being was not considered at all.

▷   **Key Learning: Nursing Care Versus Personal Care** There is an ongoing national debate about paying for older people who require residential care, much of this debate revolving around whether it is nursing care or personal care that is required. Nursing care typically refers to medical treatment like administering medication and treating health conditions such as managing pressure sores, while personal care typically refers to things like washing and bathing, dressing and undressing, getting in or out of bed, and taking medication. However, this distinction is often not as clear-cut as this in reality. One distinction that is clear is that while nursing care is free at the point of usage in the UK through the NHS, personal care in England is means-tested and assessed against the financial resources an individual or married couple have, including any property.

▷   **Key Learning: Top-Up Fee** When councils pay for a care home, they set a limit on the amount that they are prepared to pay for the accommodation. However, sometimes, service users prefer a more expensive home, and it is at the discretion of the council whether they choose to pay for the difference between their set limit and the cost of the chosen accommodation. Where the council decides not to fund the difference, families will be asked to 'top-up' this payment. Unless they do so, they will very often not be able to move into their chosen accommodation but will be required to choose accommodation that is within the council's set limit.

Effect on Carer of Partner Entering Residential Care

I felt very much alone at this time. Friends who we had been close to for many years but who had only ever known us as a couple faded away at the time when I needed them most, and my sister, upon whom I could always rely to say the right thing and who I had relied on for support, sadly died three months before Pat went away.

I had great difficulty in going from a busy life as a carer to having absolutely nothing to do, and although I was made aware of many organisations that held meetings and could offer tea and sympathy for people in my position, this was not what I needed. I needed someone who I could call on for meals out, country walks, theatre visits and in fact a normal social life, and now, six years on, I still haven't managed to satisfy that need. Making buddy friends is not easy past a certain age!

I had visited Pat every day at her care home since she was admitted, but in 2014, I was diagnosed with kidney cancer, and the surgery for this required a stay in hospital. I worried that she would not remember me, but three weeks later when I was able to visit again, I realised that she hadn't really noticed that I was missing. Perhaps a blessing in one way but a little upsetting for me because it confirmed that I was now superfluous. I was not in a very good place mentally at this time, and a few months later I was undergoing treatment for depression.

This really brings me to the present day. My health is not bad considering that I'm only a few weeks from 83 and only have one kidney. I'm about to complete cataract surgery having had one eye corrected six months ago with the other eye to be done in four weeks' time. I've finally accepted that nothing will change in my social life, so I do my best to enjoy what I've got rather than try to return to what I had.

Support for Carers

Voluntary organisations such as *Carers Careline* and *Reconnections* have been a wonderful source of support, but they are solely that, and they are not social organisations. However, I belong to an organisation called *The Catenian Association*, which is for Catholic professional men and, amongst other things, involves a lot of eating and drinking. One of the most beneficial aids has been the IMPACT service user and carers' group team at the University of Worcester. When I joined the team, I found that I could not only do the job but that I was wanted—and it was very uplifting to feel useful again. I'm very aware that at my age my time at the university is limited, but I assume that when the time comes to stop, I won't be very worried about it.

My own need for social care following cancer surgery was totally ignored. Every day in hospital I was told that a social worker would be coming to see me, but no one ever did. In the end I was discharged from the hospital and left to find my own way home to an empty house with no food in it. I was extremely tired, weak and rather traumatised.

I'm very fortunate in having no financial worries, and apart from ongoing cataract treatment, I have no health concerns at present. Having had cancer, I sometimes wonder how I'll react if it returns, but that's a bridge to be crossed if it happens.

Overall, I can't say that I'm totally satisfied with the aid provided by Social Services, though I accept that their actions are governed by prevailing financial restraints. However, more consideration for the physical and emotional needs of carers would not go amiss. I know that their priority is Pat's welfare, and I'm grateful for this, but I always felt side-lined. Even getting Carer's Allowance was a battle that took three applications!

▷   **Key Learning: Carer's Allowance/Carer's Credit/Carer Premium**   Carer's Allowance is a specific benefit for carers over the age of 16. It is available for people who spend at least 35 hours a week caring for someone, but not formally employed as their carer. This can include someone who does not live with the person they care for. 'Care' can include physically looking after someone, completing tasks for them and time spent keeping an eye on them. It is means-tested, meaning that whether a person is eligible to receive it and the amount that can be received is affected by the income that an individual or household has. The maximum amount claimable is £67.25.

Carer's Credit provides carers with employment-based National Insurance contributions so that they do not lose out on some social security benefits because of gaps in their NI record while caring and not working, such as the State Pension and contribution-based Job Seeker's Allowance.

Carer Premium is an extra payment that can be given to those entitled to Carer's Allowance who are also claiming other means-tested benefits, such as Income Support, Housing Benefit and Universal Credit. The carer premium is sometimes known as such as Carer Addition, Carer Amount or Carer Element.

Barbara's Story: Who Am I?

I am Barbara, now a widow in my 80s and the mother of Christopher, who has a learning disability. Initially, I cared for Christopher at home with my husband, but when we realised we could no longer meet his complex needs, Christopher went to live in a hospital. I have continued to care for Christopher through the years of closing institutions and into the era of community care. Attitudes towards carers have changed over this period, and my story below reflects mine and Christopher's journeys.

Dominance of the Medical Model

When Christopher was born in 1963, my husband and I had no idea he had any kind of disability, but while still a baby he began to develop slowly, and he suffered some seizures. Hospital staff didn't really know much about what was going on with Christopher's condition. We had been in the old children's hospital, and they eventually diagnosed him, aged two and a half, as having tuberous sclerosis, a form of learning disability, but they didn't tell us how to deal with it. It is only recently (55 years on!) that I have learned more about the actual condition of tuberous sclerosis. Parents weren't really involved in those days when 'doctor knows best' prevailed.

The worst part of Christopher's early life was trying to get him into some kind of schooling, because it was the old mental welfare department in those days and the senior officer there said 'well we've never had a child as young as this'. My response was 'Well, don't you think the earlier the child gets some sort of education, the better the child will be?' They eventually agreed to give Christopher a trial at the local junior training centre, and he then went on to be educated at a school attached to the local (then-called) subnormality hospital.

Christopher attended the hospital school every day, and although he didn't have much of a social life, we really felt that that was the best place for him at the time. However, as Christopher began to grow up, he became a bit more aggressive, and he did a lot of head banging which a lot of children with tuberous sclerosis do, and this is very hard to witness and cope with as a parent. Christopher's care, both medical and behavioural, was becoming too much to handle at home, especially his aggressive outbursts. In the absence of any services such as respite care, we were offered the stark choice of Christopher, then aged seven, staying at home or going to live permanently at the hospital where his medical consultant thought he would thrive better. We also felt that he would be better off at the hospital despite his young age and agreed to this course of action. We were sad but relieved at the same time, the hospital was close by, and we believed Christopher would be in capable hands.

The needs of carers, how we felt about things and how well we knew Christopher in those early years did not hold any sway against the dominance of what I now know as the 'medical model'. We certainly had no rights and no counselling/support/advocacy services, so just had to adjust to the fact Christopher was now living 'down the road' in 'the big hospital'. Apart from just going up to see him and hearing perhaps what he was doing and that sort of stuff, we were also allowed to have him home on a Sunday because it was not allowed to have him home any other day.

The two-hour 'leave' on a Sunday rule (which could not be challenged) was the hospital's maximum allowed. Parents came on a Sunday afternoon and you could take your child out; we used to take Chris for a ride in the car and take perhaps some squash or some sweets or something. Sometimes we could take him home (we lived about ten minutes away so that was handy), but those were the only things you could do. It would have been nice to have more time with Christopher, but that was the ruling so you had to abide by what they said.

Carers' Guilty Feelings

As a parent, I felt very torn about Chris moving away from home and held a lot of guilt once he became a permanent inpatient. I still recall one night, I think it was Thursday night when my husband, Nev, said 'Oh well, come on, let's go and have a drink. We have a social club, not far away', and I said 'No I won't go because if Christopher was at home, I wouldn't be able to go so I'm not coming'. It took quite a bit of persuasion from Nev to say 'Well yes, he's safe, you know where he is, and he's not going to come to any harm, so why don't you come out—let's go and have a drink?' I think I did go in the end but felt very guilty as I was going out and poor Christopher was stuck in the hospital.

Care in the Community

Christopher stayed living at the hospital until he was in his 30s when the government began to close those big old hospitals and move to care in the community. Chris was moved to a big old house near the hospital and seemed to love it on his own as he is a bit of a loner, but when other people, including women, were moved in alongside him, he did not like it, and his behaviour changed for the worse. The consultant and senior nurse next asked Nev and I if Chis could be moved to an ex-health authority house in nearby village where I had grown up. I knew a lot of people around where he was going to live and both Nev and I thought it was an ideal place for Chris.

▶ **Key Learning: Care in the Community/Community Care** Care in the Community (also referred to as Community Care) refers to a policy of caring for people in their own homes or the community that they live in rather than caring for them in institutions like hospitals or care homes. The policy's key aim was to support people to live independent lives, preferably in their own homes. It has been a longstanding policy, from the claim that care in institutions can be uncaring and impersonal when compared to care provided in the home or in their community, and also that care in the community is significantly less expensive than institutional care. There is evidence that care in the community can enable care that is more patient-centred and improve patient experience, but the evidence for cost savings is less clear (Castle-Clarke 2017).

Two other young women were also moved to the house which Chris wasn't too keen on, and then he started having chest infections and having difficulty climbing the stairs. The health authority applied for planning permission for Chris to have living space downstairs. This plan became a reality, and Chris has been happy in his self-contained accommodation, which is lovely, with all his own things. He has now been there for 25 years and hopefully he will stay there for the rest of his life. Three other men live in the same house—they don't mix much but occasionally interact, Chris preferring to be alone most of the time.

I have been able to be much more involved with Chris as his mother since his move to living in the community—I can visit when I like, as there are very few rules and regulations, a stark contrast to hospital days. The care staff are all very amenable and it's just a nice place to live for Chris now and he enjoys going out more. I ring about every other day and more often when he has not been so well. I have recently become a member of the University of Worcester's IMPACT group for service users and carers, have joined *Worcestershire Association of Carers* and begun to take part in training days at the Trust. I get far more support now than when Christopher was a child and know a lot more about his condition. I feel valued in being able to pass on knowledge as a carer, and in many ways, I did not suffer the practical problems many carers do, although the emotional and mental side of caring is always with you, regardless of where your loved one lives.

In my early years of being a carer, I was not very involved in key decisions about Christopher, and I was also unaware of any support services even existing. Although there is far more involvement of carers now in health and social care and far more services, I still don't think services are well enough advertised or made easy to access. This is a great shame because people may be struggling on as carers when some help might be just around the corner.

Commentary

The above lived experiences of Christine, Bob and Barbara illustrate a range of different experiences and degrees of satisfaction with the policies and provision for carers. As especially evident in Barbara's account, much has changed for the better since the days of large-scale, long-stay institutions, and the critical roles of carers have been increasingly recognised in social policy. This is less evident in Bob's and Christine's accounts, which detail emotive accounts of the significant emotional and financial cost of becoming and being a carer. It is noted here that an important limitation of these accounts is that the age profile of the carers means that there is no experience provided by a young carer, who do provide a significant amount of informal caring. However, within these similarities and differences, it is possible to discern some important implications for policy and practice for carers.

It is possible to discern some positive experiences of caring. This is most evident in the account of Barbara, who differs in that her care was shared with her partner, in contrast with the other accounts. This supports the observation made by Grant and Whittel (2000) that, where caring responsibilities are shared, then the ability to cope with caring is more evident. Additionally, it also makes relevant Calvo-Perxas et al.'s (2018) observation that the care setting is an important mediator of the health of the carer, wherein those with the poorest health tend to be those giving care inside the household, whereas caregivers outside the household tend to report better health. This suggests that providing support for lone carers providing care in their own home could be a specific focus of future policy and supportive practice.

The policy moves towards care in the community since the 1980s and the closure of many large-scale hospitals have benefitted the lives of many service users and carers. For example, Barbara and her son Christopher above both now have a say in their caring situations and have a lot more flexibility with regard to their caring relationship. However, the result of such policies is noted by Burns et al. (2012) as having greatly increased the numbers of hours delivered by informal carers, as evident in Bob and Christine's account of there being no respite care services available, and in Christine's case a bed only being found for her mum after Christine's breakdown. This supports Albert and Simpson's (2015) observation that the impact on informal carers' well-being is often neglected in social policy. The continuing closures of residential and respite settings under austerity policies have also very likely increased the emotional and physical risks to carers' own health.

A positive recent outcome for carers has been the recognition of carers' discrete rights in the *Care Act 2014*, through the right to a Carer's Assessment for their own support, separate to that of the person for whom they care. This ostensibly means that the needs of carers are now taken into consideration separately, as opposed to being subsumed with the need of the person they are caring for (Brooks et al. 2016). This also provides the opportunity to provide support to carers in a variety of ways, whether financial, emotional or practical. This can include respite care and creative options such as art therapy, which have been identified as having beneficial impacts on carers' mental health (Henwood et al. 2017; Pohjola et al. 2020). However, a key theme that runs through all three above accounts is the lack of voice that carers felt they had in relation to how care could be provided. Barbara's account probably exemplifies this best in detailing the overriding dominance of the medical model of care to her wishes as a carer, as well as the lack of choice in where care would be provided, an outcome emphasised in Parkhill and Wall (2019). While there has been a shift towards the social model of care for service users, this is less apparent in relation to that of carers, as the accounts of both Bob and Christine suggest that a professional dominance still exists. As a possible reason for this, Seddon and Robinson (2014) observe that there is a reliance in Carer's Assessments on the 'structured, problem-focused assessment protocols' which inevitably limit the possibilities of meeting the needs of the carer in a holistic way. This suggests the need for Carers' Assessments that enable the needs of carers to be captured and met in ways that are personalised and enduring to the carer. Additionally, Knowles et al. (2016) make the observation that long-term carers in particular are reluctant to seek support for their emotional needs and that interaction with professionals can be important to encourage them to seek such support. Again, this key type of support could be provided as a result of thorough Carer's Assessments under the *Care Act 2014*.

The above accounts also show that social policy initiatives such as the carer's right to an assessment mean very little, however, if such assessment does not lead to resource allocation. Both Bob and Christine incurred very significant financial costs in caring, and there is perhaps a need for the benefits system to play a more significant role in helping keep carers from falling into poverty themselves, many carers being unaware of such financial support or lacking the time off from caring duties to explore such avenues. Bob mentions that he was fortunate in not having had any money worries, but most poverty is experienced in old age, and there have been many examples of older people having been moved from a settled placement because 'top-up' money from a carer has run out. Analysis by Courtin et al. (2014) shows that the UK is one of the few European countries to provide both direct (in the form of Carer's Allowance) and indirect (in the form of Attendance Allowance) financial support. While Carer's Allowance is means-tested, Attendance Allowance is not, although it is limited to those over the State Pension age. Data on the number of claimants for each benefit from the DWP (2019) shows that Attendance Allowance recipients (1.571 million people) are much higher than Carer's Allowance recipients (1.303 million people), which is perhaps surprising considering that Attendance Allowance is limited to those over the State Pension age. Moreover, the take-up of Attendance Allowance is 91%, compared to 66% for Carer's Allowance. This suggests that there are a significant number of carers who are not receiving the financial support that they are entitled to. The means-tested nature of Carer's Allowance is also likely to be a significant reason for this as it is known that means-tested benefits have lower take-up for a variety of reasons (Sealey 2015). The higher take-up of universal Attendance Allowance suggests that there is a case for removing the means-testing for Carer's Allowance in order to increase take-up rates and help carers to continue caring. However, in an age of austerity, such a measure is unlikely to become government policy.

Aldridge and Hughes (2016) highlight some key policy areas that are fundamental to tackling carer poverty:

- Access to support and quality formal care.
- Personalised and flexible employment support for working-age carers.
- Support for carers to access training and improve their qualifications.
- Changes to disability benefits which consider the impact on carers.

The *Care Act 2014* did identify £5.3bn of local health and social care spending to be amalgamated into a single budget in order that the two services could make better use of resources for service users and carers. However, research from Carers UK (2016) estimated that only 25% of local authorities had actually specified any plans regarding how this resource should be spent. Carers UK (2016) also found that 50% of carers still report detriment to their own physical health due to carrying out caring responsibilities, many carers never actually getting identified by services as carers in need of their own support systems. In a further attempt to influence policy for carers, Carers UK (2016) called for:

- A new duty on the NHS and education professionals to put in place policies to identify carers and to promote their health and well-being.
- Development of education, information and training for a range of frontline professionals to increase knowledge and signposting of carers.
- Improved access to information and advice for carers.
- A public awareness campaign to improve understanding and recognition of carers.

The Carers UK (2019) report shows that, while there has been improvement in some areas, no significant strategic change in designing and delivering comprehensive services for carers has occurred yet across the UK. All three above carers' accounts highlight the 'carers' burden' in different ways, either as a physical, psychological, emotional and/or financial impact (Cottagiri and Sykes 2019). Even Barbara's more positive account talks about the 'guilt' of caring for her son. In Bob's account, he reports having experienced problems in adjusting to his wife, Pat, having moved into residential care, and one wonders to what extent his caring duties eventually took a toll on his own health. Christine reports having had a breakdown and having to give up her job as a result of lack of support in helping care for her mum. Such personal histories will resonate with the lives of the millions of carers across the UK, and in times of austerity, it can be seen that carers' needs have been marginalised, although such a policy is evidently short-sighted. If informal carers collapse because of over-demand, then the financial costs fall to the state, increasing demand on an already stretched budget, as well as bringing avoidable mental and physical illness to carers. Overall, despite an increasing range of government initiatives to better support carers in recent decades, there has been more rhetoric than action as illustrated both by the narratives of Christine, Bob and Barbara above and by the strategic work of campaigning organisations such as Carers UK (2019).

Reflective Questions

1. What are the issues regarding the appropriateness of current services with carers' needs as particularly highlighted by Christine?
2. What do the accounts above say about how Carer Assessments should be carried out? What social policies might be introduced to better engage carers in this process?
3. How might benefits policies for carers be made more accessible?
4. Does the medical model still have a part to play in helping carers to care?
5. Do the initiatives suggested by Carers UK in 2016 and 2019 indicate realistic future policy direction? Which of their suggestions do you think has the best chance of being adopted and why?

References

R. Albert, A. Simpson, Double deprivation: a phenomenological study into the experience of being a carer during a mental health crisis. J. Adv. Nurs. **71**(12), 2753–2762 (2015). https://doi.org/10.1111/jan.12742

H. Aldridge, C. Hughes, Informal carers & poverty in the UK. An analysis of the Family Resources Survey. New Policy Institute 1–30 (2016). https://www.npi.org.uk/files/2114/6411/1359/Carers_and_poverty_in_the_UK__full_report.pdf. Accessed 20 Nov 2019

J. Brooks et al., Personalisation, personal budgets and family carers. Whose assessment? Whose budget? J. Soc. Work **17**(2), 147–166 (2016). https://doi.org/10.1177/1468017316638554

T. Burns et al., Continuity of care for carers of people with severe mental illness. Int. J. Soc. Psychiatry **59**(7), 663–670 (2012). https://doi.org/10.1177/0020764012450996

L. Calvo-Perxas et al., What seems to matter in public policy and the health of informal caregivers? A cross-sectional study in 12 European countries. PLOS ONE **13**(3), e0194232 (2018). https://doi.org/10.1371/journal.pone.0194232

Carers UK, Missing out: the identification challenge (2016). https://www.carersuk.org/news-and-campaigns/press-releases/years-of-missing-out-on-support-taking-its-toll-on-the-health-and-finances-of-those-caring-for-loved-ones. Accessed 20 May 2020

Carers UK, Missing out. Research briefing on the state of caring 2019 survey (2019). https://www.carersuk.org/for-professionals/policy/policy-library/missing-out-research-briefing-on-the-state-of-caring-2019-survey. Accessed 20 May 2020

S. Castle-Clarke, Hitting home: the evidence on care in the community. Nuffield Trust comment (2017). https://www.nuffieldtrust.org.uk/news-item/hitting-home-the-evidence-on-care-in-the-community. Accessed 2 May 2020

S.A. Cottagiri, P. Sykes, Key health impacts and support systems for informal carers in the UK: a thematic review. J. Health Soc. Sci. **4**(2), 173–198 (2019). https://doi.org/10.19204/2019/kyhl11

E. Courtin et al., Mapping support policies for informal carers across the European Union. Health Policy **118**(1), 84–94 (2014). https://doi.org/10.1016/j.healthpol.2014.07.013

DWP, DWP benefits statistical summary (2019). https://www.gov.uk/government/publications/dwp-benefits-statistics-august-2019/dwp-benefits-statistical-summary-august-2019. Accessed 20 May 2020

G. Grant, B. Whittel, Differentiated coping strategies in families with children or adults with intellectual disabilities: the relevance of gender, family composition and the life span. J. Appl. Res. Intellect. Disabil. **13**(4), 256–275 (2000). https://doi.org/10.1046/j.1468-3148.2000.00035.x

M. Henwood et al., Seeing the wood for the trees. Carer related research and knowledge: a scoping review (2017). https://www.scie-socialcareonline.org.uk/seeing-the-wood-for-the-trees-carer-related-research-and-knowledge-a-scoping-review/r/a110f00000rctcnaalxxaaacommentxx-bbb. Accessed 2 May 2020

S. Knowles et al., Hidden caring, hidden carers? Exploring the experiences of carers for people with long-term conditions. Health Soc. Care Community **24**(2), 203–213 (2016). https://doi-org.apollo.worc.ac.uk/10.1111/hsc.12207

I. Parkhill, K. Wall, The journey to care – reflections of a service user. Disabil. Soc. **35**(3), 506–510 (2019). https://doi.org/10.1080/09687599.2019.1649815

H. Pohjola et al., Art intervention among Finnish older people and their caregivers: experiences of art pedagogies. Health Soc. Care Community (2020). https://doi.org/10.1111/hsc.13003

C. Sealey, *Social Policy Simplified* (Palgrave Macmillan, Basingstoke, 2015)

D. Seddon, C. Robinson, Carer assessment: continuing tensions and dilemmas for social care practice. Health Soc. Care Community **23**(1), 14–21 (2014). https://doi.org/10.1111/hsc.12115

Social Policy, Service Users and Carers: Proposals for Improving Policy and Practice

Clive Sealey, Joy Fillingham, and Peter Unwin

The aim of this book is to detail the lived experiences of service users and carers, as their specific involvement has become increasingly prominent in legislation and policy over recent years. This is evident in many recent policy initiatives such as personalisation and person-centred care, which emphasise the need for consultation, partnership and co-production on ther behalf. This book has demonstrated the need for such inclusion and the relevance of the insights and experiences of those personally and systematically impacted by policy decisions made. It is co-production principles which have underpinned the development and writing of this book, through service users and carers and academics working with each other in a way that gives equal weight and recognition to their contributions. In this respect, this book is distinctive as it represents a bottom-up approach to analysing and critiquing social policy.

What is evident in much of the lived experiences in this book is that while there have been improvements over time in involving service users and carers in health and care services, there is still a lot to be done to move services away from consultation and towards partnership and co-production. As the lived experiences in their narratives show, service users and carers are often not even informed of what services might be available, let alone given the opportunity to shape such services and the policies that underpin them. However, the lived experiences in this book demonstrate that when service users and carers are provided with the voice and means to

C. Sealey (✉) • P. Unwin
School of Allied Health and Community, University of Worcester, Worcester, UK
e-mail: c.sealey@worc.ac.uk; p.unwin@worc.ac.uk

J. Fillingham
Department of Social Work and Social Care, University of Birmingham, Birmingham, UK
e-mail: j.fillingham@bham.ac.uk

C. Sealey et al. (eds.), *Social Policy, Service Users and Carers*,
https://doi.org/10.1007/978-3-030-69876-8_13

do so, they are able to articulate cogent and coherent ways to improve policy and practice. These key areas for improvement which have emerged from the book are detailed below.

Putting the 'Social' Back into Social Work

Most contributors detailed some contact and/or statutory involvement with social workers in their accounts. While there were some positive accounts of these involvements, in the main the experiences were negative for a variety of reasons, the main one being the experience that social workers were impersonal in their practice and lacked warmth or empathy. Specific examples of these included a tick box approach to assessments and not showing particular interest in an individual. Evidence of this is provided by Lynch et al. (2019, p. 139) who observed that, while it is widely accepted that empathy is an important skill in social work, 'the majority of workers were found not to demonstrate a high level of empathy skill [which] presents concerns to be considered by the social work profession'. This deficiency should not be seen as something that is inconsequential to practice, because as the accounts in this book make clear, a lack of impersonal practice can have a major implication on the outcomes of practice, Christine Ransome-Wallis' account in Chap. 12 is an exemplar of this. There may be several reasons for this happening, such as the social workers being overloaded with cases in terms of number and complexity and the imperatives of managerialist targets which do not value the quality of relationships.

A possible more specific reason for this is detailed by Webb (2001) as occurring from the recent transformation in social work teaching in relation to its professional focus. This has meant an emphasis on both professional regulation and professional change, requiring practice that is up to date, consistent and output driven, and mainly focused on understanding the technical requirements of the profession. The prime example of this is the change of emphasis in curriculum when pre-qualifying social work training moved from diploma to degree level certification. These requirements can mean that social work is typically located in the here and now of immediate performance targets, as a huge amount of time is spent on understanding what a social worker needs to do to administratively and bureaucratically function effectively within the sometime chaotic system in which they operate. Additionally, such 'organisational defences' can also function to shield and protect social workers from the intensity of the emotional impact of their work (Dugmore 2019). Subsequently, an 'unintentional consequence' of this is that there is little time available for social workers to understand the wider social context of social work, meaning understanding the connection between what social workers do in practice and the social context and theories that govern what they do (McNay et al. 2009). Ferguson and Norton (2011) also highlight how social work has moved away from 'intimate practice', which they argue has an important role in ensuring that young people in particular feel cared about. The accounts presented here suggest that there needs to be some focus on realigning social work to focus more on the personal and social aspects of practice and less on the administrative and bureaucratic processes as currently exists. This is also the case for other professionals in health and social care.

Improving the Level of Continuity of Practice in Social Work and Other Professionals

Linked to the previous point, another recurring theme across the accounts is the lack of continuity of practice in social work and other professions, in that the majority of accounts outline not having consistent access to the same social worker and other professionals. This was related as problematic for a number of interrelated reasons, such as limiting the possibility of building a relationship or getting to know the individual, not understanding the current or developing needs of the individual and not providing relevant service provision to the individual, as identified in Le Grand (2007). More recent research supports this, with the lack of continuity of care identified as the overriding concern for service users (Wilberforce et al. 2019). In particular, the accounts here highlight the beneficial outcomes that can occur from continuity of care in relation to getting to know the individual. The ideal outcome to this issue would be to make continuity of care a mandatory requirement, but this would ignore the fact that 'care continuity is not a feature of any individual profession, but rather a system-level factor [as] individual social workers have little control over continuity, with continual pressures through new referrals in poorly resourced service settings' (Wilberforce et al. 2019, p. 14). This includes issues of poor pay, high stress and under-recruitment all leading to poor staff turnover and retainment. Moreover, this lack of retainment also has a significant cost issue in that it leads to the use of agency staff, which has the double whammy of both reducing continuity of care and also increasing the cost of the service to local authorities (Unwin 2009; Perraudin 2019). So, this is an issue than cannot be separated from wider issues detailed elsewhere in this chapter, particularly funding issues in the context of the social care being the poor relation to health care historically and especially in a time of austerity. This is not to demonise pressured professionals working in complex and challenging areas of health and social care work. The pressures and expectations placed upon all by cash-strapped and target-focused services and policies can have demonstrably negative impacts for everyone concerned.

Changing Negative Attitudes Towards Service Users and Carers

Another recurring theme is the negative and prejudicial attitudinal responses to service users and carers from professionals and wider society. These attitudes ranged from demeaning to patronising, in terms of considering the skills and abilities of individuals. As the accounts show, these attitudes can have important implication on the outcomes for individuals, in terms of their employment and wider social and economic participation with society. The account of Julia Smith in Chap. 7 is encouraging in terms of outlining an improvement in such attitudes from 30 years ago, and this is supported with evidence (Dixon et al. 2018). This positive change has been driven by the greater visibility of individuals within society, as Julia's account makes evident, and is supported by Dixon et al. (2018, p. 17) wherein:

> We have seen that where people have a relationship with a disabled person – whether as a family member or a colleague – they are less likely to hold negative attitudes towards disability in general. They are also more likely to have a perception of prejudice that matches the experiences of disabled people.

However, the account provided here shows that this is only part of what is necessary to effect real change. In particular, what is evident in the accounts of Julia Smith, Mark Lynes and Charles English-Peach is the pervading low expectations of individuals that some professionals hold. The most obvious example of this is the low educational expectations, meaning that individuals were categorised and assigned to schooling that constrained their potential educational ability. In the longer term, this has had the impact of limiting their educational outcomes, which has the impact of limiting their employment outcomes and could go a long way to explaining why disabled and disadvantaged individuals are less visible in the workplace, especially in positions of responsibility and power. So a clear message from the accounts is the need to counter the prevalent low educational expectations of individuals that exist among some professionals.

The other significant negative outcome that such perceptions caused for service users and carers is stigmatisation. This was particularly evident in the accounts of Dionne and Dorothy in Chap. 9, Francesa in Chap. 3 and Jon in Chap. 6. The key point about such stigmatisation is that it can work at two levels. The first relates to the expectations and attitudes of professionals, and the second relates to the internalised oppression many people develop when repeatedly and consistently being faced with adversity and doubting of their capacity and limited options.

As has been demonstrated above, attitudinal responses have had an impact upon every service user and carer involved in this book. The stigmatising nature of being evaluated by others on your capacity and right to support inevitably has consequences. For people facing adversity to feel that they stand alone and are judged (as many accounts within this book evidenced) is an isolating and debilitating experience which often leaves individuals feeling alone and anxious.

The attitudinal responses common to many service users and carers and evident throughout this work relate to three key areas identified by Fillingham (2013) as:

– Expectations about what an individual should know
– Expectations about how they should behave
– Debate about what is in their best interests

The expectations as to what an individual should know results in an expectation that service users and carers are able to understand and negotiate the complexities of systems and processes, which is not always the case. Conversely, service users and carers can also be expected to behave in passive ways when seeking help—consider Christine Ransome-Wallis' discussion in Chap. 12 of the submissive expectations placed upon her as her mother's sole carer, for instance. Yet simultaneously, they also encounter professionals who believe that their professional understanding of a situation is the only or primary one to be considered. For instance, the assumption that medication of Francesca's son in Chap. 3 was the only option for a young person with a diagnosis of ADHD or that Chantele's actions as a teenager in Chap. 10 were as a result of bad behaviour rather than a medical condition. Clearly there are disagreements about what a professional and a service user or carer may feel is the solution to an issue they encounter, but the repeatedly demonstrated power disparities between service users and carers and professionals cannot be underestimated. When such approaches are repeatedly encountered, the long-term impacts upon the individual can be significant. The combination of such an approach together with low expectations of service users can lead to the pathologisation of service users and carers.

The failure to recognise the skills and insights of the service users and carers considered here demonstrates a waste of extreme proportions. To negotiate with complex procedures, whilst dealing with life experiences which limit your daily activities or approach to life, requires determination, persistence and an ability to understand and relate to many institutions and individuals. Service users and carers have an array of skills, live in pressured environments and often have incompatible expectations and competing demands placed upon them. This book has demonstrated that their knowledge and understanding of their own experiences or conditions is valuable, but that these skills are seldom recognised or encouraged. The commonalities and differences between professionals and service users and carers need to be the basis for dialogue to seek to understand each other's perspectives for real improvements to occur.

Ensuring Parity Between Social Care and Health Care

Contributors to this book describe a mixture of health care needs and social care needs. There is no legal definition of health care or social care, but the Department of Health and Social Care (2018, p. 17) defines health needs as 'treatment, control or prevention of a disease, illness, injury or disability, and the care or aftercare of a person with these needs', while social care needs refer to 'providing assistance with activities of daily living, maintaining independence, social interaction, enabling the individual to play a fuller part in society, protecting them in vulnerable situations, helping them to manage complex relationships and (in some circumstances) accessing a care home or other supported accommodation'. While these definitions point to important functional differences between health care and social care, there are also important policy differences, as detailed in Table 13.1 below.

As can be seen from Table 13.1, there are clear differences in health care provision and social care provision, the most obvious of which is in relation to funding,

Table 13.1 Comparing Health and Social Care

	Health care	Social care
Level of funding	£166 billion	£34 billion
Type of funding	Primarily general taxation	Mixture: General taxation and private funding
Direct responsibility	Mainly Department of Health and Social Care	Mainly local government
Type of providers	Mainly state	State, private companies, voluntary, individual (mixed economy of welfare)
Service users	All—universal	Most needy - income tested
Principles	NHS Constitution: 'Free at the point of use, comprehensive and universal'	None

where health care spending is almost five times that of social care spending. The other key difference is in terms of service users, wherein health care is a universal service provided to all, while social care is a means-tested service provided based on a test of income. Taken together, these differences assign social care as the poor relation to health care, and it is obvious in the service users' and carers' accounts that this disparity impacts on their outcomes. For example, it was evident that the underfunding of social work led to some significant negative consequences for various contributors. Furthermore, the underlying consequences of this disparity can be seen from the fact that according to Martin Green, Chief Executive of Care England, while the NHS spends £3615 per year on staff development for each staff member, only £16 per year is spent on staff development in social care (Green 2018). It is inconceivable that this huge disparity has no impact on the quality of care provided.

There have been recent policy changes to overcome this above disparity, most notably the emphasis on integration between health and social care so that they feel like one service instead of two services (Johnson et al. 2017). Besides the *Department of Health* being renamed as the *Department of Health and Social Care*, a prominent example of this has been the *Better Care Fund*, which is where health, social care and housing funding is pooled into one fund to provide integrated care. Whilst this has led to some success in integration (HM Government 2019), the major limitation of this is that it does not involve any additional funding to either health or social care. Instead, funding is from already existing money. This ignores the more radical change required to health and social care to improve outcomes, which has to go beyond the emphasis on integration and needs to focus on parity of esteem between the two. Parity of esteem refers to viewing and treating the two services as equal in terms of value and worth and would mean that some of the differences outlined above in Table 13.1 are reduced or eliminated, particularly the funding difference. The notion of parity of esteem has come to prominence in specific relation to mental health, but mental health is just one aspect of health and social care. For parity of esteem to have a real effect, it would need to refer wholesale to social care and would require a qualitative change in policy and practice. In particular, it would require a more definitive shift away from the medical model towards the social model of health and disability, which has been occurring but is still evident in some of the service user and carer narratives in this book. The beneficial outcomes from wholesale parity of esteem would provide wide-ranging benefits linked specifically to service users' and carers' experiences, as detailed below.

A Focus on Improving the Mental Health of Service Users and Carers

A consistent theme throughout the majority of service user and carer accounts throughout this book is the impact that poor mental health had on their experiences. While for some accounts, poor mental health was an evident and primary concern, for others it was a more hidden issue which nevertheless had a significant impact on their health and well-being. A good example of this is the account of Francesca in Chap. 3, which details the long-term impact of living with undiagnosed mental health problems. Even when a mental health disorder is diagnosed, there were issues evident in relation to the treatment provided, as in Chantele's account in Chap. 10. So, there needs to be a greater focus on improving the mental health of service users and carers.

In terms of prevention, this relates to a focus on limiting the risk factors that can cause mental health problems while also improving the coping mechanisms an individual can use to cope with mental health problems (Arango et al. 2018). Risk factors that can cause mental health problems include genetic predisposition, biological factors such as exposure to drugs and medications, family-related issues such as peri- and post-natal depression and socioeconomic factors such as poverty. These are factors which are evident within the accounts detailed in this book.

The identification of specific risk factors for mental ill health suggests that a focus on the selective prevention of mental health within specific groups could be one way to prevent mental ill health. However, what the accounts show is that, notwithstanding these risk factors, mental ill health does not discriminate between groups and can affect people both within and outside these risk factors. This means that a focus on prevention requires a universal approach, wherein mental health interventions are targeted at the general public or to a whole population group that has not been identified on the basis of increased risk (World Health Organisation (WHO) 2004). This has the benefit of emphasising the importance of positive mental health within the population, rather than for some groups, and so means that the identification of mental ill health becomes easier to identify, as well as reducing the stigma that surrounds mental disorders (WHO 2004). This means that prevention of mental health should have as its emphasis the promotion of positive mental health for the entire population, and not just for some of the population.

Such an approach towards prevention would overcome one of the main limitations of current mental health policy identified by service users and carers, that of ensuring a holistic approach to the treatment of mental health, rather than a focus on medicalised treatment, as a way to improve mental health. As was evident in Chaps.

4, 10 and 11, it was only when medicalised treatment for mental health was changed to a more holistic psychological approach that treatment was effective, with art therapy highlighted in several accounts as being particularly effective. Nelson et al. (2020) argue that such a holistic approach is particularly relevant for children and young people, while Crenna-Jennings and Hutchinson (2020) argue that there needs to be a broadening of the current focus of on acute mental health towards the prevention of mental ill health for young people. There has been a focus on this in policy through the adult *Improving Access to Psychological Therapies* (IAPT) and *Children and Young People Improving Access to Psychological Therapies* (CYP IAPT). While these approaches can be helpful, the accounts throughout this book suggest that such options are not always available.

Improving the Transition from Childhood to Adulthood

Linked to the above point is the importance of improving the transition from childhood to adulthood. We already know that the transition from childhood to adulthood is problematic for young people who have linear transitions, but several service users and carers identified that the transition from childhood to adulthood is even more problematic as a consequence of lacking support to deal with issues that they encountered during this time. These included mental health issues in particular. Child and Adolescent Mental Health Services (CAMHS) is a specific service designed to deal with mental health issues in children and adolescents, but its role in enabling a smooth transition to adulthood is not as effective as it could be, as detailed in Chantele's account in Chap. 10. Part of the reason for this is that the provisions of CAMHS are variable by region, meaning that while some people are able to access services up to the age of 25, for others there is a cut-off point at 18 years. We know that the age of 24 is significant in relation to mental health as 75% of mental health problems have developed by this age (Arango et al. 2018), which indicates that access to CAMHS should be made available up to the age of 25 at least, as a way to smooth this transition. Additionally, the importance of universities in this process should not be overlooked, as several accounts, such as that of Eva in Chap. 11, detail a problematic transition within their experiences of being at university. It is also evident that universities, as access points to greater social mobility, need to do more to ensure that young people do not become lost in their transition to adulthood.

Moving Away from Austerity Social Policies

Significantly, this book has been written during a long period of austerity, which refers to the deep cuts by central government since 2010 to the funding and scope of social policy provisions. The consequences of austerity policies are reflected in much of the hardship reflected in the chapters, and even the best professional practice and determination are limited when there are no services available in local communities. Ken Loach's films *I, Daniel Blake* and *Sorry, We Missed You* have both been released during the writing of this book and paint a realistically harrowing picture of life for poor and disabled people in contemporary UK society where policies are designed to make poorer people pay for the mistakes of bankers whose investment strategies had triggered a national financial crisis. The accounts in this book make it evident that austerity has had a significant and real impact on lived experiences, either through cuts in benefits, cuts in services or cuts in support. Where the impact of austerity does not permeate directly in the accounts, it seeps thorough as an indirect cause of some of the circumstances in which individuals find themselves. What we do know about austerity is that it has failed on its own terms, as it is a false economic model (Stirling 2019) which has brought about even greater deficits than those it purported to solve. Additionally, most austerity social policy initiatives of recent years have been 'top-down' and have not reflected the lives and aspirations of poor and disabled people—real change and the adoption of social policies that include all strata of society may only be realised once 'bottom-up' approaches are valued. This means that some of the gains and improvements that have occurred for service users and carers have been rolled back or eliminated. This means that moving away from austerity social policies should be a significant priority.

Making Co-production Work

The book has been written with concept of co-production as its overarching method and aim. In Chap. 2, we outlined key features and principles of co-production, as well as some of the key challenges. Our experiences of writing this book reinforce some of these points made previously and also highlight new points of relevance as detailed below.

The purpose of this book was to identify the importance of including service users and carers in the services and systems which are intended to support them. The unique approach of this book is the incorporation of the extended lived experiences provided by service users and carers. This is something that does not typically happen in service user and carer involvement in academia. Rather, it is snippets of service users and carers experiences which are normally used, to illuminate key points that the researcher wants to reinforce. By making extended lived experiences the primary focus of the book, this has foregrounded the relevance of such an approach. It has also hopefully made others see that such an approach is feasible and practicable. The findings from the lived experiences in particular should highlight that co-production also has the potential to be a 'win-win' opportunity for all involved in the process.

Some of these wins are readily evident, such as the proposed improvements suggested by servicer users and carers. However, some of these 'wins' for service users and carers are less obvious, such as increased confidence and self- awareness, while for academic contributors there has been the greater understanding of issues and a greater willingness to consider the lived experiences of service users in their work.

This highlights the reciprocal effect of this work and the co-production approach in general, wherein the benefits are shared out between participants and also relate to wider society. This reinforces the point made in Chap. 2 that a key rationale for co-production is engendering a reciprocal relationship between all involved. This would not have been possible without the focus on co-production within this project.

Another key co-production outcome from this book is the importance of the contribution that the diversity of service users and carers have made to the project, beyond the typical tokenism of research projects in terms of their aims and objectives. The focus on the lived experiences of service users and carers has incorporated the perspectives of 'experts by experience', and this has undoubtedly provided a different outlook beyond the usual contributors to academic work. This project has emphasised that service users and carers should be seen as one of many stakeholders able to contribute to a research or policy problem (Bammer 2019), which is an important aim of co-production as a method. We feel that this approach has also led to greater validity of the accounts of service users and carers, through the corroboration between accounts that has occurred. By this is meant that there has been a reoccurrence of themes with accounts, even when accounts are not linked. The most obvious example of this is the significance of mental health distress among accounts, even where the account was not specifically focused on this aspect.

We observed in Chap. 1 that this book is a unique example of co-production between service users and carers, distinguishable from other similar examples due to the level of involvement and co-production between service users and carers and academics. This leads to three relevant observations.

The first is that, in terms of relevance to the key features outlined in Chap. 2, the primary rationale behind using co-production for this book is the expected beneficial outcomes from co-production, for both service users and carers and academics. These beneficial outcomes relate to the design, commission and delivery of services. We would hope that the combination of the lived experiences of service users and carers and the analysis provided by the academic writers presents specific ways in which the design, commission and delivery of services might change. As an example of this, in Chap. 9, the discussion of child protection provides a specific service user recommendation as to how this could be improved (see Table 9.2).

The second is that for co-production to work, there needs to be a huge element of flexibility in ways of working, especially from an academic perspective. What we have seen is that while for academics the processes of writing and editing are normal experiences, for service users and carers this is a new experience that presents unique challenges. As an example of this, for most chapters, the writing process was not a 'single point in time' process, but something that occurred over a longer period. Additionally, the continual process of editing and requiring additional information from service users and carers meant a significant imposition of time and resources. Academics are also used to working to deadlines, but again the imposition of such deadlines for a project with such a level of co-production has neither been possible nor been desirable, as service users and carers have responsibilities and real-life concerns that prevent such strict deadlines. Had we tried to progress this project in the way that an academic project is normally expected to progress, then it clearly would not have been completed. Rather, as Hickey et al. (2018, p. 12) observe:

> a co-produced research project should provide opportunities for an iterative, fluid, open ended, experimental and interactive process; there should be opportunity for solutions and innovations to emerge from the relationships developed.

The quote above reinforces a key point that was evident in this project, which is the need for flexibility as a key component of a successful co-produced project. It is evident to us it that, without such flexibility, the book would not have been completed.

The third point, as observed in Chap. 1, is that there is no one specific method for co-production. Instead, our experiences reinforce the point that co-production is a fluid process, which can be changed and adapted depending on the circumstances. As an example of this, while we set out with the aim that all service user and carer contributors would write their own chapters, it soon became evident that this would not be possible. So, we modified our approach to include where chapters could be co-written or dictated by participants. This emphasises the point made by Durose et al. (2017) that with co-production, it is more important to have a 'good enough' methodology that works than one that is too fixed but does not work. By 'good enough' is meant one that enables the aims and objectives of the project to be met, as reflected in the methodology used in this project.

References

C. Arango et al., Preventive strategies for mental health. Lancet Psychiat (2018) Published Online May 14, 2018

G. Bammer, Key issues in co-creation with stakeholders when research problems are complex. Evid. Policy **15**(3), 423–435 (2019). https://doi.org/10.1332/174426419X15532579188099

W. Crenna-Jennings, J. Hutchinson, *Access to Child and Adolescent Mental Health Services in 2019* (Education Policy Institute, London, 2020)

Department of Health and Social Care, *National Framework for NHS Continuing Healthcare and NHS-Funded Nursing Care, October 2018 (Revised)* (Department for Health and Social Care, London, 2018)

S. Dixon et al., *The Disability Perception Gap* (Scope, London, 2018)

P. Dugmore, *Acknowledging and Bearing Emotions: A Study into Child and Family Social Work Practice*, Dissertation (University of Sussex, 2019)

C. Durose et al., Generating 'good enough' evidence for co-production. Evid. Policy **13**(1), 135–151 (2017). https://doi.org/10.1332/174426415X14440619792955

H. Ferguson, J. Norton, *Child Protection Practice* (Palgrave Macmillan, Basingstoke, 2011)

J. Fillingham, *Changing Needs and Challenging Perceptions of Disabled People with Acquired Impairments*, Dissertation (University of Birmingham, 2013)

M Green, *Care England Calls for Parity of Esteem Between NHS and Social Care Workforce* (Care England, London, 2018). http://www.careengland.org.uk/news/care-england-calls-parity-esteem-...3. Accessed 17 June 2020

G. Hickey et al., *Guidance on Co-producing a Research Project* (INVOLVE, Southampton, 2018)

HM Government, *2019–20 Better Care Fund: Policy Framework* (Department of Health and Social Care and the Ministry of Housing, Communities and Local Government, London, 2019)

L. Johnson et al., *Integration 2020: Scoping Research Report to the Department of Health* (Social Care Institute for Excellence, London, 2017)

J. Le Grand, *Consistent Care Matters: Exploring the Potential of Social Work Practices* (Department for Education and Skills, London, 2007)

A. Lynch, F. Newlands, D. Forrester, What does empathy sound like in social work communication? A mixed-methods study of empathy in child protection social work practice. Child Fam. Soc. Work **24**, 139–147 (2019). https://doi.org/10.1111/cfs.12591

M. McNay, J. Clarke, R. Lovelock, The journey towards professionalism in social work: the development and assessment of practice learning. J. Pract. Teach. Learn. **9**(3), 72–91 (2009). https://doi.org/10.1921/146066910X541647

P. Nelson et al., What makes a looked after child happy and unhappy? Adopt. Foster. **44**(1), 20–36 (2020). https://doi.org/10.1177/0308575919900665

F. Perraudin, Councils spend millions on agency social workers amid recruiting crisis. The Guardian, 8th April 2014 (2019). https://www.theguardian.com/society/2019/apr/07/social-work-recruiting-woes-see-councils-pay-millions-to-agencies?CMP=Share_AndroidApp_E%E2%80%A6. Accessed 17 June 2020

A. Stirling, *Austerity Is Subduing UK Economy by More Than £3,600 Per Household This Year* (New Economics Foundation, London, 2019). https://neweconomics.org/2019/02/austerity-is-subduing-uk-economy-by-more-than-3-600-per-household-this-year. Accessed 17 June 2020

P. Unwin, The role of agency social work, in *Modernising Social Work*, ed. by J. Harris, V. White, (Policy Press, Bristol, 2009)

S. Webb, Some considerations on the validity of evidence-based practice in social work. Br. J. Soc. Work **31**, 57–79 (2001)

WHO (World Health Organisation), *Prevention of Mental Disorders. Effective Interventions and Policy Options* (World Health Organisation, Geneva, 2004)

M. Wilberforce et al., What do service users want from mental health social work? A best–worst scaling analysis. Br. J. Soc. Work, 1–21 (2019). https://doi.org/10.1093/bjsw/bcz133

Index

© The Author(s), under exclusive license to Springer Nature
Switzerland AG 2021
C. Sealey et al. (eds.), *Social Policy, Service Users and Carers*,
https://doi.org/10.1007/978-3-030-69876-8

T
Timebanking, 20
Top-up fee, 201
Toxic Trio, 35
Transition to independent living, 62
Tuberous sclerosis, 204

U
*United Nations Convention on the Rights of
the Child* (UNCRC), 76, 81
Universal Credit, 6, 86, 203

V
Visibility of disabled people, 120
Voluntary and Community Services, 93

W
Well-being, 207
Whole family approach, 159
Work coach, 89
*Working Together to Safeguard
Children*, 47
Working with service users and carers, 2

9 783030 698751